SOVEREIGNTY, RIGHTS AND JUSTICE

SOVEREIGNTY, RIGHTS AND JUSTICE

INTERNATIONAL POLITICAL THEORY TODAY

CHRIS BROWN

polity

First published in 2002 by Polity Press in association with Blackwell Publishers Ltd

Editorial office:
Polity Press
65 Bridge Street
Cambridge CB2 1UR, UK

Marketing and production:
Blackwell Publishers Ltd
108 Cowley Road
Oxford OX4 1JF, UK

Published in the USA by
Blackwell Publishers Inc.
350 Main Street
Malden, MA 02148, USA

ISBN 0-7456-2302-6
ISBN 0-7456-2303-4   (pbk)

A catalogue record for this book is available from the British Library.

Library of Congress Cataloging-in-Publication Data

Brown, Chris.
  Sovereignty, rights, and justice : international political theory today / Chris Brown.
    p.   cm.
  ISBN 0-7456-2302-6 (acid-free paper) – ISBN 0-7456-2303-4 (pbk. : acid-free paper)
  1. International relations.   I. Title.
  JZ1305 .B758 2002
  327.1'01—dc21

                                                                    2001006335

Typeset in 10 on 12 pt Palatino
by SNP Best-set Typesetter Ltd., Hong Kong
Printed in Great Britain by TJ International, Padstow, Cornwall

This book is printed on acid-free paper.

Contents

Preface

One way to situate *Sovereignty, Rights and Justice* is by reference to two earlier books: it is a very distant successor to *International Relations Theory: New Normative Approaches* (1992) and a kind of companion to *Understanding International Relations* (1997/2001). *International Relations Theory* was written at a time when international political theory was still searching for recognition, and, as a result, has somewhat of a defensive character; in *Sovereignty, Rights and Justice* the legitimacy of the discourse is assumed, and the focus is much more on the content of international political theory rather than meta-discursive matters. Also, the 'cosmopolitan-communitarian' classification of international thought employed in the earlier volume is de-emphasized here – this was never more than a very crude aid to thought and can now be dispensed with. *Sovereignty, Rights and Justice* is complementary to *Understanding International Relations* in so far as the latter examines the conventional discourses of international relations theory, while the former examines a number of roads not taken by those discourses; both can serve as introductions, but *Sovereignty, Rights and Justice* presumes rather more in the way of background knowledge than the earlier work and is addressed to political theorists as well as to scholars of international relations.

Perhaps closer in spirit to this book than either of these earlier volumes are the various essays, articles, reviews and chapters I have published on a range of topics in international political theory over the last decade, and which are listed in the bibliography. None of the following chapters is a reprint of earlier work – apart from anything else my views on many issues have changed over time – but many phrases and sentences have survived; pity to waste a good line so I have not tried too hard to avoid auto-plagiarism.

Although the book is not formally divided into two, still chapters 2–4 are somewhat different from chapters 5–12. The former are intended to tell what is by now a fairly well-known story of the development of international thought in order to bring us to the point where we can examine contemporary problems; in order that this story can be told efficiently and quickly, these chapters are lightly sourced with relatively few references. The thinkers who are the subject of chapters 2 and 3 are anthologized with extensive extracts and introductory material in a volume co-edited with Terry Nardin and N. J. Rengger to be published in 2002. The twentieth-century discipline of International Relations, the subject matter of chapter 4, is covered more extensively, albeit from a different angle, in *Understanding International Relations*. Chapters 5–11, the remaining two-thirds of the book, cover material in much greater detail and, I hope, depth, and are more extensively sourced – although I have still tried to avoid breaking up the text with too many references. The final chapter provides a kind of conclusion.

For a book of this nature, one's intellectual debts are legion, and what follows can do no more than scratch the surface. In the 1990s I have had the privilege of becoming a kind of 'country member' of the political theory community in Britain, attending such annual rituals as the Oxford Political Theory Conference each January. I am grateful for the hospitality of the community towards someone whose background is very different from their own. In terms of individuals, my first acknowledgement must be to Brian Barry for his support and to Brian and Anni for their friendship; I find I disagree with Brian on many theoretical issues – although much less so on matters of practical politics – but, agree or disagree, it has been a privilege to have been in regular contact with this important political thinker over the last decade. Second, thanks to the very strong group of political philosophers at the University of Southampton – Russell Bentley, Peter Johnson, the late Liam O'Sullivan and, particularly, Andy Mason and David Owen. Andy and I were only together at Southampton briefly, but for long enough for me to regret the lost opportunity of more frequent discussions; fortunately the cost of housing in London means that we remain neighbours and can exchange thoughts regularly in the John Arlott and at St. Mary's. David is a truly remarkable political theorist and a good friend – I owe a great deal to his intellect and his enthusiastic willingness to engage. Finally, by way of specifics, I have had the privilege to join the LSE's International Relations Department at more or less the same time as David Held joined Government and Anne Phillips the Gender Institute; add existing colleagues John Charvet and Paul Kelly and, another recent addition, Cecile Fabre, and LSE's strength in the area of political theory is assured. In addition to the above, thanks for reading papers, inviting me to seminars, coming to my seminars and so on to David Boucher, Simon Caney, Margaret Canovan, Terrell Carver, Peter Jones, Preston King, Cecile Laborde, Raymond Plant and Albert Weale.

Britain has an extremely active community of international political theorists and scholars of IR more generally, and to acknowledge all of those who have influenced my thinking would be impossible – those not mentioned below should pencil their names in the margin. A few figures stand out as particularly influential – Tim Dunne, Mervyn Frost, Andrew Linklater; thanks to them and to Ken Booth, Mick Cox, Alex Danchev, Toni Erskine, Fred Halliday, Christopher Hill, Mark Hoffman, Richard Wyn Jones, Richard Little, James Mayall, Nick Rengger, Steve Smith, Hidemi Suganami, Peter Sutch, Paul Taylor, Nick Wheeler, John Williams and Michael Yahuda. In North America, Molly Cochran, Terry Nardin, Michael J. Smith, Joel Rosenthal and colleagues at the Carnegie Council for Ethics and International Affairs and the International Ethics section of ISA have been important influences, seminar hosts and readers of drafts; likewise in Germany, Lothar Brock, Friedrich Kra-tochwil, Klaus-Dieter Wolf, Michael Zuern and, in particular, my friend Mathias Albert, one of the most interesting theorists of his generation, and a relentless organizer – I have lost count of the number of Albert-sponsored conferences, seminars and edited volumes I have been involved with in the 1990s.

Brian Barry, Andrew Linklater and David Held read the manuscript and made helpful suggestions for its improvement, most of which I have adopted; thanks to them, my secretary, Barbara King, the folk at Polity Press – David Held again, Gill Motley, Sue Leigh and Louise Knight – and, as always, to the students at Kent, Southampton and LSE who have heard most of it before.

Chris Brown
London,
August 2001

Prologue:
September 11th, 2001

The final manuscript of this book was delivered to Polity Press in late August 2001, two or three weeks before the attacks on the World Trade Center and the Pentagon, attacks that many believe have brought about a fundamental change in world politics. In the circumstances, it is reasonable to ask whether an account of 'international political theory today' completed before September 11th has not been overtaken by events – the fate, for example, of so many books on US-Soviet relations in the late 1980s? I think not: the big questions addressed by international political theory, and discussed in *Sovereignty, Rights and Justice*, are the same today as they were on September 10th, while the chapters in this book that discuss the ethics of war, violence and terrorism, cultural diversity and international political theory and global social justice are more relevant than ever, and do not require development in the light of the crimes of '911'. Still, there are two issues addressed in the main body of the book where it is widely, although I think for the most part wrongly, believed that things have changed fundamentally, and where some brief additional remarks may be helpful – the so-called 'clash of civilizations' and the future of 'globalization'. In addition, the role of the US in world affairs – and, perhaps especially, of contemporary anti-Americanism – deserves a little more consideration than it receives in the main body of this work.

There is no doubt that Samuel Huntington's thesis that the future of world politics will be characterized by a clash of civilizations, one feature of which is likely to be a deep hostility between Islamic civilization and the West, has been given a new lease of life both by the events of September 11th, and, most especially, between the contrasting reactions to these events in the West and the Arab world. The deep sense of solidarity with the people of New York that was felt throughout Europe contrasted sharply with the scenes of rejoicing in Palestine, and the general satisfaction expressed in the street and the bazaar elsewhere in the Middle East; the leaders of the Arab world – who knew that the al-Qaeda network's action was directed at them as much as, if not more than, at the Americans – did not share this satisfaction, but at the level of popular culture the contrast was clear enough and is further attested to by the way in which Osama Bin Laden's picture has become iconic to many Muslims, ironically given Islam's general attitude to portraiture. Huntington's thesis, which was widely rejected when first elaborated, now appears prophetic; his original 1993 article 'The Clash of Civilizations' is widely referenced, and, indeed, has been reprinted in the London *Sunday Times*, where it was described as 'uncannily prescient' (14 October 2001).

So, was Huntington right all along? It seems to me that the intellectual case against his, at times ad hoc, at times essentialist, notion of what a civilization is remains strong, and his spatial account of the 'fault-lines' between civilizations, allegedly lying in places such as Bosnia, is misleading. On the other hand, whether or not there is to be a clash of civilizations will not be decided in the seminar room or in academic journals. Popular attitudes are the key here; the 'West' and 'Islam' are complex, multi-layered social formations and the most important dividing lines run within rather than between such broad categories as civilizations, but if Westerners come to think of all Muslims as potentially suicidal fanatics, and Muslims of Westerners as godless hedonists, then the clash of civilizations will become a reality and the world will become an even more dangerous place than it is today. All the more important then that the kind of issues concerning cultural diversity and international political theory addressed in chapter 10 of this book should be taken on board as widely as possible. One, possibly desirable, alternative to a clash of civilization is cross-cultural dialogue – but only if it is understood that dialogue is not an easy option. The only dialogue that is worth having, that is not simply an exchange of clichés, is one in which all the parties examine critically, as well as set out, their own values. 'Westerners' must examine their role in the various conflicts that poison Middle Eastern politics, and must address the demands for global social justice that emanate from the losers in today's world economy, but, equally, Muslims must ask themselves whether it is really plausible that all the woes of the so-called world of Islam are the responsibility of America, and, in particular, whether the savage theology of the al-Qaeda network and the Taliban deserves the respect it receives in many mosques and in the independent Arab mass media. We must hope that the young men who so readily wave Bin Laden posters do not really want a world in which their sisters would be subject to persecution or worse for wearing lipstick; if they do, then 'clash' rather than 'dialogue' is not just inevitable but actually desirable.

Has the era of 'globalization' been brought to an end by the Fall of
the Towers, as suddenly as a previous era of economic interdependence
was ended by the outbreak of war in August 1914? The world economy,
unhealthy before September 11th, may well be pushed into recession
by the crisis of confidence that day has engendered, and, certainly,
anyone who took seriously the notion of a 'borderless world' will find
that, for the foreseeable future, borders will be even more heavily
policed than they have been in the past. The war against terrorism will
place in the hands of state authorities all sorts of powers of surveillance
and regulation; moreover, it seems likely that the general public will
accept, and perhaps welcome, this extension of state control – so far,
the popular reaction to the fear that global terrorism has generated has
been to look to the state for protection, and I see no reason to think that
this will change as time goes by, although the consensus that now exists
in support of the detailed strategy of the war against terrorism may
gradually disappear. On the other hand, the political, social and economic forces that created globalization in the first place have not gone
away, and there is no reason to think they will go away. The tension
between these forces and the territorially based political structure of
the Westphalian order, a tension that is a major theme of this book,
seems likely to continue for the foreseeable future.

Part of this tension can be seen in the nature of the al-Qaeda
network, who may endorse a pre-modern theology, but have themselves a very modern, post-modern even, organizational form. The fact
that they are a 'network' and not an hierarchically organized terrorist
group is in itself of significance, and not just because it makes them
more difficult to combat. The loose network – rhizomorphic rather than
arboreal, root-like rather than tree-like, to use the language of Gilles
Deleuze – is becoming the characteristic organizational form of globalization. As Michael Hardt and Antonio Negri have suggested, power
in the modern world is distributed in networks rather than concentrated, which is why, on their account, we have a genuine *Empire*
emerging today, rather than the competing imperialisms of the past
two or more centuries (Hardt and Negri, 2000). In a parallel development, the groups that oppose the emerging global order – the so-called
'anti-globalization' coalition as well as terrorist groups such al-Qaeda
– operate as networks rather than under a clear chain of command. But,
still, it is striking that these groups find it impossible actually to campaign against the empire in its real form as a network – instead they
feel they have to give it a name, 'America'.

The hatred of America which is so apparent in much of the non-
Western world, and which, sadly, has infected so many Western intel-
lectuals, is, for the most part, a product of this process of reification.
The peoples of the world do not actually seem to hate American music,

television, films, clothes, food or soft drinks; millions of them wish to relocate to the US, while even those who do not would mostly be glad to see the kind of democratic institutions and respect for individual rights characteristic of the US in their own countries – although this point does not, of course, apply to the supporters of radical Islam. On the other hand, many of the same people who, implicitly, endorse American values in this way, are only too conscious of their own lack of power and wealth in a world in which the US appears to have so much of both; it is easy to see how this consciousness can turn into an overestimation of US power and the belief that this power is always used against the interests of the wretched of the earth. The turn towards a unilateralist American foreign policy, which has been characteristic of the US since the end of the Cold War, but which was intensified in the first few months of George W. Bush's presidency, has reinforced this belief.

Along with Hardt and Negri, I think the demonization of America is a mistake – there may be an emerging empire today, and US firms and politicians may have more influence in that empire than any others, but the US *as a state* does not have the same kind of imperial role that, for example, Britain and France had with respect to their empires a century ago; power today is diffused in networks rather than concentrated in places like the Pentagon or the World Trade Center – although, in a sense, the people who died in the World Trade Center did indeed represent the system as a whole, in so far as all nationalities, classes, races and socio-economic groups were to be found amongst the thousands of victims. But, as against Hardt and Negri, and for reasons that are set out in chapter 12 of this book, I am not convinced that the 'empire' that is emerging will act against the long-run interests of the wretched of the earth. Global capitalism has not yet delivered an adequate standard of living for the majority of the world's inhabitants, but I am not convinced that it will be unable to do so; more to the point, it is difficult to see any decent alternative to the present system – as opposed to a falling back on the nationalism that has served the world so badly over the last centuries. In any event, the ambiguous attitude of so many 'progressive' intellectuals to the events of 11 September, the belief that America in some sense deserved this slaughter of the innocents, is difficult to understand – whatever one's attitude to the emerging empire, I cannot see how the homicidal fanatics who committed these acts could be mistaken for the harbingers of an alternative world order with which decent people could identify.

At a deeper level, the problem here is one identified throughout *Sovereignty, Rights and Justice*, namely the lack of an adequate conceptual and moral vocabulary for dealing with the changes that have taken place in the world in recent times, and especially over the last half century. So much of our thinking about politics and society is rooted within a framework in which the bounded community is taken for granted, that we have difficulty getting straight in our own minds what our attitude should be to cataclysmic global events which now, for the first time in human history, can be experienced live, in real-time, and throughout the world. My hope is that what follows, by clarifying the various conceptual debates that make up international political theory today, will do a little more than simply identify this problem.

London, November 2001

Introduction: Sovereignty, Rights and Justice

Consider: homeless people sleep in doorways in the Strand in central London while single mothers in 'sink' estates in greater Glasgow bring up their children in poverty, British citizens of Black or Asian origin report that they regularly experience racial discrimination and the life-chances of British women remain significantly different from those of British men. Also: villagers in parts of South Asia routinely tread the fine line between malnutrition and starvation, the inhabitants of Central Africa struggle to survive the civil wars which have wrecked the Congo basin, gender differences in infant mortality are striking in many parts of the world, and national minorities in the Balkans and elsewhere face persecution and oppression.

How is the relationship between the two grim situations summarized by these sentences to be understood? The author of this book is a British citizen (non-British readers will find it easy to provide their own local examples) and so the ills related in the first sentence are experienced by fellow citizens; this fact is generally taken to be significant, indeed to provide a valid reason for responding to such ills – the British welfare state and a range of anti-discrimination legislation are such a response, inadequate though they may be. Obligations are recognized here, but how do things stand with respect to the ills of those who are not one's fellow citizens and who live in faraway places? Some kind of obligation is recognized here too, but, seemingly, of a very different kind. All of the wealthy, constitutionally secure liberal democracies have foreign aid programmes of one kind or another, and subscribe to international organizations part of whose remit is to relieve global poverty; the same democracies have been at the forefront in the development of the international human rights regime over the last half-century. Still, even the most generous aid budgets are no more than a small fraction of the internal transfers between rich and poor that take place within these democracies, and the willingness of those countries where human rights are generally respected to take active steps to enforce such rights elsewhere is somewhere between non-existent and very lukewarm. Foreigners, it seems, are different from our fellow nationals; 'they' have different claims upon us, 'we' have different obligations towards them.

Such a distinction between 'us' and 'them' seems well established in popular thought, but what of scholarly discourse? Here the situation is rather more complex. It is certainly the case that for much of the last century 'government' and 'political theory' were seen as occupying different disciplinary spaces from 'international relations' (IR) and 'international theory'. Domestic politics was seen as a realm where questions of political obligation were central; liberals, conservatives, social democrats and socialists may have differed as to the kinds of society that they wanted to see emerge within their country, but no one doubted that co-nationals had some kind of obligation towards each other and that social life was impossible without this fact being recognized. International relations, on the other hand, concerned relationships between states, and the most important strand of theorizing of this relationship – realism, of which more below – stressed the extent to which whatever obligations states had towards each other rested ultimately on contingent factors, most importantly mutual self-interest.

That there was a clear distinction between domestic politics and international relations was more or less taken for granted by scholars in both fields – IR scholars in particular believed this distinction to be a defining feature of the modern 'Westphalian' system of sovereign states. However, in reality, it was only during the inter-war years, and then, even more emphatically, after the Second World War, that IR came to be seen as a distinct field of study with its own characteristic concepts and theories, drawing upon older disciplines such as philosophy, history, law and political science, but melding these disparate discourses into something distinctive and different. It was only in these years that it came to be widely held that 'international relations', the subject matter of the discipline IR, were *sui generis*, different from other kinds of social relationship by their very nature, and thus that they had to be studied in an equally distinctive way. The 'theory of international relations' then came to be seen as something very different from 'political theory' as that term was usually understood, but this is a position that would not have been recognized for much of the nineteenth, let alone the seventeenth or eighteenth centuries – and, more to the point, it is increasingly challenged today, in the twenty-first century.

It is with this latter challenge that this book is primarily concerned – although some consideration will be given to earlier patterns of thought about these matters. Over the last twenty years or so, a dis-

tinctive discourse has emerged which does not treat international relations as a separate subject for theorizing from political science, and
which refuses to think of the issues of obligation raised in the opening
of this chapter as falling naturally into categories such as 'domestic' or
'international'. The creators of this discourse come from, and sometimes consider themselves still to be located in, a variety of backgrounds in political and social theory, moral philosophy, economics as
well as international relations, but together they have made something
new – or perhaps rediscovered older insights from the time before the
'disciplining' of international relations.

Knowing what to call this new discourse presents problems. Some
adherents of the new discourse have employed the term 'normative
theory' to describe what they do, the contrast being with those vari-
eties of IR theory which claim to be purely explanatory (e.g. C. Brown,
1992a; Frost, 1996; Cochran, 2000). However, this is clearly somewhat
unsatisfactory; it rests upon a distinction between 'normative' and
'positive' theory that, as will be argued below, is ultimately unsustain-
able, and also 'normative' as a word has unfortunate connotations of
'preachiness'; the implication is that normative theorists are going to
tell everyone else what they ought to do about pressing moral issues
such as global poverty. This is not usually the main intention of this
work, which is more oriented towards the task of interpretation. For
similar reasons the term 'international ethics' is somewhat unsatisfactory, although a great deal of good work is done under the rubric of
this term, supported, for example, by the Carnegie Council for Ethics
and International Affairs with its journal *Ethics and International Affairs*,
or under the auspices of the 'International Ethics' section of the
(American) International Studies Association, and it has been used in
a number of important collections and books (Nardin and Mapel, 1992;
Frost, 1996; Rosenthal, 1999). If 'ethics' had today the kind of general
implications conveyed by the title of Aristotle's *Ethics* this would be all
well and good – but for the most part it does not. Rather, the usual con-
notation is with moral codes and prescription.

After eliminating these two possibilities, we end up with the term
used in the subtitle of this book and throughout for the new discourse
– 'international political theory'. International here is intended to
connote a specific focus rather than to imply a separate discourse; of
course, what that focus actually is will require a certain amount of
meditation on the term 'international'. Three terms seem particularly
central to this meditation – sovereignty, rights and justice, the main title
of this book. Most of the rest of this introductory chapter will provide
an initial overview of the relationship between these three terms, in the
process providing a kind of preview of the argument of the book taken
as a whole. Further preliminary reflections on 'us' and 'them' and on

the relationship between international relations and international political theory will follow, and then a chapter outline of the book along
with a brief explanation of some exclusions and omissions.

Sovereignty

It might seem strange to begin the title of a book that is trying to escape
from conventional IR with 'sovereignty' since this notion is so central
to the conventional discourse, and international political theorists such
as Thomas Pogge and Charles Beitz have been so dismissive of its
merits (Beitz 1979/2000; Pogge, 1994a). It provides, however, a very
important bridge between the old and the new. The notion itself
emerges out of political theory; when Jean Bodin and Thomas Hobbes,
amongst others, developed the outlines of the modern notion of sovereignty in the sixteenth and seventeenth centuries respectively, the
'international' was not their primary concern but they were immediately aware of the international implications of what they were doing
– and the prototypical 'international lawyers' of the next hundred years
who worked through these implications, from Grotius to Vattel, were
themselves political philosophers as well as, sometimes instead of,
lawyers. Moreover, the current literature on sovereignty is itself of a
much higher quality than was characteristic of, say, twenty years ago.
Spurred on by European integration, the putative onset of globalization, and such challenges to the notion of sovereignty as the emergence
of an international human rights regime, it is not simply constructivist
international political theorists such as Friedrich Kratochwil and
Alexander Wendt who are breaking new ground – one of the most
interesting recent studies of sovereignty has come from the realist
Stephen Krasner (Kratochwil, 1995; Krasner, 1999; Wendt, 1999). All in
all, sovereignty has plenty of life left in it as a focus for study.

Highlighting the term sovereignty is designed to draw attention to
the distinguishing feature of international political theory, as opposed
simply to political theory, which is that it deals with the implications
of a world in which there are multiple political units, each claiming to
be, in some strong sense, autonomous – and the term 'sovereignty' is
a useful shorthand way of referring to this claim. Sometimes this claim
is cast in legal terms, as a refusal to recognize that there is any external person or body who may legitimately exercise authority within a
particular realm. Alternatively the claim may be to possess certain
kinds of capabilities or powers which can be exercised without the
approval of another; Krasner helpfully suggests it may be sensible to
distinguish here between claims concerning the capacity to act within

a territory and to be able to regulate relations across borders (Krasner, 1999). In any event, the claim to autonomy means something more than, for example, the right to exercise delegated powers, which could be taken away in a perfectly legal manner. The key point is that, whatever the exact nature of the claim to autonomy may be, a world in which such claims are made has a different politics from a world in which such claims are not made.

We can see this very clearly when we compare the politics of a world of autonomous units with those of, on the one hand, an empire, and on the other, a federal system. An imperial system has a centre of authority and a chain of command. Distant provinces of an empire may have quite a high degree of actual autonomy – in the era before modern communications the governor of a distant province might have the title 'Vice-Roy' precisely in order to convey his capacity to act independently on behalf of the ruler, taking decisions as though he were king, but 'on behalf of' is the key term here. There is no actual *claim* to autonomy; autonomy is a practical response to problems of distance and far from being claimed as a matter of principle, it is denied as a matter of principle. Relations between the metropolis and provinces in such an empire are very different from those between genuinely autonomous units; the political focus is always upon the centre and upon the effectiveness of the transmission belt between centre and periphery. The central point here is that it is not simply the *fact* of autonomy which makes a difference; the *claim* to autonomy symbolized by the terms 'sovereign' and 'sovereignty' is itself important. To put the matter in different terms, in the former case autonomy is contingent, in the latter it is built into the rules of the game, it is a constitutive rule which defines the nature of the relationship (Kratochwil, 1995).

A federal system provides a different, and perhaps more ambiguous, point of comparison. The essence of federalism is a political/legal arrangement in which both the central authority and its component units are able to claim autonomy in respect of certain spheres of competence. Thus, it is not simply the case that a province actually possesses a degree of autonomy but that it is acknowledged to possess this autonomy as of right. Some cosmopolitan international political theorists (Thomas Pogge, for example) have suggested that this situation shows what is wrong with Hobbesian notions of sovereignty, asking, rhetorically, where sovereignty resides in, say, the United States (Pogge, 1994a). Is the relationship between the units of a federal system analogous to the relations between states in an international system? Not on traditional accounts of sovereignty, which stress the absoluteness of the term – since the lower units can in certain areas be overruled by the higher this produces a different politics from an international system in which this is not the case. On the other hand, since modern thinking on actual sovereign powers stresses the extent to which they have always been limited, there may be fruitful points of comparison here, as Daniel Deudeny has emphasized in his account of the 'Philadelphia' System – pre-1860s federalism in the US – as a kind of international system (Deudeny, 1996). In any event, federal systems provide a good reason to investigate and cross-examine the notion of sovereignty, as contemporary discussions on 'post-sovereignty' in Europe illustrate, but they are still different in kind from systems based on the politico-legal notions of autonomy summarized by the idea of sovereignty (Wallace, 1999). The key difference is that disputes between the units and the centre and among the units are ultimately settled by constitutional-legal means, which is clearly not something that can be guaranteed to be the case in a system of sovereign units; the latter may agree to resolve their differences in such a way, but, as Hegel put it in the context of a discussion of Kant's scheme for a perpetual peace, any such agreements are tainted with contingency (Hegel, 1821/1991, §333).

Extending this latter point, a defining characteristic of a sovereignty-based system is the absence of authoritative central institutions. If we assume that 'politics' is necessarily connected to 'government', or that politics is about the authoritative allocation of values, then such a system is not properly political, and 'international political theory' becomes a misnomer. It was for some such reason that Martin Wight famously declared there to be no 'international theory' (Wight, 1966). Political realists, classical and neo-, similarly emphasize the importance of the lack of authoritative institutions by their stress on the 'anarchy problematic' (e.g. M. E. Brown, et al., 1995). There are two reasons why these are overreactions to the lack of authoritative central institutions. First, as Alexander Wendt has admirably demonstrated, there are different kinds of anarchy (Wendt, 1992 and 1999). The simple absence of authoritative central institutions does not of necessity lead to the kind of anarchy charted by Kenneth Waltz and his neo-realist colleagues, or to relationships locked into the eternal return of recurrence and repetition described by Wight (Wight, 1966; Waltz, 1979 and 1990). Wendt suggests that anarchy is 'what states make of it', and although we might want to suggest that there are limits to this process of construction, the basic point is valid (Wendt, 1992).

Perhaps more directly to the point, it is by no means clear that the original argument that politics requires government, that authoritative allocation is central to the political process, ought to be accepted. If, for example, we take the basic question to be Lasswell's 'who gets what, where, when' (or Lenin's 'who, whom') then it is by no means obvious that *authoritative* allocation is central to the political. Questions about the justice of a particular allocation arise whether the allocation is made by a government or in some other way. For example, even if we are unwilling to follow some feminist writers and subsume private life wholly into public by asserting bluntly that 'the personal is the political', we do not need to deny that the process whereby gender roles are allocated is profoundly political. The idea that because a particular order is 'anarchic' therefore the kinds of questions political theorists characteristically ask cannot be asked in this case is either unfounded – or, more sharply, founded in the desire to protect the interests of the strong, for whom questions of justice and right are generally embarrassing, and to be avoided if at all possible. From an international political theory perspective such questions are central – hence the second and third terms of the main title to this book. But, whose rights, which justice?

Rights

Liberal political theory, drawing on the natural law tradition, and certain aspects of medieval political practice, asserts that individual human beings have rights, and since the Second World War, a quite elaborate international human rights regime has been developed to give body to this proposition. In the past, on the other hand, international lawyers have generally declined to see individuals as subjects of international law, save in very restricted circumstances, stressing instead the rights of states. Nowadays the international human rights regime is accepted as part of international law, and lawyers extend still further the notion of rights by addressing the 'rights of peoples' – the right, for example, to national self-determination, or the specific rights of indigenous or nomadic peoples. However, some non-Western critics of the notion of universal rights stress the parochial origins of such a universalist position, and some feminists agree that the international human rights regime has implicitly taken the paradigmatic rights-holder to be a Western male – although feminists and advocates of, for example, 'Asian values' tend not to agree on anything else. Meanwhile, realist IR theorists do not employ the language of rights at all, although their basic position could easily be turned into a defence of the rights of states (although not of the rights of political communities).

All this suggests two things: a system based on sovereignty by no means excludes talk of rights, but it complicates such talk to a very high degree. Of course, many of the debates about rights that exist internationally are mirrored domestically (or vice versa). Thus, for example, the claim that states have the right to manage their own affairs independently of international standards of behaviour is paralleled by the claims to autonomy of indigenous peoples, endorsed by some theorists of 'multiculturalism'. The difference between these two situations is, however, quite clear. In the domestic case, the rights of indigenous communities will ultimately be settled by authoritative, political-legal, constitutional processes; things are rather different in a system based on sovereignty. The International Court of Justice has jurisdiction in some circumstances over inter-state conflicts, but its capacity to decide between the competing claims of states, individuals and groups is decidedly limited, and its capacity to enforce its decisions is more or less non-existent. The new International Criminal Court (established by the Rome Treaty of 1998 and likely to come into being in 2002) will have the capacity to judge individuals, but again only in limited circumstances, and again, with few powers of enforcement. With one or two exceptions – most notably in Europe, where the sovereignty system is most under pressure at the moment – the international politics of rights takes place under very different circumstances from the politics of rights within a country.

In a sovereignty system, the politics of rights is about the exercise of political influence rather than legal decisions. States uphold their rights by attempting to exclude foreign influence over their decision-making procedures. Compliance with international human rights legislation is similarly determined by the exercise of influence; most states do not want to be seen by their own publics, or by world public opinion as mobilized by the international media, as violators of human rights. On the other hand, when important issues are at stake, states are unlikely to allow this kind of reputation to be decisive, and, crucially, states themselves determine what are the important issues. However, it should be noted that in recent decades the growth in the number of non-governmental organizations with an interest in human rights has been quite striking, leading some to think in terms of the emergence of a 'global civil society' oriented towards individual rights. As against this, the increasing willingness of non-Western countries to describe the international human rights regime as neo-colonialist and based on a form of cultural imperialism should also be noted. The rights of states and of individuals are put into the starkest relief when allegedly humanitarian interventions take place – that is to say, when one state forcibly, possibly violently, violates the sovereignty of another putatively on behalf of the citizens of the latter. Such interventions have always been few and far between – although they are not unprecedented even before the twentieth century – but in the last decade or so they have become, if not common, then at least no longer quite so exceptional. An interesting question is whether, if such interventions became commonplace, the system of sovereign states could survive. This, and the other questions raised above, will be examined in much greater depth below.

The classical liberal conception of human rights was largely political and personal, covering such matters as freedom of speech, assembly, religion and so on. Now, these 'first-generation' rights are often said to be accompanied not just by the rights of peoples, 'third-generation rights' as they are sometimes called, but by social and economic rights – the second generation. Again, such a move raises all sorts of issues in a sovereignty system. Within a domestic political order it may make sense to speak of a right to an old age pension or to unemployment assistance, because the state with its powers of taxation has the ability to deliver on such a right. What does a right to subsistence mean in an international system? From whom is such a right claimed? Clearly it would be possible for an international authority to be established to tax the rich and redistribute to the poor, but why would states – especially rich states – take such as step? Here issues of justice are raised.

Justice

What can justice mean in a system based on sovereignty? Nothing, say the realists, but the traditional answer, provided by lawyers and theorists of international society, is clear – justice means respect for the rights of sovereigns. It concerns the procedures of international relations, the practices that are necessary to allow sovereigns to relate to one another, preferably peacefully (Nardin, 1983). It means 'impartial rules, impartially applied'. But, with increasing force from the 1960s onwards, the modern international system has seen the emergence of claims for international *social* justice, for international redistribution between rich and poor on the basis of international distributive justice. The different meanings of the idea of the social are interesting here. Theorists of international *society* – the so-called 'English School' – contest with harder-nosed realists who prefer the term international *system*, denying the social nature of inter-state relations, but when the former use the term society they mean simply to convey the idea that relations between states are minimally norm-governed; the wider implications of the term social are rarely considered (Bull, 1977/1995; C. Brown, 1995a and 2001a; Dunne, 1998; Jackson, 2000).

For 'international social justice' to make sense there would have to be an international society in a deeper sense of the term – indeed, it would be rather less confusing if the term global were to be substituted for international. It would then be clear that we are speaking not of a relationship between separate secondary units but between human individuals – international (global) social justice requires that we ask what is owed to individuals qua individuals, not simply by 'their' sovereign but by all other individuals. It is, of course, a moot point whether the depth of relationships between individuals on a global scale could be such as to sustain such a system of rights and duties. It is not simply traditional IR theorists who think not – the most important theorist of justice of the last century, John Rawls, is clear that his highly influential account of distributive justice could not be applied internationally (Rawls, 1971/1999 and 1999b). However, it is equally moot whether a conventional division between procedural and distributive justice can be sustained in the face of the move to globalization through which we are currently living. The growth of international interdependence does not necessarily create the sense of community that may be required to make a scheme of redistribution work, but it does mean that any account of the inappropriateness of distributive justice that relies upon the separateness of societies is going to have to be revised quite considerably.

Theorists of international social justice characteristically concentrate on issues of distribution, but what is to be distributed is less the subject of consensus. We might think in terms of global wealth, and a redistributive international tax system, but there are other forms of inequality that are only indirectly connected to wealth generated by the sovereignty system. Sovereigns claim the right to police their borders, determine their own membership; this is clearly a matter that has enormous social implications and not just because of poor people attempting to enter rich countries. For political refugees a border may be a matter of life and death, something that distributes life-chances very directly and dramatically. Questions of membership are clearly issues of international social justice. Who is included, who excluded can be a matter of life and death.

Inclusion and exclusion: 'us' and 'them'

This gets to the heart of the matter. A political arrangement of the world's surface based on sovereignty rests on processes of inclusion and exclusion which may well cut across considerations of rights and justice (Walker, 1993). A certain amount of care is required here. All political arrangements rest on inclusion and exclusion in one form or another, and the vision of a politics that is literally all-embracing would imply the absence of any kind of scarcity, which hardly seems to be a sensible starting point. But the sovereignty system imposes a particular form of inclusion and exclusion which has dramatic consequences in all directions, and breaking this form down can be hard, not just in analytical terms but in terms of political values. Herein lies one of the distinctive features of international political theory. Consider, for example, the way in which the free movement of refugees and economic migrants into the advanced industrial world is characteristically supported by libertarian political philosophers and neo-liberal economists as well as by many progressivist liberals, while opposed by an equally unlikely coalition of social democrats, trade unionists and right-wing, authoritarian nationalists. The point is that a political geography based upon a system of autonomous sovereign units encourages a particular mode of thinking about the world in which notions of 'right' and 'justice' are particularized and parochialized, and this is particularly striking in a world in which government is seen as representative and responsible. The 'subjects' of an autocrat have few rights, and justice is another word for the will of the ruler, but once subjects become 'citizens' then the issue of what they owe to each other as opposed to non-citizens becomes real. Giving priority to the interests of fellow citizens or co-nationals inevitably involves downsizing one's obligation to everyone else.

To summarize: international political theory shares with political theory a concern with rights and justice, but it focuses this concern on the particular problems thrown up by the implications of sovereignty for these key notions, sovereignty being taken as shorthand for a particular system of inclusion and exclusion. The existence of bounded political entities is a backdrop to most conventional political theory, something that political theorists are aware of but do not allow to impinge too radically upon their consciousness. For international political theorists, this bounded quality of politics is foregrounded; it becomes the key feature of political life. The existence of a boundary between the domestic and the international is taken for granted by conventional political theory, but is contested and cross-examined by international political theorists.

International political theory and international relations

International political theory is different from, although related to, political theory, but it is also different from, and related to, international relations theory – although in rather different ways. In the twentieth century, the model for what IR theory ought to be generally involved a set of linked propositions designed to explain the regular patterns that were perceived to exist in international relations. Opinions might differ as to the extent to which such propositions could be expressed in formal terms, but both the builders of formal models and the more modest 'barefoot empiricists' employed the same general account of the nature and role of theory (Knorr and Rosenau, 1969; Nicholson, 1996; C. Brown, 1997/2001).

What is the purpose of this kind of theorizing? For the majority of theorists in this area, the answer is clear – explain in order to predict, predict in order to control, or if control is impossible, then at least to minimize the consequences of undesirable states of affairs and take advantage of whatever opportunities exist. In other words the goal is to solve problems; the assumption is that the more we know about the way the world works the more likely we are to be able to make it work to our advantage – although empiricists might argue that prediction without explanation can also be effective. Of course, who 'we' are in this context is contestable – many political scientists with this way of looking at the world have been concerned to promote the interests of their state (or, often, their side in the Cold War); there have always also been figures on the left with similar epistemologies, whose 'we' is the wider global interest, and whose work has characteristically appeared in outlets such as the *Journal of Peace Research*. This contest between competing political perspectives establishes a role for so-called normative theory. Positive knowledge tells us how to manipulate the world, but a different kind of knowledge is required to set down the purposes of such manipulation. The – explicit – model here is economics where 'positive economics' tells us what policy mixes of, say, unemployment rates, wage rates and inflation rates are possible, and 'normative' considerations determine which of these possible combinations is to be actively pursued. It is at this point that the 'normative' theory or 'international ethics' referred to at the opening of this chapter finds a respectable niche within contemporary IR, as an essential adjunct to the main business of producing explanatory theory.

Much of the impetus for international political theory comes in reaction to this way of setting up the relationship between the normative and the positive. In the first place, there is the political point made with great force by Robert Cox, that a 'problem-solving' approach to the role of theory takes the world as it is, and normative theory that fits within a problem-solving framework is obliged to do the same (Cox, 1981). The underlying assumption is that the world throws up a series of problems which it is the task of the theorist to solve – the explanatory theorist provides the tools for this task, outlining possible solutions, while the normative theorist attempts to suggest which of these possible solutions is the most desirable. The problem with this division of labour is that no room is left for a critique of the starting point; the underlying assumptions of the nature of the problem remain unchallenged. This leads to a more fundamental point; the explanatory theorist, and his or her normative associate, assume that they are attempting to describe the world as it is, to read off from the legible face of social reality the patterns and regularities that are to be found there. But this way of looking at the world misconceives the nature of these patterns and regularities, ignoring the differences between social facts and the 'brute facts' of nature (Searle, 1995).

An alternative perspective stresses that we live in 'a world of our making' – to use Nicholas Onuf's helpful phrase (Onuf, 1989). It is not so much that conventional IR theory takes the world as it is, which is Cox's point, rather that it fails to realize that any account of how the world is can only exist within a framework of shared ideas and concepts. Rules, regularities and patterns are not found within the world, and norms are not imposed upon it; rather they are all products of theory and constitutive of the world (Kratochwil, 1989). Thus, to take the most potent example from conventional IR theory, the neo-realist model of international relations is self-validating to the extent that it accurately works through the implications of the world that it has created, a world in which egoists seek to survive under conditions of Hobbesian anarchy (Waltz, 1979; Mearsheimer, 1994/5). But by taking this world as given, failing to recognize that it is a creation, the neo-realist is locked into an unchanging, timeless conception of international relations in which relevant and important pieces of information – such as the nature of the state, its history, identity and particular interests – cannot be conceptualized.

Some critics of conventional IR theory understood, at least in part, the implications of this critique. The 'English School', exemplified by writers such as Hedley Bull and Martin Wight, understood clearly that the contemporary international system had an origin, had changed over time and might change in the future – all, one might have thought, fairly straightforward positions of some significance, but regarded as irrelevant by many contemporary conventional theorists (Bull, 1977/1995; Wight, 1977). But their positions were also problematic, albeit in a different way. Wight and Bull were steeped in a tradition of statecraft and diplomacy that required them to explain international relations in terms of a particular language and style of reasoning that was divorced from the more philosophically informed terms that later international political theorists would employ. Thus it was not until Terry Nardin worked through the implications of international society as a kind of Oakeshottian civil association, or Friedrich Kratochwil exposed the logic of international law and norms in quasi-Wittgensteinian terms, or Mervyn Frost set out the legal reasoning behind the notion of a 'settled norm', that many of the ideas of writers such as Bull and Wight could be situated within a broader, more fruitful, context (Nardin, 1983; Kratochwil, 1989; Frost, 1996). The point about the latter three writers is that they are *not* 'normative' theorists in the sense in which the term is used above – although they all write about norms (and Frost, unhelpfully from my point of view, actually describes himself as a 'normative theorist'). They are not normative theorists because their positions are, in different ways, profoundly anti-positivist, denying the possibility of the conception of knowledge upon which the positive/normative divide rests.

In short, taken as a whole, 'international political theory' is not an adjunct or supplement to conventional international relations theory, but an alternative project starting from a fundamentally different ontology and epistemology. Not, it should be stressed, that only constructivists or anti-positivists produce international political theory. Many of the analytical political theorists who have contributed to the creation of the new discourse come from a very different background and have no particular interest in IR's 'culture wars'. What these figures share with the refugees from mainstream IR is above all a commitment to the idea that 'international relations' is not *sui generis*, an activity that is so different from other areas of social life that it requires the development of patterns of thought specific to its peculiar circumstances.

Outline and structure of the book

These remarks on the nature of international political theory are, of course, radically incomplete – it is the aim of the rest of the book to give substance to the positions sketched above. The next two chapters provide a certain amount of necessary historical background to contemporary international political theory. A genuinely historical survey of international political theory would be obliged to range very widely over Chinese, Indian and Islamic sources as well as the more conventional beginning of the discourse in the thought of classical Greece and Renaissance Italy. This is a thoroughly worthwhile project, the more conventional part of which has been addressed with some success by writers such as Fred Parkinson, Thomas Pangle and Peter Ahrendorf, and, most effectively, David Boucher (Parkinson, 1977; Boucher, 1998; Pangle and Ahrendorf, 1999). Collections of texts such as that of Terry Nardin, N. J. Rengger and the present writer make the raw materials for such a project more widely available than before (C. Brown et al., 2002). But this volume is not intended to be a historical survey and the aim here is simply to provide the kind of background that will allow the reader to make sense of contemporary writings. After a few preliminaries, chapter 2 therefore begins with the modern states-system, conveniently known as the Westphalia System in honour of the treaties that, more or less, ended the Thirty Years War in 1648 and are generally, if somewhat inaccurately, regarded as installing the ground rules of the European international system for the subsequent three centuries. This chapter will examine the two characteristic discourses associated with Westphalia, the 'law of nations' and the 'society of states'. These two discourses were set in place in the seventeenth and eighteenth centuries and are thus essentially pre-Enlightenment; on the other hand, many if not most of the categories of contemporary political theory emerge one way or another from the Enlightenment, and the international thought of Enlightenment and post-Enlightenment theorists is the subject of chapter 3 – post-Enlightenment in this case being extended to cover not simply the romantic reaction to the Enlightenment and figures such as Hegel, but also nineteenth-century writers on the state and the nation. Chapter 4 brings the historical background more or less up to date; this chapter is devoted to 'realism' and 'liberal internationalism' in their various manifestations; these are the two mainstays of international relations theory in the twentieth century, and this chapter will elaborate some of the more gnomic comments about IR theory made above.

Contemporary theory proper begins in chapter 5, with a consideration of the various cases that might be made in favour of self-determination and non-intervention, two key, but controversial, norms of contemporary international relations. This chapter will examine the justifications for these norms provided by IR theorists and by those international political theorists who stress the rights of political communities, such as Mervyn Frost, Terry Nardin and Michael Walzer – although each of these writers qualifies these rights (albeit in different ways). A central issue to be examined here is the relationship between states and communities; are the rights of political communities transferable to states, and if so, under what circumstances? Chapter 6 continues this story by examining the potential for violence that exists within a sovereignty-based system. Can the rights of political communities be seen as encompassing the right to employ violence in pursuit of political ends, and if so, under what circumstances and with what restrictions? This chapter will examine contemporary 'just war' theorizing, and also the – strangely neglected – subject of pacifism. It will also examine the relationship between 'force' and 'violence' and the apparently paradoxical phenomenon of non-violent force in IR.

Chapter 7 shifts the emphasis to the individual and rights, with an overview of the emergence of the international human rights regime. The story here is one of the emergence of a very extensive body of international legislation conferring upon individuals rights by virtue of their humanity, along with, in the 1990s and into the twenty-first century, the development of the first hesitant steps towards an effective international mechanism for compliance and enforcement of rights, with the Rome Statute of 1998 establishing an International Criminal Court to the fore. At the same time, the notion of universal rights has been under attack as a Western, male project, and the politics of international human rights protection becomes ever more complicated. The idea of an effective, enforceable international human rights regime must involve a breach with the norm of non-intervention, and the possibility of humanitarian intervention – humanitarian war even – is the subject of chapter 8. Here, the record of the last decade is examined, in the context of the competing norms outlined in the previous two chapters.

Chapter 9 shifts the focus of concern towards global economic inequality, examining theories of international distributive justice and various accounts of the duties owed by rich (states, individuals) to poor (states, individuals). This discussion draws upon earlier considerations of universal rights, since it is clear that modern notions of rights cannot be restricted to the purely political. The issue of borders, touched upon above, is examined here. Central to the theory and politics of redistribution and international social justice is the extent to which the world can be seen as a single social system, and one of the key issues here concerns cultural diversity and international political theory, the subject of chapter 10. Again this chapter draws upon earlier discussions – it is here, for example, that the East Asian challenge to human rights will be examined. International political theory is centred upon the 'international', but increasingly the very notion of the international is put in question by 'globalization'. Chapter 11 sketches the way in which a post-Westphalian political theory might differ quite markedly from the Westphalian theory that is, for the most part, the subject of the rest of the book, although it should be noted that throughout the text the tension between the norms of Westphalia and actual international political practice will be a consistent theme. Chapter 12 examines the recent rise of an active opposition to globalization, and attempts to pull together many of the general themes of the book.

The intention is that the various topics covered in this book will feed into one another; all international political theory revolves around essentially the same set of problems concerning the relationship between the individual and the community, and topics such as international human rights and the norm of non-intervention, global justice and cultural diversity, are different sides of the medal rather than the discrete subjects that any method of presentation is likely to make them. This means that, although some chapters could be taken in isolation, there is much to be said for reading them in the order in which they are presented. There is, I hope, a coherent story here, but this coherence will only be apparent if the text is treated as a conventional narrative, with a beginning, a middle and an end.

Two general comments are worth making about the various topics examined. First, the temptation to organize the text around a central classification of international thought has been resisted. In an earlier work, the distinction between 'cosmopolitan' and 'communitarian' thought was employed to organize material (C. Brown, 1992a). Although these terms will turn up quite frequently in what follows, this distinction is not, in fact, a suitable basis for classification. It obscures more than it clarifies; too many writers who seem to be in one camp cross over to the other at crucial points. There is a real distinction to be made between cosmopolitan and communitarian thought, but it cannot be made to bear too much weight – and there is no other classification that does much better in this respect. The best strategy seems to be to present arguments and make connections but not to try to impose a classification scheme on the reader – who on past form seems likely to spend more time picking holes in the scheme than thinking about the issues it is supposed to illuminate.

Second, this book does not address in detail the ontological and epistemological issues which have become so important to a certain kind of international political theorizing. One of the features of the literature of international political theory in recent years has been the emergence of very sophisticated and intelligent discussions of the epistemological and ontological implications of constructivism, scientific realism, post-structuralism, Lacanianism and so on for the study of international relations (Ashley, 1984; Walker, 1993; Edkins, 1999; Edkins et al., 1999; Guzzini, 2000). Some of this work is certainly valuable, but, on the whole, it is regrettable that it has come to play so prominent a role. When difficult and complex ideas genuinely illuminate important topics they must be confronted, but difficulty for its own sake is not a virtue and the narcissistic, hermetic quality of much of this work limits its relevance. There are, of course, 'late modern' theorists who have made important contributions to the understanding of the agenda set out above, and whose work is considered in the following chapters, but the temptation to allow the new learning actually to set the agenda has been resisted. Feminist writings have been treated in the same spirit. Feminist writers such as Jean Bethke Elshtain, Catherine MacKinnon and Martha Nussbaum have made important contributions to the literature on global inequality, human rights, cultural diversity and the nature of community and their contributions are recognized, but the idea that there is necessarily a distinctive feminist contribution to be made to all the topics under discussion has been resisted, and, similarly, the option of a separate chapter explicitly devoted to feminist thought has been rejected.

It has been difficult to decide how much knowledge to assume on the part of the reader, at least partly because it is hoped both political theorists and IR theorists at all levels will find the book of value. Inevitably some presentational compromises have had to be made to avoid either losing the attention of, or talking over the head of, one group or the other. As a result, if occasionally the account of some particular topic, theory or theorist seems either overdone or underdeveloped, the hope is that the reader will make allowances.

2

The Westphalia System: the Law of Nations and the Society of States

Introduction: inclusion and exclusion before Westphalia

Political life is impossible, it seems, without some kind of bordering, some distinction between 'insiders' and 'outsiders'. All political entities whether formal (cities, states, empires) or informal (tribes, guilds, universities) find it necessary to distinguish between members and non-members. But this says nothing about the nature of relations between insiders and outsiders, members and non-members (C. Brown, 2000b). There are at least two sets of questions here: first, on what is the distinction between insiders and outsiders based? Is it regarded as, in some sense, natural, the consequence of a fact about the world that is, to all intents and purposes, unchangeable, or is it acknowledged to be essentially artificial? Or, perhaps most plausibly, is it seen as based on non-natural, but nonetheless real, characteristics? And, how permeable is the boundary – can outsiders become insiders easily, or only with great difficulty, if at all? Second, is the relationship between insiders and outsiders *normatively* charged? Are outsiders regarded as morally inferior to insiders, or simply as different? Indeed, are they thought about in moral terms at all? Do insiders acknowledge that they have moral duties towards outsiders, and if so, are these duties the same as, or more limited than, those that they acknowledge towards each other?

Many accounts of the relationship between insiders and outsiders are possible in theory, and, indeed, many different relationships have been experienced in practice. Systems of inclusion and exclusion can be very complex and can produce results that are sometimes counter-intuitive. The classical Greeks, for example, drew a clear distinction between themselves and 'barbarians' based on religion, culture and, perhaps especially, language (barbarians were so called because they did not speak properly, but made noises that sounded something like 'barbar'), and yet the external relations of the Greek cities seem not to have been unduly influenced by this distinction. Being Greek appears to have been of little advantage to the inhabitants of cities which found themselves at the mercy of one or other of the major players in the Peloponnesian War, as the Melians most famously discovered at the hands of the Athenians (Thucydides, 1998, p. 294). The reason why inter-*polis* relations were so fraught seems to have been rooted in another – tribal – system of insiders and outsiders which took precedence over the distinction between Greeks and others. The cities were composed of extended kin-groups sharing certain religious rites and, perhaps, a commitment to certain political forms; beyond this restricted confraternity, cultural affinity might be recognized but moral obligation was more problematic.

There is an interesting parallel to the Greek experience on the other side of the world. The tribes of Aotearoa (New Zealand) were kin-groups for whom genealogy (*whakapapa*) was central – each member of a sub-clan claimed descent from a particular individual; wider groupings traced descent from mariners who made the original voyage from the ancestral homeland, Hawaiki, to Aotearoa in the same canoe (Belich, 1996). Relations between the various tribes were frequently violent, and there was no collective term for the inhabitants of Aotearoa until the arrival of the Europeans in the late eighteenth century. At that point 'Maori' emerges as such a collective term, and meant 'normal' as distinct from the 'Pakeha' ('whites' or Europeans). Some such terminology is common among 'aboriginal' peoples: most of the familiar names of the tribes of native Americans of the Wild West translate as 'the people', or 'human beings'. What is interesting is that the arrival of this term, and the need it obviously signified for a new system of inclusion/exclusion, did nothing to lessen the degree of inter-tribal violence. In the New Zealand Wars of the 1860s some tribes fought with the British and the colonists against other Maori, and even today it is difficult for the Maori to speak with one voice. The category 'Maori', like the category 'Greek', has real cultural meaning but does not readily translate into political terms.

Systems of inclusion and exclusion may work in a more generous way. Within medieval Christendom there were borders between the various political authorities, but these borders existed in a context where the overriding identity was, in principle, universal and religious. Individuals were discouraged from thinking of their secondary identities as natural, or as conveying more than limited and conditional moral obligations. Rulers ruled where they could and sought to extend their power, often through violence, but the influence of the church – which was material as well as spiritual, since religious foundations owned much of the wealth of the continent – was, for the most part, exercised to limit the scope of the resulting conflict, and sometimes successfully. Christendom was, of course, based on the distinction between Christians and non-Christians, and the medieval era is characterized by wars with pagans, pogroms against Jews – the 'enemy within' – and the struggle with Islam. However, even these divides between insiders and outsiders were not quite as sharp as had been the case in the Greek world. Borders could be, and were, crossed – by conversion or apostasy – and even some outsider groups had a place in the scheme of things; for example, the Jews played an important role in Christian theology, as the people who had rejected the Messiah, and whose eventual conversion was an important long-term goal that would herald the Second Coming. This did not prevent atrocities committed against the Jews, but a universal religion such as Christianity is, at least in principle, capable of recognizing actual outsiders as potential insiders.

The purpose of these very brief sketches is to highlight the point that there is nothing inevitable, much less natural, about the understanding of systems of inclusion and exclusion which has been promoted, explicitly or implicitly, by the discourse of (Western) political theory over the last three or four hundred years – that is, since the passing of the world of medieval Christendom. As noted in chapter 1, this discourse is associated with the idea of a system of sovereign states, that is, legally autonomous, territorial, political entities that are 'hardshelled', with clearly defined and effective borders, but which engage in regular, systematized relations one with another. This is the 'Westphalia System' and its internal rules have peculiar features. On the one hand, the divide between insiders and outsiders is all-important; a sharp distinction is drawn between the realms of the political and the international, and the former ('domestic politics') is characterized very differently from the latter ('international relations'). On the other hand, relations between states are nonetheless generally taken to be law- and, perhaps, norm-governed; institutions exist (international law, diplomacy) which regulate international relations, and the rights and duties generated by these institutions bind across borders, although they apply to states not to individuals (Bull, 1977; Nardin, 1983). The rest of this chapter will examine this peculiar relationship in more detail, via an examination of the 'law of nations' and the 'society of states', although it should be noted that the distinction between these two discourses is by no means rigid. Whereas today 'international law' is characterized differently from international political theory, with its own characteristic modes of argument and professional standards, this was not the case in the seventeenth and eighteenth centuries; figures such as Grotius, Pufendorf and Vattel were recognized as political theorists as well as jurists. In any event, before moving to these discourses, some comments on the historical foundations of the Westphalia System may be helpful.

The Peace of Westphalia and the Westphalia System

In their memorable history of England, *1066 and All That* (1930), Sellar and Yeatman opine that there are only two dates of which the student need be aware, 55 BC and AD 1066. Students of International Relations have been taught to add AD 1648. In that year the Treaties of Münster and Osnabrück were signed, bringing to an end, at least nominally, the Thirty Years War in Germany. These treaties (which taken together are known as the Peace of Westphalia) are conventionally taken to inaugurate a new era of international relations – thus the 'Westphalia System'. But of course, as is pointed up by Sellar and Yeatman's admirable book, dates as such have no meaning save as shorthand – ways of referring briefly to complex periods of change – and such is certainly the case with 1648. It would be little exaggeration to say that the Westphalia treaties changed almost nothing; at best they registered changes that had taken place over the previous 150 years, and even then did so ambiguously. It could well be argued that the Peace of Augsburg of 1555 was more 'Westphalian' than the Peace of Westphalia. Clearly there is a story to be told here before we can move to examining the discourses of law and political theory, although those discourses are, themselves, part of the story, which makes for a complicated narrative.

The story is one of transition from one system of inclusion and exclusion to another. In the medieval world territory was an important, but not the only or even the most important, basis for inclusion and exclusion, whereas in the world of Westphalia it becomes certainly the most important, and, for a while, virtually the only, basis. The best way to understand the old system is in terms of a composite notion invented in the 1990s to convey the diverse impact of globalization, namely 'glocalization', which is meant to convey the idea that the focus of social action has moved from the state to both the global and the local level (Robertson, 1995). Making suitable adjustments to the meaning of the term 'global', the transition with which we are concerned here could be seen as a process of reverse glocalization, from a 'glocal' medieval world to a world in which one political authority, the territorial state, comes to dominate both the local and the global. And it is worth noting that the association of modern conditions with the medieval has been picked up before – see, for example, Hedley Bull's notion of neo-medievalism (Bull, 1977/1995).

It is perhaps unwise to generalize too freely, but it seems clear that the basis for medieval glocalism was twofold – an economy that could not sustain mid-size political units let alone very large ones, and a framework of ideas that, on the contrary, promoted universal categories and discouraged particularism. Conversely, it was economic growth in Braudel's long sixteenth century (c.1492–1648), combined with the decline of this framework of ideas, that undermined the old world (Braudel, 1972). Emphasis on the economy and the world of ideas is important here because it is clear that the impulse to create what came to be known as territorial states actually pre-dates the sixteenth century. Many medieval rulers attempted to create larger political units; on the whole they failed because circumstances were against them, but the ambition was there – and some succeeded in this ambition, at least in the short term. The Norman conquerors of England created an effective political unit – or perhaps inherited and improved one – that can claim to be the first Westphalian state ahead of its time, while in early thirteenth-century Sicily the Emperor Frederick II created the first absolutist monarchy, but was unable to hand it on to his heirs. In short, as writers as diverse as Michael Mann and Benno Teschke have stressed, the shift to a Westphalian world did not take place because rulers suddenly desired it to happen; it took place because the factors that previously had sabotaged their ambitions were slowly removed (Mann, 1986/1993; Teschke, 1998).

The importance of material as opposed to ideational factors here has been a subject of debate for a century or more; both were clearly involved and fed off each other (Tilly, 1975). To begin with the material, a key feature of medieval Europe was its comparative poverty – comparative to what had gone before and what was to come. The worldwide economy of the Roman Empire, which had sustained and been sustained by the political authority of Rome, was replaced by an essentially local economy in which the vast majority of people lived in villages or small estates or religious foundations, and grew the food which they ate; likewise small towns were fed by their surrounding countryside. Long-distance trade was minimal and based on luxury goods of one kind or another; the communications/transportation system that would have allowed more extensive trade did not exist and could not be created in the absence of a wider political authority: a kind of vicious circle was in place because the absence of such an authority was a function of the poverty of this world. The local economies were not creating the kind of surpluses that would allow rulers to build up an efficient apparatus for coercion and tax-gathering. The dominant military technology of the day was based on heavy, armoured, stirrup-using cavalry; sustaining such a force was expensive (the cavalryman needs a horse, remounts, armourers and grooms) and the standard way of paying for it was to give land to the cavalryman in return for service – which reinforced localism, because the local 'lord' ensconced within rudimentary but effective fortifications was able to determine when and if he would provide such services. Small towns had a similar capacity to defy nominal overlords – in the absence of efficient siege engines or the ability to keep a military force in the field for reasonable periods of time, rulers were generally unable to coerce effectively the walled medieval cities.

Medieval historians would, of course, qualify this general picture, pointing quite correctly to the enormous variation in conditions in medieval Europe at different times and in different places, but as the broadest of broad generalizations it remains the case that for much of the medieval era there are strong material obstacles to the creation of medium-sized let alone large political units. It is noteworthy that the two examples given above of proto-Westphalian polities were both the result of conquest. In Norman England and Norman Sicily the new rulers were able to impose duties upon the vassals to whom they gave the land they had conquered, not least because the new landlords were well aware that they were surrounded by a hostile local population – even so, within a relatively short period of time the kings of England were engaged in the same kind of contest with local landowners that their continental cousins were accustomed to.

The way in which Europe broke out of this vicious circle is still a matter for debate – with the respective roles of improvements in agricultural technology, the impact of the Black Death and, later, the effects of the European voyages of discovery as key issues – but break out it did, and a virtuous circle set in from the twelfth century onwards, with gradual economic growth over the next few centuries quickening in the 'long' sixteenth (Wallerstein, 1974). Greater wealth gave greater opportunities to rulers. The new larger surpluses that could be extracted from the villages enabled rulers to build up their coercive capacity, by, for example, the employment of professional soldiers and the development of gunpowder-based field artillery and siege engines. Anglo-Welsh longbowmen and Swiss pikemen between them undermined the supremacy of heavy cavalry. Even very rudimentary cannon were able to penetrate most medieval fortifications, and cannon-proof defence-works were beyond the financial capacities of most cities and local noblemen. Rulers of medium-sized territories became able to tax effectively in order to make war, and successful war-making increased the areas available to be taxed. As Charles Tilly has noted of the sixteenth century, war made the state and the state made war (Tilly, 1975). 'Medium-sized' is an important qualification here; the conditions did not exist to allow the re-creation of an imperial system in Europe – as the careers of the Emperor Charles V and King Philip II of Spain demonstrate, distance is still the enemy of the virtuous circle described above. Thus it is that, out of the medieval world, states, and not just one state, emerge.

The ideational component of both the medieval world view and the transition to Westphalia is, as always, a matter of dispute. As to the former, there can be no dispute that the church promoted an account of inclusion and exclusion that was based on religious identity and the idea of Christendom. Serf, lord, king and clergy were all, in principle, members of the one true church and no loyalty at any other level could be allowed to undermine that first premise of medieval Catholicism; the Pope, possessor of the authority of St Peter, could, again in principle, exclude from everlasting bliss anyone who tried to undermine this first premise. Moreover, the church as the largest landowner in Europe possessed a great deal of secular power to back up the spiritual. In addition, as the next section of this chapter will establish, medieval philosophy and notions of natural law, in so far as they could be divorced from theology, largely backed up the universalist notion of Christendom. What is much less clear is the extent to which the authority of the church was generally recognized. Medieval discussions of the matter concern the big issues of principle, and highlight key moments such as Henry IV's submission to the Pope at Canossa, but what of more mundane affairs? When England's King John was placed under interdiction by the Pope the people of England were unable to marry in church or to be buried in consecrated ground. The chroniclers tell us that this was a disastrous state of affairs, and John has been the archetypal 'bad king' ever since, but he ruled apparently successfully under the ban for many years and was eventually brought to heel as a side-effect of losing a struggle with his secular enemies, which suggests, not implausibly, that the clerical chroniclers may have had their own axe to grind.

As will be seen below, the Renaissance recovered the Roman heritage of active, republican citizenship, which was at odds with clerical universalism, and, crucially, the Protestant Reformation broke the unity of the church. The material and the ideational go together here; it does seem to have been the new commercial classes who became Protestants perhaps as a side-effect of literacy and the desire to read the Bible in the vernacular – although these tendencies were snuffed out where the Counter-Reformation was successful, in Italy and Flanders. Many rulers regarded Protestantism as an opportunity to confiscate church lands, and welcomed the freedom from external influence that it offered – it was, of course, England's Henry VIII who moved from being 'Defender of the Faith' to 'Supreme Head of the Church in England', famously as the result of the unwillingness of the Pope to give him an annulment of his first marriage. Even Catholic rulers welcomed the independence that the Reformation generated for all princes.

During the sixteenth century, the Reformation generated wars of religion out of which the Westphalia System emerged. The Westphalian territorial state involved a double-headed notion of 'sovereignty'; rulers were sovereign in so far as they accepted no internal equals and no external superiors, and to get to this point the claims of universal rulers had to be undermined (Hinsley, 1966). The Peace of 1648 was of some significance in this respect because it formally recognized the rights of the various elements of the Holy Roman Empire to conduct their international relations without reference to the Emperor, but this was not of great moment because the power of the Emperor had been divorced from ideational factors for a long time; emperors based their power on the material resources they could command, and would continue to do so for that matter. More important was the Peace of Augsburg of 1555, which (temporarily) brought to an end the first series of wars of religion in Germany. Here was established the principle – horrifying to the medieval mind – that the ruler (Catholic, Lutheran or Calvinist) was entitled to enforce religious uniformity within his realm (*cuius regio, ejus religio*). This is the key break with medieval political practice; the most anti-papalist ruler would not have made such a claim even fifty years before, and, for that matter, neither Lutheran nor Calvinist would willingly concede such a principle. Indeed, the revival of religious wars over the next eighty years suggested a very general reluctance to allow secular rulers this kind of power, and, as Stephen Krasner has recently emphasized, it is a striking – albeit little-noticed – feature of the Westphalia settlement of 1648 that it backs away somewhat from the implications of this claim and contains provision for the protection of religious minorities (Krasner, 1999).

The significance of the Peace of Westphalia is not so much that it established new principles, rather that after 1648 challenges to the principles that had been established over the previous century became few and far between. The wars of religion ended, perhaps as a result of exhaustion, possibly because, as the Thirty Years War had already demonstrated, power-political considerations frequently overrode religious concerns. Protestants and Catholics had found themselves occasional allies on both sides of the war, and the Pope himself had, on occasion, found it necessary to align with Protestant powers; this tendency became more advanced as time went by. By the end of the seventeenth century, the Pope was part of a broad anti-French coalition that encompassed Protestant and Catholic powers (including such staunchly Calvinist figures as William of Orange). In short, the universal claims of church and empire were no more, although the latter would continue in name until ended by Napoleon a century later, and F. H. Hinsley has argued that it took as long for the idea of Europe as essentially one finally to fade (Hinsley, 1963). *Pace* Hinsley, after the mid-seventeenth century we enter into a new world and it is time now to examine some of the thinkers who helped to create that world.

Sovereignty, natural law and the law of nations

Another broad generalization: with perhaps one important exception, the notion of sovereignty as absolute power does not feature in medieval thought. Certainly there are struggles between church and empire, but even the most extreme papalist does not deny that there should be some kind of secular sphere, and the imperialists similarly have no objection to spiritual authority where it is appropriate. Practical feudal politics are all about the dispersal of power, and this position is endorsed by Aquinas and the Schoolmen, who saw natural law and their inheritance from Aristotle as supportive of mixed forms of government and opposed to any concentration of power, much less territorially based concentrations of power. And yet, during the long sixteenth century the doctrine of sovereignty as absolute power does emerge from the pens of Jean Bodin and Thomas Hobbes, and the intellectual descendants of Aristotle and the Schoolmen gradually transform themselves from natural lawyers in the medieval sense of the term into proponents of the 'law of nations', and, eventually, after a renaming by Jeremy Bentham, to 'international lawyers' (Hobbes, 1946; Bentham, 1960, p. 426; Bodin, 1992). How and why does this shift come about?

One possible materialist answer is that the emergence of the doctrine of sovereignty is a response to the troubles of the time – Bodin explicitly advocates political sovereignty as the only remedy for the wars of religion in France, and Hobbes is equally obviously influenced by the troubles of his era, the Civil War in England and the Thirty Years War in Germany. The problem with this, apparently rather plausible, explanation is that it is clearly incomplete; times of trouble were not uncommon in the high Middle Ages, nor was the solution of a strong leader who would establish order, but in, say, the twelfth century such a state of affairs did not produce the doctrine of sovereignty, whereas in the sixteenth it did. There is something else going on here that needs to be pinned down. What is different about this period in the realm of ideas?

One factor of possible significance has already been alluded to in passing – the single exception to the medieval rejection of the notion of sovereignty as absolute power, which, as might have been anticipated, concerns the sovereignty of God. For the Christian, God is omnipotent – all-powerful – by definition, but the scholastic tradition holds that God exercises this power in accordance with natural law and right reason; God is not arbitrary in His commands, although we may not always understand His reasoning. In the early fourteenth century, William of Ockham proposed an alternative account of God's commands as an expression of his sovereign will, and rejects the notion that this will can be in any way contained by natural law or reason (Coleman, 2000). God's will is the law not because it is right but because it is His will; we should not obey because we think we understand God's will or because, supreme presumption, we agree with his commands as consonant with the supreme good, rather because it is His will that we should obey and we trust that He is good. The parallel between Hobbes's argument in particular and William's is striking: it is central for Hobbes that there is no supreme good, *'summum bonum'*, as the (Aristotelian) philosophers had argued, and therefore we rely upon a sovereign to issue commands (Hobbes, 1946, p. 63). It is not too much of an exaggeration to say that the tradition of legal positivism – law as the command of the sovereign – owes much to William of Ockham (Connolly, 1988).

For all the importance of William's 'nominalism' for political thought in this period, the main factor in shaping the discourse of sovereignty and reshaping the notion of natural law stems from a different source, namely the reception of Roman political and legal thought associated with the Renaissance and the rise of humanism (Carroll, 1993; Tuck, 1999). The great medieval philosophers largely drew on Greek thought – especially Aristotle – albeit via Latin translations, but in the late fifteenth and sixteenth centuries a newly literate non-clerical group of intellectuals began to read the Romans in much greater depth, especially Roman republicans such as Cicero, but also Roman jurists and historians. This reading is influential in two important respects.

First, the Roman legal notion of property was highly influential. For the Romans property was absolute. If you owned something that meant it was yours to do what you like with – unless you use it to harm someone else, in which case there might be a lawsuit. For example, infamously, in Roman law the father of the family has this kind of *dominium* over its members, the landowner over the land he owns, and, later, the Emperor over the Empire itself. This is dramatically different from the feudal notion of property where every piece of land is, in principle, held subject to the performance of duties and cannot be disposed of without the approval of the overlord. The point about the Roman notion of property – *dominium* – is that it provides a model of sovereignty for the new princes of the Westphalia era. As Friedrich Kratochwil has argued in an important paper on non-intervention, the new sovereigns regarded their territory as their property, and the system as a whole as a system of property ownership (Kratochwil, 1995). On the one hand, this meant that they claimed the right to do what they wanted within their territory without external interference; on the other, it meant that as property-owners they also defended in principle the rights of other property-owners to do what they wanted with *their* property. What we have here is a new set of rules of the game; the medieval approach to political power stresses that rulers have rights and duties – they are, in principle, stewards of the land and their use of their stewardship is subject to external evaluation in accordance with natural law and right reason. The new rules remove these restrictions, although they still require of property-owners that they respect each other's property.

The Roman influence makes itself felt in a second, less legalistic, way. For the medievals, influenced by Greek thought and, especially, notions of natural law, violence between political communities is always to be regretted, although it may occasionally be necessary. It is normal for peoples to live in peace and under conditions of justice, and violence is only justified under very limited circumstances – essentially, if and only if the innocent are protected, and there is a reasonable prospect that, by violence and in no other way, a wrong can be righted. The 'Just War', theorized by Aquinas and others, fleshes out this account, and will be discussed in greater detail later in this book. It was clear that medieval rulers frequently flouted these principles, but the latter were believed to be endorsed by philosophical authorities such as Plato and Aristotle, as well as by the requirements of Christianity – indeed, for some Christians the issue was whether war could ever be seen as just given the apparent pacifism of Jesus and the early church. The general view, post-Augustine, was that the proper authorities had the authority, in certain circumstances, to make war, but that these circumstances were defined in a very restricted way.

The Romans saw things rather differently, as was apparent from their historians, Livy and Tacitus. The Roman Republic was an expansionist polity, and although, in principle, the Senate and people required a reason for war and unprovoked aggression was condemned, militant patriotism meant that what constituted a sufficient reason for war was defined very loosely. In particular, pre-emptive and perhaps preventative war was justified – in other words, it could be right to make war even if there was no immediate cause, save that it seems likely that in the not too distant future the city or state in question would pose a threat to the security of the Republic. In general, Rome placed more emphasis on the military virtues than Greece – although if the Spartans had produced books of philosophy a different picture might have emerged.

By no means every 'humanist' – as those Renaissance figures whose attention was drawn away from God towards a more earthly focus of interest by their reading of the classics were termed – picked up this bellicose lesson from Rome, but Richard Tuck has recently made a compelling case for the proposition that some did, and that during the long sixteenth century and beyond there was a running contest between natural lawyers, who preserved the scholastic notion of the common interest in peace and justice as a starting point, and the humanists, who were much more favourable to the particularistic claims of the new sovereign states (Tuck, 1999). The key figures who usually feature as the founders of the law of nations in this period appear on both sides of the divide. Thus, in the sixteenth century, the Dominicans of the Salamanca School – Francisco di Vitoria and Tomas Suarez – broadly defend the rights of the original inhabitants of Spanish America against the claims of the Spanish Crown on the basis that it is not simply relations between Christian rulers that are bound by natural law. This makes them important figures in the history of the law of nations, inadvertently contributing to its secularization, but they cast their defence in terms which are essentially medieval and pre-humanist. Their near-contemporary, Alberto Gentili, an Italian Protestant who, for health reasons no doubt, found himself a professorship at Oxford, is much more supportive of the idea that the sovereign is entitled to make war if he thinks it appropriate, a position that derives from Roman thought and is much closer to what will become the Westphalian norm.

A similar position, argues Tuck, is taken by Hugo de Groot – Grotius – the figure who, more than any other, is most often identified as the father of international law. Grotius is a natural lawyer, but the foundations of natural law are, for Grotius, to be found in the right of self-preservation and the right to own property. Natural law is not about human sociality and the common good, except in so far as the latter is defined in terms of the mutual possession of these rights. These rights are possessed by individuals, and, by extension, by states. When individuals enter into civil society they do not give up these rights – indeed, the role of civil society is to protect these rights, and if it fails to do so, individuals may act on their own behalf. States, in any event, are not in civil society and therefore possess the untrammelled right to protect themselves. It is customary to contrast Grotius's notion of the pre-civil 'state of nature' with that of Hobbes, the argument being that the former is a rather less daunting place than the latter, and thus can more easily be seen to support rules and norms. It is on this basis that some 'English School' theorists identify a Grotian approach to international society as a kind of middle way between realist and revolutionary thought (Wight, 1991). Tuck, on the other hand, argues that Grotius and Hobbes are in substantive agreement on such issues – only the terms they use are different, the underlying meaning is the same. Both reject the older notion of natural law as the expression of a common good for humanity, turning it instead into a set of natural rights.

For Grotius, natural law is a morality based on coexistence between self-regarding individuals (Nardin, in C. Brown et al., 2002).* Non-interference in each other's affairs is the basic tenet here and this is transferred to international relations in *The Laws of War and Peace*, one of the founding texts of the Westphalia System. States have a right of self-defence in all circumstances, not simply a right of defence against direct attack, but a more general right to preserve their security, which might involve pre-emption, and the right to punish offenders. On the other hand, Grotius does not regard all wars as just, and does not make a distinction – which would become important at a later stage – between *ius ad bellum* and *ius in bello*. An unjust war, one not fought for reasons of self-defence broadly defined or to punish wrongdoing, cannot be fought justly. In this at least, Grotius remains distant from later Westphalian thinking. On the other hand, he has gone a long way from medieval conceptions of natural law – too far, according to the lawyer Samuel Pufendorf. Pufendorf accepts the shift of natural rights, but stresses duties as well as rights including, crucially, a duty of bene-volence. The moral law, he asserts, cannot simply rest upon a selfish understanding of rights – there must be some other factor if the rela-tions of persons, and states, are not to be understood as taking place in a moral vacuum.

Vitoria, Suarez, Gentili, Grotius and Pufendorf are often taken to be the founders of international law, but none would have seen them-selves in quite this way, although the last three wrote extensively on international topics. They saw themselves as natural lawyers, albeit each understanding something different by that term, and their work on the relations of states emerged from their wider interest in natural law. They were succeeded, however, by figures who were much more directly concerned with the law of nations, which they regarded as dif-ficult to divorce from the idea of a 'society of states'.

The law of nations and the society of states

On most accounts – and here – the next two names on the above list will be those of Christian Wolff and Emeric de Vattel. These two figures complete the story of the foundation of the law of nations, but they do

* For extended extracts from the work of the founders of the law of nations – Grotius to Vattel – readers are referred to C. Brown et al. (2002); the commentary that follows draws heavily on Terry Nardin's introductions of the relevant chapters of that volume.

so from a somewhat different position from that of their predecessors. Wolff is a philosopher, Vattel a publicist, and each is concerned with the philosophy and practice of international relations in a way that their forerunners are not. Wolff applies natural law, but natural law as applied to nations, which he sees as a separate branch of natural law; Vattel sets out the law, but is also concerned with diplomatic practice. He more than any other sets out in formal terms the nature of the Westphalia System and is widely regarded as the key figure in the study of international society (Bull, 1977/1995).

Wolff's major contribution is his conception of foundations of 'international' law – this term was still to be coined by Bentham fifty years or more after Wolff wrote, but is no longer unsuitable as shorthand – the construct of a universal state (*civitas maxima*). In the words of Terry Nardin, 'we must imagine that states comprise a society governed by natural law, and that this natural society of states constitutes a universal state . . . [in] other words, all states, considered collectively, must be imagined to hold a kind of sovereignty over each state considered individually' (C. Brown et al., 2002, p. 321). International law is an authoritative body of rules that govern the relations of individual states, and in the absence of a real sovereign who could declare and interpret these rules, it is necessary to posit a fictional collective sovereign. This is an ingenious solution to what might otherwise seem a very difficult problem, and a solution that, as we will see, Edmund Burke was to pick up on later in the century.

Vattel's *Law of Nations* is a different sort of enterprise, still connected to the project of natural law but less philosophically oriented, more attuned to diplomatic practice. The natural law element remains present because he is unwilling simply to rest the foundations of international law on diplomatic custom and state treaties. There must be, he argues, some reference point beyond this against which custom and treaty can be judged – it is only when this requirement is abandoned that international law will become positive law, a development that does not take place till the nineteenth century. However, in many respects Vattel leaves conventional natural law further behind than any of his aforementioned predecessors. The equality of states, the legitimacy of the balance of power and thus of anti-hegemonic warfare, and the distinction between *ius ad bellum* and *ius in bello* are all central features of Westphalian international political discourse that are absent in previous discussions but present in Vattel's work. The legal principle of sovereign equality, still enshrined in bodies such as the UN, is established by analogy with the natural equality of persons ('a dwarf is as much a man as a giant is') and reflects diplomatic practice and protocol whereby ruling princes are accorded respect and address each other as fraternal equals, irrespective of the size of their domains. The prin-

ciple of sovereign equality is preserved by the prevention of the hegemony of any one state, hegemony is prevented by the balance of power
and the balance of power may justly be preserved even by preventive
war. International law is not suspended by the outbreak of war; legal
equality implies that the laws of war apply to all, regardless of issues
of *ius ad bellum* – the soldiers of an unjust ruler are as entitled to its protection as those of the just. All this is very much the basis for Westphalian thought, and a codification of Westphalian practice.

Vattel provides the first full-scale, philosophically informed defence
of what came to be known at the end of the twentieth century as the
'morality of states' – an approach which posits that the states which
make up the Westphalia System relate to each other in moral terms
and not simply as fellow power-holders (Vincent, 1986). His is also the
last such defence of this position for 200 years. After Vattel, the dominant position of international lawyers is to codify state practice and
treaty law; international law becomes a positive discourse, reflecting
what states do rather than providing either a justification or a critique
of state practice. Until recently, most textbooks on international law
have begun with a quick run-through of the sources of international
law in which natural law is mentioned in passing, and generally contained an equally brief consideration of whether, in the absence of an
international sovereign, international law was really law – but that
has been the extent of concern with the philosophical issues involved.
Neither have such philosophical issues migrated to political philosophy proper, at least not in the form of a discussion of the morality of
states. As will be established in the next chapter, there have been a great
many philosophical critics of the notion of a society of states, but far
fewer defenders.

Perhaps the major figure of the next 200 years who does provide an
elaboration of Vattel's picture of a society of states is Edmund Burke.
Towards the end of his life Burke became the most articulate of British
opponents of the French Revolution, and in this role in his *Letters on a
Regicide Peace* he set out an account of international society in strikingly
Vattelian terms (Burke, 1906; Welsh, 1995). Prior to the Revolution, he
argues, the states of Europe formed 'one great republic' under what
was, in effect, a common system of laws and custom – this the French
revolutionaries have undermined, and hence intervention against them
is justified. Here Wolff's philosophical construct of a *civitas maxima* is
treated as though it were a reality. Burke is, of course, well aware of
the frequent wars that characterized the society of states in the eighteenth century but seems to regard them as of little consequence to the
main argument. The victims of these wars might have demurred, but
there is some justification for this position, in so far as private citizens
of the aristocratic and bourgeois classes did regard war as a matter for

kings and no concern of theirs. The ultimate expression of this attitude is to be found in the comic novelist Laurence Sterne's *A Sentimental Journey*, where the narrator turns up at Dover for a trip to the Continent claiming to have forgotten that France and Britain were at war. He makes the trip to Paris anyway in the entourage of a French nobleman who has been visiting London (Sterne, 1967). Perhaps Burke realizes that this sort of relaxed attitude will not survive the arrival of a people's war (although it is noteworthy that throughout the Revolutionary and Napoleonic Wars a packet-boat maintained a regular service under a flag of truce between Dover and Calais, and scientific congresses were held in Paris at which British participants were given safe-conducts to attend, so the old civilities were not entirely lost).

Burke is an interesting figure in so far as he links the possible existence of a society of states to a common background culture. On his account, international society works in the eighteenth century because the states who make up its members share a common cultural and religious background. 'Christendom' is still a reality; the shared values of Christian princes (and well-behaved republics such as Venice and the United Provinces) provide the basis for a degree of sociality that the rules of the system taken on their own cannot. In this sense, even if the French revolutionaries were sincerely to commit themselves to the rules of diplomacy and international law, their commitment would be of little value because they did not share the presuppositions upon which those rules and that law are based. Co-existence and non-interference are possible only for those who share such presuppositions. This is an interesting position which will become of much greater significance in the twentieth century; for all Burke's protestations, the French revolutionaries were as European as he was, as much steeped in European culture, even Christian culture, as their opponents. The real test of Burke's position would come when the European states-system became a global system and multicultural – at this point the issue of whether a system of co-existence could operate in a world where there are genuinely radically different conceptions of the Good would become a live issue.

Conclusion: was the Westphalia System really 'Westphalian'?

With the exception of Burke, the writers who fill out the notion of a society of states in the eighteenth and nineteenth centuries do not raise new issues or highlight old problems. By the mid-eighteenth century the norms and principles of the Westphalia System have been identi-

fied, and the most interesting work in international political theory
is coming from writers who reject these norms, or support them on a
different basis – these Enlightenment and post-Enlightenment figures
will be the subject of the next chapter. Here it may be helpful first to
summarize these norms, and then to examine the extent to which these
norms were actually operative in the international relations of the
period.

The Westphalian norms are easy to summarize. The actors in the
Westphalia System are sovereign states – territorial polities whose
rulers acknowledge no equal at home, no superior abroad; except in
very exceptional and restricted circumstances, individual human
beings have no standing in international society. States are legally
equal, differing in capabilities ('Great Powers, Medium Powers, Small
Powers') but with the same standing in international society, which
means that the norm of non-intervention is central – no sovereign has
the right to intervene in the affairs of another. Non-aggression is a norm
of the system; states are, however, entitled to defend themselves
directly and, by extension, to act collectively to prevent any one state
from achieving dominance. Procedural rules exist in international
society governing the practice of diplomacy and such matters as the
making of treaties, and these rules are authoritatively binding upon all
members of international society. Two factors immediately come to
mind about these norms. First, they are unique; no previous 'international' system developed an elaborate set of norms of this kind. Second,
they still largely dominate the official self-understanding of the twenty-
first-century international system. As we will see, contemporary international law is more willing to assign legal status to individuals than
the above summary would suggest, and the UN Charter restricts the
right of self-defence to a right to respond to a direct attack – preserving the balance of power is no longer even a semi-official norm of international society – but in other respects the above list describes the
official normative basis of contemporary international relations. This,
of course, is why this book has begun with this period of international
thought rather than any other.

Given this contemporary relevance, a question that might otherwise
seem academic is actually of considerable significance. Were these
norms ever actually the guiding principles of Westphalian political
practice? These might be the way the system described itself, but did
they actually correspond to the way in which the system worked?
Recently a number of writers have suggested that they did not, most
vehemently Stephen Krasner, the title of whose recent book laconically
summarizes its thesis: *Sovereignty: Organized Hypocrisy* (1999). Krasner
helpfully distinguished a number of different meanings of sovereignty,
arguing for example that the ability to control cross-border transactions

is rather different from the ability to govern domestically. However, his central point is that the norm of sovereignty and its corollary, the norm of non-intervention, contradict the *actual* first principle of the system, which he takes to be the realist notion of 'self-help'. Rulers are motivated above all else to preserve themselves and will do whatever they need to do to achieve this end, including violating the so-called norm of non-intervention if this is what self-preservation requires. The idea that sovereignty constitutes a norm of the Westphalia System can only be taken seriously if the actual practice of the system is ignored. States have always intervened in each other's affairs whenever they have felt the need to do so, whether for 'humanitarian' or purely selfish reasons – a proposition that is backed up by a wealth of detail.

It is difficult to deny that intervention as opposed to non-intervention has been the underlying theme of actual state conduct in the Westphalia System; apart from Krasner's empirical work, there have been a number of other studies making the same basic point (for example, Barkun and Cronin, 1994). The question is whether or not these empirical observations are to the point, whether they capture the nature of norms in this, or for that matter any other similar, social situation. One fruitful approach to norms is to treat them as the equivalent of the rules of a Wittgensteinian game; Friedrich Kratochwil's brand of constructivism, already met above in the context of sovereignty as *dominium*, is particularly relevant here (Kratochwil, 1989 and 1995). On this account, sovereignty is a *constitutive* rule of international society, rather than a rule that is supposed to regulate a pre-existing society of states, which is, roughly speaking, the basis upon which Krasner criticizes the concept. To claim to be sovereign is to assert a claim to valid authority in accordance with rules without which international society could not exist; hence, even when actually intervening, the rulers of states are obliged to explain how their behaviour can be understood in terms of the rules (for example, as misunderstood, or as a justified exception). They offer such explanations, not, as Krasner suggests, as a matter of hypocrisy, but because failure to do so would, as it were, end the 'game', and, at the same time, end their capacity to claim the status of sovereign since this status only exists by virtue of the existence of international society. Since most rulers do not wish to surrender their claim to sovereignty, they cannot simply declare that they could and would do anything they could get away with in order to further their interests. There have been rulers who have made such claims, but figures such as Adolf Hitler are, fortunately, unusual and exceptional. More usually, such declarations are not made, and this is why international society can be seen as norm-governed.

Krasner's response to this line of reasoning is that the Westphalia System is not a game and therefore has no constitutive rules (Krasner,

1999, p. 229). This is somewhat to miss the point; the game-like quality of the Westphalia System is not an attribute that could be observed in the real world, which seems to be how Krasner wishes to treat it – rather the Westphalia System is a game because it is played as such. There are basic epistemological and ontological questions being raised here, but, perhaps fortunately, it is not necessary to go into much further detail on this matter. The discursive force of the norms of the Westphalia System is not ultimately dependent upon the extent to which they guide actual practice, although if they had no influence at all it would be hard to hold this position. Such is not the case – there is certainly enough connection between the norms of the system and state conduct to allow us to move on.

3

Enlightenment and Post-Enlightenment International Thought

Introduction

The transition to the Westphalian political order was accompanied by shifts in thought that moved from a critical stance to a general acceptance of the legitimacy of a system of sovereign states. Natural lawyers such as Grotius and Pufendorf preserved a degree of distance from the norms of the new system even while validating some of the underlying presuppositions of these norms, but by the time of Wolff and Vattel there is no longer much in the way of a critical edge to the writings of the international lawyers. Vattel presents an idealized picture of the actual diplomacy of his era (the early/mid-eighteenth century) in a more or less uncritical manner, while Wolff's account of the *civitas maxima* is designed to explain the underlying rationale of the system rather than to expose the extent to which the society of states falls short of a morally desirable world. Similarly, Burke's critique of the international politics of republican France rests on the supposition that pre-revolutionary international society was, more or less, the best of all possible worlds. There might be some disagreement as to whether the society of states constituted a 'second-best' solution to world order, or was actually the best way to preserve the 'liberties' of Europe, that is, to allow states to develop in their own way within a common framework of values, but, either way, a critical edge was not much in evidence (C. Brown, 1995a).

With the thinkers of the Enlightenment and their successors, this rather self-satisfied acceptance of the status quo disappeared, and a critical edge was restored to international thought. Many, perhaps most, Enlightenment figures regarded the society of states as a poor kind of substitute for a proper society of all human beings, and the defenders of international society as 'sorry comforters', to use Kant's phrase, whose thought is designed to reconcile us to suffering (Reiss, 1970, p. 104). Other thinkers accepted the basic idea of a system of independent units but wished to reshape the units in question to respond to a new ordering principle, that of 'nationality'. Still others responded to the changes in material life that were so obvious to contemporaries in the nineteenth century and after, and contemplated the apparent lack of fit between a system of independent states and an increasingly interdependent world economy; this lack of fit has, of course, become even more apparent in the late twentieth and early twenty-first centuries. And yet, the Westphalia System endures; in spite of two centuries of critiques from all directions, it is fascinating that an essentially Vattelian account of international society is still one of the major schools of thought in the discourse of International Relations. How is this resilience to be understood?

It may seem strange to address this question at this stage of the argument, but there seems little point in pretending ignorance of the system's survival when presenting the critical positions set out in what follows; in any event, there is one particular point about the survival of the system that will not come up in discussion. Most of the debates between, for example, Kant and his critics, or Cobden and his, focus on whether the Westphalia System *deserved* (and deserves) to survive, whether it was/is the best way of arranging human affairs or meeting basic human needs. However, the most important reason for the survival of the system may be simply the fact that once this particular way of organizing the world's surface is established it is very difficult to shift – there is, in short, a 'lock-in' effect, whereby an initial arrangement effectively maintains itself over time, even in circumstances where the reasons for the arrangement no longer apply, because the costs of change are prohibitively high. A nice example is the 'qwerty' keyboard, which has now survived for 150 years.* This particular layout of keys dates from the time when typewriters were mechanically unreliable; the 'qwerty' arrangement of letters was designed to *slow down* the speed of typing in order to prevent jams. Such an arrangement is no longer necessary, mechanical keys being long gone, but the arrangement survives because, once established as the industry standard, it is virtually impossible to shift.

A similar line of reasoning might be applied to many proposals for international reform. When Frederick the Great of Prussia remarked of the Abbé de St-Pierre's proposal for a system of perpetual peace, that all it requires for its success was the 'consent of Europe and a few similar trifles', he was drawing attention to the extent to which the Westphalia System was locked in – and, of course, making the kind of

* I owe this example to Stefan Rossbach.

smart remark designed to encourage intellectual friends such as Voltaire to overlook the despotic nature of his rule (Hinsley, 1963, p. 45). More prosaically, many of the debates about the relationship between industrial capitalism and the Westphalia System assume that the former, in some sense, chose the latter, or, perhaps, was chosen by it, whereas in fact the Westphalia System was a 'given' for capitalists. Capitalism developed within a system of independent states because that was the only system there was in Europe at the time in question (Lacher, 2000). There was no element of choice involved. Similarly, in the late twentieth century it was often said that the system of sovereignty was not appropriate for many of the new nations created after the fall of colonialism – but again there was no effective choice here, given the way in which the sovereignty system had eliminated alternative ways of politically organizing the surface of the earth.

In short, in examining the international thought of this period it is important not to assume that ideational factors are more important than they actually were. Ideas were important in the establishment of the Westphalia System, but once the system was up and running it took on a life of its own – as is still apparent in the twenty-first century. Nonetheless, the effective running of the system did depend on the extent to which it was regarded as legitimate, and although the basic outline of the system was a 'lock-in', there were still many other features that were open to change.

The Enlightenment and cosmopolitanism

Defining the Enlightenment is notoriously difficult. In the late twentieth century, talk of the 'Enlightenment Project' was commonplace, the general idea being that the core Enlightenment belief was in human emancipation via the growth of knowledge – a belief encapsulated in Kant's famous answer to the question 'What is Enlightenment?': 'humanity's emergence from self-immaturity' (Reiss, 1970, p. 54; cf. Foucault, 1986). However, if understood politically, the progressivist implications of 'emancipation' give only a partial account of the thought of the period. Enlightened figures such as David Hume and Edward Gibbon certainly were opponents of superstition, but they were hardly concerned with emancipation in any political sense; in the same way Wolff and Vattel, conservative theorists of international society, were also as much figures of the Enlightenment as their more radical contemporaries and successors, such as Voltaire or Immanuel Kant.

The factor common to all of these writers – including, interestingly, Wolff and Vattel – and common to the Enlightenment as a whole, is a basically *cosmopolitan* attitude to international affairs and the West-phalian division of the world into sovereign states. A brief historical digression is necessary here. The original 'cosmopolitans' were a product of post-Aristotelian philosophy in the Hellenic world; Dio-genes the Cynic was, apparently, the first person to describe himself as a *cosmopolites* (citizen of the world), and the Stoics famously also adopted this label – including the Stoic Roman Emperor, Marcus Aure-lius (Nussbaum, 1997). This original self-designation emerged in a period when the form of political identity previously dominant in the Greek world, that of a citizen of a *polis*, had been rendered meaningless by the rise of the Macedonian Empire, and later Rome, and the conse-quent loss by the cities of the capacity for self-rule (C. Brown, 2000c). To be the citizen of a Greek city had meant being part of a self-governing fellowship which defined one's identity not just as a political animal, but indeed as a human being. Once this identity was no longer open, the way was clear for a counter-assertion – that one was a citizen of the whole world, regarding all humanity as one's fellows, although it is important to notice that this fellowship is *not* self-governing. The world of which one is a citizen is not like a city in this crucial respect; in so far as there is a world government it is not one in which citizens govern themselves and each other, and a cosmopolitan perspective on world affairs does not require that it be so – the fact that one of the leading cosmopolitans is an emperor makes this point very clearly. Marcus considers himself to be ruling in the interests of the world as a whole, but the world as a whole does not rule; he does. The opposite of a cosmopolitan is not so much the citizen of a city in the old sense of the term – because such cities no longer exist – but rather the patriot, the figure who gives his loyalty to some sub-division of humanity, although in the age of the Antonines the scope of the Roman Empire was so all-inclusive (in Europe at least) that to be a Roman patriot and a cos-mopolitan was a more plausible stance than it would become later.

The dominant attitude of the clerical elite throughout the Middle Ages was, in principle, cosmopolitan, partly for doctrinal reasons, but also because of the absence of any practical alternative, given the gen-erally unattractive nature of the rulers thrown up by feudalism. A certain local pride might be possible, but it was not until the rise of the Italian city-states and the concurrent revival of humanism that a serious alternative to cosmopolitanism emerged. The republican tradition, exemplified by Machiavelli, placed local, particularistic loyalty – to Florence or, perhaps, Italy – above the general good, and, albeit in a somewhat modified form, the theoretical defenders of sovereignty continued this tradition. As noted in chapter 2, the contest between scholastic and humanist conceptions of the requirements of natural law eventually brought forth the idea of a society of states, which combines both republican and cosmopolitan elements. The endorsement of sovereignty was clearly anti-cosmopolitan, but the cosmopolitan element was present in the notion of a *civitas maxima*. Figures such as Wolff and Vattel were clearly cosmopolitan in their promotion of the social element of a society of states, and the more conservatively Enlightened, such as Hume and Gibbon, approved of this endorsement.

Nonetheless, the cosmopolitanism of the majority of the Enlightened was not satisfied by the idea of a society of states; acceptance of such a society involved acceptance of the legitimacy of inter-state war, and, *pace* the allegedly civilized nature of mid-eighteenth-century warfare, war was still a destructive force which was rightly regarded with horror by the majority of right-thinking folk. From out of this rejection of war came one of the characteristic Enlightenment approaches to international affairs, the 'Peace Project' – a blueprint for international peace and harmony which usually involved the creation of a European-wide assembly at which representatives of the peoples of Europe, or perhaps of their rulers, would resolve the issues of the day without resort to war. The most famous of these projects, the *Project for Perpetual Peace* of the Abbé de St-Pierre, a French cleric and diplomat, was produced in 1713, and was the subject of commentaries by many of the key figures of the Enlightenment (C. Brown et al., 2002). The most important of these commentators was also the most important cosmopolitan thinker of his era and one of the key figures in international political theory, Immanuel Kant. We will return to the general subject of cosmopolitanism below, but first a somewhat more extended consideration of Kant's work, so important for late twentieth-century cosmopolitanism, is required.

Kant and *Perpetual Peace*

The feature of Kant's work that makes him one of the two or three most important figures of the Enlightenment is also the feature that makes him central to the development of international political theory, and that is his aspiration to formulate a coherent and consistent account of the moral and social world, taken as a whole. This entailed providing an account of: the moral law as it applied to individuals in their personal behaviour and in their social relations; the political framework within which social relations based on the moral law could take place; and, crucially, the relations *between* polities that needed to exist if a moral life is to be possible. It is this last stage of the argument that is distinctive; Kant is the first great modern political philosopher to realize that the question of international relations cannot be sidestepped. Whereas Hobbes, Locke and even Rousseau develop accounts of politics within bounded polities, and deal with the relations of these polities via asides, *obiter dicta* and minor works, Kant realized that this was not good enough. His thoughts on international relations are central to his thoughts on politics in general, and his works of international political theory completed his system (Bohnman and Lutz-Bachmann, 1977; Riley, 1983; Williams, 1983; Rengger, 1988; Hurrell, 1990).

The importance of Kant's thought on international relations is often underestimated because of the format he chooses for some of his key works on the subject – see, for example, F. H. Hinsley's generally dismissive account, and Martin Wight's misdescription of Kant as a 'revolutionary' (Hinsley, 1963; Wight, 1991). The most famous of these – *Perpetual Peace: A Philosophic Sketch* – appears on the surface to be simply the latest in a long line of eighteenth-century peace projects, complete with a series of 'provisional' and 'definitive' articles laying down the law for the princes of Europe; others, such as the *Sketch for a Universal History from a Cosmopolitan Point of View*, seem to be occasional and somewhat lightweight (Reiss, 1970). These impressions are misleading; these texts are remarkably subtle pieces of work, but the subtlety can only be discerned once they are read in the context of Kant's wider project. To understand this it is necessary to take a step or two back from these overtly 'international' texts in order to grasp the general features of Kant's political theory, beginning with his account of the moral life.

For Kant, morality is a matter of employing reason to choose principles of action ('maxims') that reflect the demands of duty. We can tell what those maxims are, and distinguish them from mere rationalizations of our interests, because we have within us an innate knowledge of the moral law, the 'categorical imperative'. The content of this imperative is outlined in the *Groundwork of the Metaphysics of Morals*; it ought to be possible to universalize moral maxims, that is, they ought to form the basis for a universal law; they must involve treating humanity (other humans and oneself) as ends and not simply as means to an end, and they must form the basis for a political order in which rational agents are subject to laws they themselves make – the first of these three formulations, Kant believes, actually contains the others, and so 'act on the maxim that can at the same time be made a universal law' is the shortest summary of the categorical imperative. The moral law, it should be noted, binds *all* rational beings, laying the same obligation on all. Morality is about the exercise of good will, doing the right thing and for the right reason; because of this latter point, the political realm cannot make us behave morally, but a properly constituted political and legal order can make it *possible* for us to behave morally, and, by obliging us to obey just laws, can produce a world in which human beings behave as they would behave if they were, indeed, governed by the moral law. Morality is a matter of choice, and if people do the right thing simply because it is the law rather than because they know it is the right thing to do, they are not behaving morally – but the end result is much the same. In this world, a true 'kingdom of ends' could not be achieved – Kant holds traditional Christian views on 'original sin' – but a properly constituted political order can provide the context for a life lived in accordance with morality.

A properly constituted political order is 'republican', that is, based on justice (*Recht*, a combination of the English notions of justice and law), political equality and the rule of law; despotism – including the despotism of the majority in a democracy – takes away from the individual their position as co-legislator, co-creator of the law that binds them, and the only restrictions on freedom permissible are those required in order that freedom can be general. To avoid despotism, the separation of powers, the legislature from the executive, is crucial. The state's role is important, but essentially negative – it cannot make people moral, or happy, but it can provide the framework within which morality and happiness are possible. Much of this represents a quite standard Enlightenment political programme, but what is more unusual is Kant's insistence that the rule of law must be extended to the relations of states if it is to be operative domestically. War is the consequence of the absence of the rule of law internationally and war undermines a properly constituted political order both directly, by the human misery it causes, and indirectly, because war promotes despotic rule. Hobbes is quite wrong to think that the implications of an international 'state of nature' can be mitigated by effective domestic governments alone (Hobbes, 1946, p. 83). International relations must be brought within the framework of law.

One way of doing this would be to create a single world republic, but Kant rejects this step for a variety of reasons, the relative importance of which are still debated (Laberge, 1998). Sometimes it seems that Kant argues that a world republic would be unmanageable (laws losing their force at a distance) and, in any event, unnecessary, but the main argument he offers is that it would be unachievable, because it is not currently the 'will of nations' – which, perhaps, is another way of recognizing the 'lock-in' effect noted in the introduction to this chapter (Reiss, 1970, p. 106). In any event, Kant's solution is essentially statist; the rule of law internationally is to be achieved in a world of states, but states of a particular kind. The argument of *Perpetual Peace* can now be presented. The first part of *Perpetual Peace* sets out the appropriate legal principles for a non-ideal world in which war is still a feature of international relations; these Provisional Articles are designed to nudge relations in a peaceful direction by interdicting the kind of practices in war which create continuing enmity between peoples and outlawing the sort of provisions in peace treaties that provide the reasons for the next war – in fact, they are very much the principles upon which the UN is founded and our contemporary international legal order is based. The innovation comes in the second part of *Perpetual Peace*, where the Definitive Articles are set out; there are three of these only: 1. that the civil constitution of every state shall be republican (in the sense noted above), 2. that the international order shall be based on a federation of free states, which would abolish war amongst themselves, and 3. that cosmopolitan obligations should be limited to universal hospitality, the right of the stranger not to be treated with hostility.

On the face of it this may seem a strange set of articles, but it is, in fact, complete. The three relationships which need to be covered are covered thereby; the relationship of the individual to their own state (*ius civitatis,* civil right/law, sc. *Recht*), the relationship of polities to each other (*ius gentium*, international right/law), and the relationship of states and individuals to each other that follows by virtue of their common membership of the universal state of mankind (*ius cosmopoliticum*, cosmopolitan right/law) (Reiss, 1970, p. 98). As to *ius civilis*, a republican constitution is required because only a republican constitution is compatible with the requirements of the moral law, but Kant also argues that republicanism is conducive to peace, because the people will not be as profligate with their own lives and treasure than will a monarch who treats war as a sport. This argument has been criticized as psychologically flawed; on the other hand, Michael Doyle has called Kant in aid of the so-called 'Democratic Peace' thesis, that constitutionally secure liberal democracies do not go to war with each other (Doyle, 1983 and 1986 – see also Russett, 1993; Cohen, 1994; MacMillan, 1996; Gowa, 1999). This is hotly contested, but in any event it should be noted that Kant's 'republics' are, in crucial respects, not modern 'liberal democracies'; they do not have welfare states and they accept no responsibility for economic management – this is one of the reasons why citizens will not be bellicose: they have no interests that it would be legitimate for the republic to pursue (C. Brown, 1992b).

Since republics are non-violent they ought not to have too much difficulty forming a federation based on the rejection of war, but until all states are republics such a federation will be not be universal; republics will still need armed force to protect themselves from non-republican regimes, which leaves open the possibility of war – one reason for thinking that this is a second-best solution for Kant. The 'cosmopolitan' article in *Perpetual Peace* is interesting because it is apparently so limited in scope; individuals do not even have the right of asylum, let alone free movement between republics – all that can be said is that although they may be turned away, they may not be treated with hostility. The limited nature of this right is striking given that this article contains Kant's strictures on the Europeans who have despoiled the non-European world in pursuit of wealth, and also the very broad statement of cosmopolitan principle that a wrong suffered anywhere is felt everywhere. The apparent contradiction here is possibly explained by remembering that the parties to the Definitive Articles are republics which, by definition, do not persecute their citizens, and so a right of asylum as between republics would not be necessary.

Kant was a 'statist' in the sense that his system did not involve the creation of even a rudimentary world government – the 'Federation of Free States' has no institutions – but Martin Wight was not altogether wrong to see Kant as a 'revolutionary' thinker, although placing him in the same category as Lenin does require a certain amount of intellectual gymnastics (Wight, 1991). Kant certainly wished to see the existing international order transformed into something very different, although he anticipated this happening gradually as human beings learnt by trial and error that they must create a federation of republics. He also marked a very clear break with past thinkers by his insistence that the domestic political order of a state and its international behaviour are linked *in both directions*. His cosmopolitanism remains influential with modern international political theorists such as Charles Beitz and Onora O'Neill (Beitz, 1979/2000; O'Neill, 1986 and 1991). What they take from him is not so much his thoughts on cosmopolitan right in *Perpetual Peace*, but the implications of the universalism of his account of the moral law. The categorical imperative requires us to treat each other as ends and never solely as means, and it mandates truthfulness in human relations, and, as O'Neill stresses, this forms the basis for a critique of many aspects of contemporary international relations, in particular of global economic inequality. If all rational beings are governed by the same moral law which enjoins them to create republican constitutions and the rule of law, then a cosmopolitan commitment to universal human rights need not be excessively sensitive to the arguments of those who claim that rights are a specifically European way of understanding human dignity. Kant himself seems to have held 'savage' peoples in some contempt and was certainly personally anti-Semitic, but his principles are a different matter, Eurocentric perhaps, but not overtly racist.

Cosmopolitanism and its critics

If Kant is the inspiration for one group of modern cosmopolitans, the man who is usually regarded as his intellectual opposite – Jeremy

Bentham, the founder of utilitarianism – plays a similar role for another. For Bentham there are no moral categorical imperatives; behaviour is judged according to its consequences, specifically whether it promotes 'utility' or not, and likewise social institutions (Bentham, 1960). Bentham himself made some studies of international law – indeed invented the term – and concluded that the system of multiple sovereignties was actually conducive to maximizing utility, on the grounds that if every political system looked after the interests of its own citizens the general good would be served (Bentham, 1962). But utilitarianism is a critical doctrine, and the same kind of reasoning could, in different circumstances, lead to different results. Such has been the case in the late twentieth century, with utilitarians such as Robert Goodin and Peter Singer concluding that under present circumstances international anarchy does not serve to maximize utility (Singer, 1985; Goodin, 1995). Singer has argued that global inequality is such that utility would clearly be maximized if extensive resources were to be transferred from rich to poor, although the complexity of utilitarian reasoning is also revealed in the work of Garrett Hardin who, from more or less exactly the same staring point, concludes that such transfers are pointless because they could not have the desired consequences (Hardin, 1974). More on these arguments in chapter 9.

If cosmopolitanism was the dominant theme of Enlightenment thought, it is also the case that there was an undercurrent of anti-cosmopolitan thought that grew stronger at the end of the eighteenth century and became dominant in the nineteenth. In part, this reflected a continuation of the patriotic, republican strain of thought identified above, a strain of thought associated with the notion of popular government. Today it has become common for cosmopolitanism to be associated with progressive politics, and Dr Johnson's adage that 'patriotism is the last refuge of a scoundrel' is quoted approvingly by those who associate love of country with jingoistic flag-waving. In fact, many people today who are not usually thought of as particularly progressive – business executives, media moguls and WTO bureaucrats, for example – are reliably cosmopolitan in outlook, while Johnson's 'patriots' were those Whigs and Radicals who sought to check the power of the Crown in Britain, and supported their fellow patriots in what would become the United States. The love of country was endorsed by Jean-Jacques Rousseau, and eventually, largely as a side-effect of the French Revolution, became associated with the romantic movement's critique of the Enlightenment to become the nineteenth-century doctrine of nationalism.

The 'romantic' critique of the Enlightenment focused attention on the allegedly cold, rationalistic, calculating nature of Enlightenment thought. Figures such as David Hume and Immanuel Kant stood apart from their contemporaries and fellow citizens, living lives alienated from their respective communities. Kant's was a life of the mind, spent entirely in the smallish town of Königsberg and lived to inflexible routines; Hume was a rather more gregarious man of the world, but someone whose views could hardly have been more at odds with those of his Calvinist fellow Scots – both had, in different ways, chosen internal exile. The counter-position to this stressed the importance of belonging to a living community. A key figure here in Germany was Johann Gottfried Herder, a folklorist and opponent of Kant's cosmopolitanism. For Herder, language defined a people, and shaped its thought; every people with its own language has its own way of life, and something to contribute to humanity, and Kant's belief that there could be some kind of universal cosmopolitan culture could only mean the dominance of one culture over all others, and the destruction of all those things which give meaning to the lives of ordinary people (Barnard, 1965 and 1969).

Herder did not give a specifically political twist to these ideas, but some of his successors in Germany and elsewhere did. Herder's folklorism combined with the patriotic republicanism of the French revolutionaries, and the resistance that this republicanism provoked once it turned into a justification for empire, to create the doctrine of 'nationalism' – the belief that the world (or at least its 'civilized' element) is composed of discrete peoples who, in the form of nations, are entitled to rule themselves. Without doubt, this has been one of the most successful political ideas of the last two centuries, to the point where the terms 'nation' and 'state' are widely regarded as synonymous, and the composite 'nation-state' is frequently used to describe all the current members of the international system, despite the quite obvious fact that the vast majority of states could by no stretch of the imagination be seen as coterminous with any particular nation. Gradually, over the nineteenth and into the twentieth centuries, nationalism came to be seen as the underlying principle of contemporary political legitimacy, replacing dynastic legitimacy in this role.

Initially nationalism was associated with popular rule, and in the mind of figures such as Giuseppe Mazzini and John Stuart Mill the right to national self-determination was a simple, unthreatening aspect of the right of a people to determine their own form of government (Mazzini, 1907; Mill, 1984). Mazzini explicitly sees love of country as wholly compatible with love for humanity. In the case of the great historic nations of Europe there might be some justification for this belief – though irritating problems emerged in places such as Alsace and Lorraine or the South Tyrol – but the 'historyless' peoples of Europe and the world insisted on becoming involved (in spite of being told not to by Mill), and as the history of the twentieth century would demonstrate, nationalism is an enormously divisive force, by no means immediately compatible with cosmopolitan thought. The importance of nationalism is that it provided (and, for that matter, still provides) a justification for the existence of sovereign states which is not simply based on the property rights of kings and princes. Some such justification was certainly required in so far as dynastic legitimacy was hardly likely to be an acceptable long-term principle for the kind of educated, secularist populations that emerged in Europe in the nineteenth century; the peacemakers of 1815 who attempted to place dynastic legitimacy on a firm footing were obviously deluding themselves as they rearranged the map on purely strategic grounds and invented the 'legitimate' claims of the new rulers on an ad hoc basis after the event.

The romantic critique of cosmopolitanism was, perhaps, a side-effect of a wider 'revolt against reason', and nationalist ideas are similarly tainted with a degree of irrationalism; as Ernest Renan famously remarked, nationalism necessarily involves bad history, since the actual historical record rarely supports the account of past events upon which most nationalist programmes are based (Renan, 1939, p. 190). On the other hand, not all defences of particularist politics are irrational in this way; the Hegelian account of the rational, ethical state was so designed that it took on board the romantic critique of cosmopolitanism and the view that human beings needed to be part of a community, without falling into irrationalism (Pelcynski, 1971; Taylor, 1975; Plant, 1983). G. F. W. Hegel is a notoriously difficult writer who offers a very ambitious, indeed total, system which claimed to comprehend everything of philosophical significance. Of particular importance for his political views are his *Philosophy of History* and his *Elements of the Philosophy of Right* (Hegel, 1956 and 1991). Hegel understood history as the growing self-understanding of *Geist* which takes place through the emergence of ever more complex and ethically rich institutions and ideas, culminating in the rational, ethical state of the modern age – *Geist* is best translated as spirit, although mind would also be acceptable; the term has strong religious connotations. How spirit or mind can be said to achieve self-understanding has puzzled many very capable thinkers, and it is fortunate that it is possible to present an account of Hegel which does not rely too heavily on this notion. We can instead think of his work as an account of the development of freedom and the conditions required to create autonomous, self-determining individuals. Such a strategy misses much that was important to him, but produces a story more accessible to modern readers.

For the emergence of free individuals, Hegel argued in the *Philosophy of Right*, three dimensions of ethical life are necessary. The ethical family should provide unconditional love, a context within which the individual comes to have a sense of his or her own worth. This is a necessary foundation for autonomy but not sufficient; individuals must leave this arena of unconditional affection and make their way in a wider world in which they must earn respect. In this wider world, which Hegel termed 'civil society', individuals encounter each other as potential opponents and rivals, but also as rights-holders in a context where relations are governed by law. In civil society are to be found many of the institutions that from the perspective of Anglo-American liberalism are thought of as part of the state – public administration and the judicial system for example, or 'the police and the corporation' as Hegel put it. But, just as the family needs to be accompanied by civil society because autonomous individuals cannot be created in a world governed by unconditional love, so civil society on its own would be a realm of strife and tension were it not to be accompanied by a third ethical institution, the state. For Hegel, the state was not to be understood primarily as the site of decision-making on policy matters, its role in conventional liberal thought; instead the role of the state was to reconcile individuals to each other. As members of civil society individuals compete fiercely – albeit under terms governed by law – and inequality and a degree of civil strife is the inevitable result, but as fellow citizens they meet as equals, and differences are reconciled; such at least was Hegel's claim.

Before moving to consider the implications of this position for international relations one or two points need to be clarified. First, this set of institutions – family, civil society and the state – is, in its ethical form, a product of modernity. In the world of classical Greece, freedom was available in the *polis*, but for some only and in an unreflective form. The Romans created universal legal categories, but under the Empire free institutions disappeared and the Roman family was based, indefensibly, on the untrammelled power of the father. It is only in the modern, post-Reformation, post-Enlightenment world that all the preconditions of freedom come together. At times, Hegel seems to suggest that a fully ethical state has been achieved already, and 'Right Hegelians' draw conservative lessons from this position, but 'Left Hegelians' argue – with at least equal plausibility – that Hegel's thought offers not a defence of the status quo but a call to reform; the ethical community is a possibility towards which we should strive rather than an achievement to be defended. These are divisions that are still of some importance in our own age. A second, very important, point concerns the nature of the state itself. Hegel regarded the state as a critically important institution which overshadows every other aspect of communal life, in the process using language which has led many to accuse him of worshipping the state, and of preparing the way for totalitarianism. However, what is crucial to remember here is that Hegel's ethical state, like Kant's, is characterized by the rule of law and the separation of powers. Hegel favoured monarchy, but always constitutional monarchy in a *Rechtstaat* – a state governed by law and devoted to justice.

What kind of international relations might one expect to find in a world of Hegelian states? The final sections of the *Philosophy of Right* (§330–40) address this issue. Hegel believed that states need other states in order to function properly. Just as individuals cannot develop their individuality except by rubbing against other individuals (metaphorically speaking) so states can only develop *their* individuality by living in a world of other states; whether this is a helpful analogy can be disputed, but for Hegel it followed that states cannot surrender their sovereignty. War must always remain a possibility, and projects of 'Perpetual Peace' – Kant was specifically referred to – cannot succeed. Such projects rely on states agreeing to limit themselves and any such agreement will always be 'tainted with contingency', liable to collapse when and if circumstances change. Moreover, Hegel was prepared to envisage a positive role for war in providing a context within which individuals can demonstrate self-sacrifice and the civic virtues – although it should be noted that he saw war as a public act, in which harm to civilian life and property was excluded.

The Hegelian ethical state might also be a national state, but this is not a necessary connection, and Hegel ruled out any account of particularism that implies that there are fundamental differences between human beings (*Philosophy of Right*, §209). Cosmopolitanism must not be set in opposition to the 'concrete life of the state', but human beings are in a fundamental way equal and Hegel was, for example, a strong supporter of Jewish emancipation, a key issue of the nature of political inclusion and exclusion in the politics of his own time. For Hegel there is an element of affection and commitment required on the part of the citizen, but directed to the concrete institutions of the ethical state and not to the myth of the 'Nation'. Therein lies part of his significance for the international political theory of our time; he provides a justification for the division of the world into separate polities that does not rest on fictions about the nation, a justification taken up by, for example, Mervyn Frost; modern defenders of 'civic nationalism' such as Michael Walzer and David Miller also owe a great deal to his arguments. Moreover, the Hegelian account of the states-system can be employed to give substantive ethical content to the notion of international society.

Industrial society and international relations before 1914

The central features of the Westphalia System were in place in the seventeenth century and given a full justification in the work of Vattel in the early eighteenth, while major ethical critiques and defences of a system of sovereign states were developed in the second half of the eighteenth and early nineteenth centuries. Or, to look at these matters from a different angle, we might say that most of the concepts which are still employed to understand international relations were developed *before* the great changes that transformed the lives of all human beings in the nineteenth century – changes in manufacturing, communications, transport and general life-style that resulted from what used to be called by economic historians the 'Industrial Revolution'. Perhaps this makes a certain sense; given the 'lock-in' effect noted in the introduction to this chapter, industrial society had no choice other than to adapt itself to a system of sovereign states, and the fact that the 'fit' might not be very close is neither here nor there. On the other hand, the possibility that the rise of industrialism warrants a new look at notions such as sovereignty should not be dismissed out of hand – apart from anything else, it seems plausible that the nationalist ideas outlined in the previous section owed a great deal of their appeal to the conditions created by the Industrial Revolution, and, conversely, twentieth-century liberal internationalism, to be examined in the next chapter, rests firmly on the international thought of earlier liberals.

A great deal here hangs on the increasing importance of international trade and finance in the international system. Prior to the rise of industrial society, international trade was a relatively unimportant feature of the economic life of most states, and was widely regarded as a political as much as an economic activity; trade was seen as 'zero-sum', with winners and losers, and the aim of mercantilist policy was to win out in trading relations with foreigners. It was for this reason that Rousseau declared that in his ideal world states would be autarchic – because contact with foreigners promotes conflict (Hoffmann and Fidler, 1991). The founders of liberal political economy, especially Adam Smith and David Ricardo, effectively removed the intellectual foundations for this point of view; although mercantilism still has a great deal of popular support, the intellectual case in favour of there being general gains from trade is very strong, and as the importance of international trade grew in the nineteenth century, so it was more or less inevitable that this would be the basis for a new look at inter-state relations. So it proved with the thought of Richard Cobden, the most important English advocate of free trade and a tireless publicist and writer on the subject, who asked the most basic question: 'Can the "States System" which was applicable to the international affairs of Europe a century ago be suited to the circumstances of today?' (C. Brown et al., 2002, p. 522).

Cobden's answer was a resounding 'no!' He was an active campaigner in the peace movement of his day, whose particular contribution was the firm belief that the old forms of international interaction had been made outmoded, in so far as they meant anything in the first place. His hyperbolic description of the balance of power will be familiar to students of international relations: 'it is not a fallacy, a mistake, an imposture; it is an undescribed, indescribable, incomprehensible nothing: mere words conveying to the mind not ideas but sounds' (C. Brown et al., 2002, p. 523). He is also highly critical of the idea that the protection of commerce could be a legitimate reason for state action; the arguments here are similar to those used by later liberal internationalists – commerce rests on the cheapness of commodities, which is compromised by high spending on the military; war would be a disaster for the nation; many successful trading nations have very low military expenditures; we cannot be the policeman of the world; the most important way in which we can exercise influence is by being a moral example to the rest of the world; and so on. The sense of familiarity his writing evokes is fascinating, given its early provenance.

Unlike some later campaigners, or Kant for that matter, Cobden was not an advocate of world government or even a pacific union of republican states; on his account the forces of modernity will create a peaceful world if left to their own devices – there is no necessity for institutional innovation, all that is required is for governments to allow the beneficial effects of trade to be felt. Non-intervention is the key to peace, and in the long run autocratic governments will be undermined by trade and economic growth. This somewhat Panglossian approach to international trade was not shared by neo-mercantilist critics. The most intelligent of these, especially Friedrich List in Germany in the 1830s and 1840s, regarded free trade as an appropriate strategy for the dominant economic power, but highly disadvantageous for everyone else. The international division of labour that would be instituted thereby would leave Britain, the first industrial power, unchallenged in its monopoly of manufactures, while the US and the German states would be the hewers of wood and the drawers of water for the 'workshop of the world'; even if such a position would be profitable in the long run, which seems unlikely, it would undermine the power of the latter states. Moreover, Britain did not adopt this strategy *until* it was the dominant power. In a compelling metaphor, List remarks that 'it is a very common device that when anyone has attained the summit of greatness, he kicks away the ladder by which he has climbed up, in order to deprive others of the means of climbing after him' (List, in C. Brown et al., 2002, p. 525).

List recommended a policy of tariff protection for 'infant industries' to prevent them from being stifled by British manufactures. He was also a strong supporter of a customs union for the German states, on the principle that successful industry required a larger domestic market than could be provided by the individual German states. The notion that there is a particular optimal size for sovereign states as *economic* units is an interesting development – previously, in so far as it was discussed at all, optimality had been associated with communications and efficient government. It is also interesting that, whereas in the nineteenth century optimality involved the creation of nation-states in Europe that could serve as domestic bases for national economies, in the twentieth the development of productive capacity has been such that only much larger, continental-sized units would serve. Some, at least, of the advantages of being a 'middle-sized' economic power have disappeared, and small-scale 'city-states' such as Singapore and Hong Kong have been very effective in the new global economy.

Protectionists and liberals shared a generally favourable approach to industrial capitalism, however much they might disagree about trade policy. Less favourably disposed were the socialist (and, later, Marxist) critics of the new economic order, although it was not until late in the nineteenth century that these critics developed a distinctive account of international relations. This is not to say that mid-nineteenth-century socialists, including Marx and Engels, did not have a great deal to say about international relations, rather that they did not employ any distinctively socialist ideas. When, for example, Marx and Engels wrote about the Eastern Question – which they did frequently, and from an anti-Russian perspective – they employed the conventional categories of power politics to explain state behaviour (Marx, 1969). They were cosmopolitans in the sense that they were committed to the cause of workers everywhere, and judged international affairs according to the impact they might have on the prospects for revolution – which, of course, was why they were so bitterly anti-Russian, the Czars being the most powerful supporters of reactionary politics in Europe. What was missing from their analysis was any sense that, for example, the policy of the British state reflected the interests of the British bourgeoisie.

The reason for this omission lies in the nature of capitalism in their time. When Marx and Engels were in their hey-day, most manufacturing concerns were small-scale operations where the owner was also the manager, and the possibility of such enterprises capturing the state was remote, Later in the century, and especially in Germany and the US, the arrival of new large-scale industries based on steel and chemicals, with professional managers and funded via close links with equally large-scale banks, made the possibility of the state being seen as representing the interests of national capital much more plausible. At this point a distinctive socialist account of international relations does emerge, expressed most clearly in the masterwork of the Austrian Marxist, Rudolf Hilferding, *Finance Capital* (Hilferding, 1981; C. Brown et al., 2002). On Hilferding's account, the national economies of the advanced capitalist powers are now dominated by interlocking oligopolies in such a way that capitalists no longer compete with each other within the national economy, but instead compete predominantly with foreign capitals which have also formed into national blocks. The new monopolies are vulnerable only to external competition and they recruit the power of the state to restrict this competition via tariffs. At the same time, they seek to extend the area over which they can extract monopoly profits (their 'economic territory') and this leads to 'imperialism' in the sense of a general tendency to expand. A country's economic territory does not have to be under direct political control – Britain's 'informal empire' might well at this stage have included countries not ruled from London, such as Argentina, or even, at an earlier period, the United States. Tariff policy is not seen simply as defensive in the manner of List, but also as a tool that can be employed aggressively to expand the national territory. Hilferding sees imperialism/ expansionism as the foreign policy of finance capital, and, along with other Marxist writers of the time such as Rosa Luxemburg, is concerned by the increasing militarism of contemporary international relations (Luxemburg, 1951). This was, it should be recalled, the period of arms-racing and alliance-building that led up to the First World War. He, rightly, sees this militarism as alien to the liberalism of the old competitive capitalist bourgeoisie. International conflict is more or less guaranteed by the expansionist tendencies of 'finance capital' (the union of bank and industrial capital), although it is worth noting that Hilferding – unlike Lenin who, after 1914, popularized his ideas – did not assume that this conflict will always and necessarily lead to war.

Although Hilferding's intellectual world is a long way away from the world of nationalist thought, which also comes into its own in this period, they share the notion of the state as the expression of the nation or national economy; in fact the kind of reasoning Hilferding employed could easily be used to back up a programme of economic nationalism. He provided a good reason for taking the state as the key actor in international relations, even though on his account the state is a place-holder for the monopolies that dominate its economy. His conflict-ridden account of international relations contrasted strikingly with the liberal position associated with Norman Angell in the same, early twentieth-century, period. Angell argued in *The Great Illusion* that a condition of international interdependence now exists in the world economy such that it no longer makes sense to think that states could possibly improve their position by violent conflict with one another (Angell, 1909). There is a debate here that will reappear frequently in twentieth-century international thought, and still has not been resolved in the early twenty-first century – although now it is 'globalization' that is said to generate the great illusion that national economic policies could be profitable. However, these late twentieth-century debates have taken place within a different context. Thinking about international relations is no longer, as it were, a free-lance activity to be undertaken by interested philosophers, publicists, economists and so on. Of course, such folk can continue to express their views, and have done so, but alongside this informal band of international thinkers there now exists, at least in aspiration, a group of scholars who profess a disciplined body of knowledge on the subject. This constitutes a genuine change in the nature of discourse on international relations, and the theoretical underpinnings of this change are the subject of the next chapter.

4

Realism, Liberal Internationalism and Twentieth-century International Political Theory

Introduction: disciplining international relations

The most striking feature of international thought in the twentieth century is not so much any innovation in content – perhaps surprisingly, there are actually very few new ideas that have emerged over the last hundred years – but rather the change in intellectual context marked by the arrival of 'International Relations' (or 'International Politics/Studies') as a discrete field of academic study, perhaps even an academic discipline. This is a genuinely new development. None of the writers discussed in the previous two chapters thought of themselves as primarily students of something called 'International Relations'. They were natural lawyers, philosophers, social critics, sometimes politicians, who for one reason or another felt obliged to address avowedly international topics in some depth but who did not imagine that by so doing they were engaging in a different discourse from their starting point. Nor did they think of International Relations as a suitable subject for a university degree – it should be noted that the same could be said of most of the social sciences, and although 'political science' can claim Plato and Aristotle as its first practitioners, it was not accepted as an academic discipline until the late nineteenth century.

In the twentieth century, this changed. Immediately after the First World War a number of university chairs in International Politics or International Relations were established – in particular in the US and the UK, for reasons that will be discussed below – and within a few years these chairs became the focus for academic departments, admitting and teaching undergraduates and postgraduates. After the Second World War there was a further expansion of study in the field, and again in the 1960s and after. Nowadays the various national professional associations in the field – the (American) International Studies Association, the British International Studies Association, the Japan Association of International Relations, the Scandinavians and Germans – can boast a combined membership of well over 10,000 scholars, and simply in quantitative terms it can safely be said that most sustained thinking about international relations takes place within universities, or in specialized think-tanks and research institutions with close connections to the university sector.

This change came about largely in response to the horrors of war, especially to the shock of the 1914–18 war, and involved the coming together of legal, philosophical and historical studies in order to address and promote the prospects of peace. Until recently this simple judgement would have been almost universally accepted, but Brian Schmidt's history of the discipline has caused a few second thoughts (Schmidt, 1998). His thesis is that International Relations has its origins in the nineteenth-century American discipline of Political Science rather than in a melange of other discourses, and that 1919 was much less of a turning point than the conventional account suggests. This is helpful in so far as it firmly establishes International Relations as a sub-field of Political Science – a position that is widely accepted in the US but still contested in some circles in the UK – but the de-emphasizing of the impact of the First World War is less convincing, partly because there clearly was a major expansion associated with that event, but also because the peculiar features of International Relations, and particularly its Anglo-American leanings, can only be explained if this context is taken into account.

The Anglo-American nature of IR as an academic discourse is still quite striking; the major non-English-speaking contributors to the discourse are Scandinavian, Dutch and German scholars who, largely, publish in English, and the Japanese and (South) Koreans whose university systems were reformed post-1945 on American lines. Since 1945 in this, as in every other aspect of the US–UK relationship, the American side has been dominant, but before the Second World War the relationship was less one-sided. How is all this to be explained and what have been the consequences of this English-language dominance? Leaving aside the US, why were the chairs in International Relations founded in London, Oxford and Aberystwyth rather than Paris, Berlin and Munich? A comment drawn from the Inaugural Lecture of the second Woodrow Wilson Professor in Aberystwyth, C. K. Webster, in 1923 is apposite here:

This is the first Chair of International Politics founded in this country, and though in other countries there are professors whose duties are akin to mine, there is no general acceptance of the principles of the study. Indeed, even if such principles had existed before the Great War, that event has so sapped the foundations of international order, and *changed so remorselessly our conceptions of IR*, that a recasting of our ideas would be necessary. But, of course, no ordered and scientific body of knowledge did exist in 1914. Perhaps, if it had, the catastrophe might have been averted. (Cited from Olson, 1972, p. 10; emphasis added)

This is revealing, especially as it comes from a writer who was a hard-nosed diplomatic historian, and not one of those thinkers of the twenty years' crisis who would later be castigated by the fourth holder of the Wilson Chair, E. H. Carr (Carr, 1939).

The throw-away line that the Great War 'changed so remorselessly our conceptions of IR' repays further attention, because, on reflection, this is by no means as obvious as Webster implies. It could well be argued that the Great War actually vindicated the conceptions of international relations which had dominated thinking about the subject for the previous 100 – if not 300 – years. The war was fought by states exercising their sovereign right to resort to violence in accordance with principles of international law which had been in operation since at least the early eighteenth century. It was fought (and won) by a coalition of states united only by their determination to prevent one state from achieving military dominance over the continent, again, a motivation which would have been understood at any time in the previous three centuries. It was a war that was initiated by the conflict-generating propensities of nationalism, as had been virtually every major war of the previous century. In terms of outcomes, the war certainly brought about the overthrow of three imperial regimes, changed radically the distribution of world power, and provoked social revolution in a number of countries, but much the same could be said of previous European-wide wars. So then, what was the conception of international relations that had been, apparently, changed so remorselessly?

The answer seems to be that what was changed by the war was the view that modern industrial society had outgrown such violent and irrational patterns of behaviour. What the events of 1914–18 allegedly demonstrated was that the approach to international relations characteristic of *bien-pensant* British liberals in the early years of the twentieth century – a belief in the atavistic nature of military force as a problem-solving mechanism, a belief in the peace-generating qualities of international economic relations – had been based on a fundamental misunderstanding. Moreover, this misunderstanding may actually have contributed to the outbreak of war, which is the, perhaps unintentional, implication of the final sentence of Webster's cited above. Thus it is that the need to create an ordered and scientific body of thought about international relations arises: the argument is that, while before 1914 we thought we understood the nature of international relations, the events of 1914–18 have proved to us that we did not, and so we need to create the discipline of International Relations in order to fill this gap in our knowledge (a gap which, previously, we did not know existed).

As always, it is worth asking who the 'we' are in this sentence. The answer appears to be a relatively small number of liberal thinkers, most of whom were to be found in the English-speaking democracies. Writers on the socialist left in Europe were not surprised by the coming of war. As was noted in chapter 3, the most important and influential pre-1914 work of socialist international political economy, Hilferding's *Finance Capital*, identified imperialism as the foreign policy of finance capital, and predicted that modern industrial economies would be more, rather than less, conflictual in their foreign relations than the free-trade capitalist states of the mid-nineteenth century (Hilferding, 1981). What surprised socialist theorists in 1914 was not so much the outbreak of war, rather the fact that all the European socialist parties, save the Serbian and the Bolshevik faction of the Russian, found themselves obliged by their working-class membership to support the national war effort. Even this shock was not inexplicable; socialist writers were well aware of the force of nationalist sentiments, even if sometimes inclined to write off this phenomenon as the product of false-consciousness or of the treason of a labour aristocracy. Neither the Leninists in charge of the new Soviet Union and their followers elsewhere nor the old Social Democratic left in Europe had much sense that the Great War had over-turned previous conceptions of international relations – although they did hold, reasonably enough, that the war demonstrated the bank-ruptcy of the old order.

The forces of conservatism and nationalism in Europe seem to have been equally unimpressed by the allegedly unprecedented nature of the Great War. From the point of view of the German *ancien régime*, the Great War unfolded as expected, except that, in the end, they lost. In 1918 at Brest-Litovsk they imposed a traditionally harsh peace treaty on the defeated Russian enemy. The post-1918 German government attempted to use Wilson's liberal agenda to mitigate the consequences of Germany's defeat, but the commitment to the underlying principles of liberal internationalism on the part of those, quite sizeable, elements of the new republican order who remained rooted in the imperial past must be doubted. The French political class in the years immediately after the war thought in pre-1914 patterns and made no secret of the contempt in which they held the new liberal internationalist thinking. God himself was satisfied with Ten Commandments, remarked Clemenceau of Wilson's Fourteen Points.

In short, it was only those who took (Anglo-American) liberal principles seriously who felt greatly in need of the new academic discipline of International Relations – the qualification to 'liberalism' here is required, as will be noted below. Opponents of the new thinking, whether from the left or right, were reasonably happy with the current state of their knowledge. They believed themselves to be in possession already of more or less reliable knowledge of international relations and saw no great need to engage in a recasting of their ideas. The dissatisfaction that Webster drew upon was not as widespread as he seems to have believed it to be. Instead, it was largely confined to liberal circles in Britain and America, and whereas American leadership in liberal internationalism was initially established by a president who believed in the new ideas in a way that no British leader ever did, the failure of the US to ratify the Versailles Treaty and the Covenant of the League of Nations meant that the torch passed, for a generation, to the British liberal establishment.

The significance of all this is considerable, not least because the new discourse was shaped by specifically *Anglo-American* liberal thinking. To an extent this thinking shared features with continental liberalism, such as the belief there are no real conflicts of interest, that the 'people' always really want peace even if they are sometimes misled into thinking otherwise, but, at root, Anglo-American thinkers had a different view of the nature of the state, and this has had a deep impact on the discipline. For these thinkers, the state was understood to be an institution designed to solve the problems of collective action rather than an institution which was central to the constitution of the collectivity itself, and to individual personality. To put the matter differently, liberal internationalists rejected the Hegelian notion, shared by many continental liberals, that the state is an institution which brings meaning into the lives of individuals, giving them a sense of their worth as equal citizens, a function which the institutions of civil society cannot perform alone. From the point of view of English-speakers who take their liberalism from John Locke (or Thomas Hobbes, David Hume, Adam Ferguson, Adam Smith and Jeremy Bentham) the state is an entity which exists in civil society rather than beyond (much less above) it – indeed, most of the time, such liberals do not use the term 'the state' at all, preferring a more administrative term such as 'the government'. There certainly was a neo-Hegelian tradition in the English-speaking world, attached to pragmatism in the United States and to 'idealists' such as Green, Bosanquet and Bradley in Britain, but one of the consequences of the First World War was the emergence of a strong line of attack on the so-called 'Hegelian theory of the god-state' (Hobhouse, 1918; Boucher, 1997). In the years after the war liberals in the US and Britain were very much attached to 'negative' as opposed to 'positive' conceptions of liberty (Berlin, 1969). In Britain the state was more or less taken for granted as a necessary social institution, even though the term itself was not much used, and patriotism was certainly not exceptional, but the idea that the state ought to be the subject of an affective identification was much less prevalent; indeed, loyalty to the Crown or even the Empire was more common than overt loyalty to the British state. In the US, then as now, metonymic patriotic symbols such as 'the Flag' or 'the Constitution' carried more weight than 'the state', which, again, then as now, is a term rarely used in political discourse.

This orientation towards the state continues to have considerable significance for the discipline of IR, and the liberal presuppositions that underlie the field can be found in realist as well as liberal internationalist modes of thought. However, it is now appropriate to leave these meta-disciplinary considerations on one side, and focus a little more closely on the characteristic ideas that have been produced by the academic discourse of IR. Classifications of twentieth-century international thought can be quite complicated, but two strands of though dominate: 'liberal internationalism' and 'realism'. The latter has been dominant for most of the last century, and, perhaps, has an older pedigree than the former, but it was liberal internationalism that dominated the field in the early years, and therefore is the appropriate starting point.

Liberal internationalism

It is somewhat of an exaggeration to suggest that liberal internationalism was some kind of official ideology for the emerging academic discourse of IR after the First World War, but there is little doubt that most of the philanthropists who funded chairs in the subject, and many of the early holders of these chairs, subscribed to most elements of the liberal internationalist package (C. Brown, 1997/2001). That package will be reasonably familiar to readers of the last chapter – although, interestingly, there are some elements of international thought characteristically seen as liberal which do not appear in 1919. Liberal internationalism consists of the application of broadly liberal principles to international affairs, and in the aftermath of the First World War this application was oriented towards two tasks, determining what had produced war in 1914, and devising mechanisms and principles that would prevent its occurrence.

The first element of this diagnosis and prescription concerned domestic politics. A firm liberal belief (shared, as we have seen, by Kantians and Manchester School liberals) was that the 'people' do not want war; war comes about because the people are led into it by militarists or autocrats, or perhaps – and here J. S. Mill can be seen in the background – because their legitimate aspirations to nationhood are blocked by undemocratic, multinational, imperial systems (Mill, 1984). The events of 1914 could be read as bearing out this analysis; the crowds that bayed for war in all the European capitals were led astray by undemocratic rulers. An obvious answer here is to promote democratic political systems, that is, liberal-democratic, constitutional regimes, and the general acceptance of the principle of national self-determination: if all regimes were national and liberal-democratic, there would be no war. This position leads to the second component of liberal internationalism, its critique of pre-1914 international institutional structures. The basic thesis here was that the anarchic pre-1914 system of international relations undermined the prospects for peace. Secret diplomacy led to an alliance system that committed nations to courses of action that had not been sanctioned by parliaments or assemblies. There was no mechanism in 1914 to prevent war, except for the 'balance of power' – a notion which liberals associated with unprincipled power-politics (Cobden's fulminations come to mind here). What was deemed necessary was the establishment of new principles of international relations, such as 'open covenants openly arrived at', but, most of all, a new institutional structure for international relations – a League of Nations.

The aim of a League of Nations would be to provide the security that nations attempted, unsuccessfully, to find under the old, balance of power, system. The balance of power was based on private commitments of assistance made by specific parties; the League would provide public assurances of security backed by the collective will of all nations – hence the term 'collective security'. The basic principle would be 'one for all and all for one'. Each country would guarantee the security of every other country, and thus there would be no need for nations to resort to expedients such as military alliances or the balance of power. Law would replace war as the underlying principle of the system. The debt that this kind of thinking owes to the Peace Projectors of the eighteenth century and to Kant's thought is apparent; although the League of Nations was an institution while Kant's pacific union was simply a treaty, the rather weak enforcement provisions of the League meant that, in practice, it rested on much the same foundation as Kant's scheme – the putative commitment to peace of the populations of 'republics'. There was, however, this important difference: *pace* some rhetoric to the contrary, League membership was not restricted to constitutional, democratic states, which undermined whatever force might be found in the Kantian route to peace.

These two packages of reforms – to domestic and institutional structures – were liberal in two senses of the word. In political terms, they were liberal in so far as they embodied the belief that constitutional government and the rule of law were principles of universal applicability both to all domestic regimes and to the international system as such. But they were also liberal in a more philosophical sense, in so far as they relied quite heavily on the assumption of an underlying harmony of real interests. The basic premise of virtually all this thought, from Kant and Cobden to Woodrow Wilson, was that although it might sometimes appear that there were circumstances where interests clashed, in fact, once the real interests of the people were made manifest it would be clear that such circumstances were the product of distortions introduced either by the malice of special interests or by simple ignorance. Thus, although liberal internationalists could hardly deny that in 1914 war was popular with the people, they could, and did, deny that this popularity was based on a rational appraisal of the situation. On the liberal view, national interests are always reconcilable; international politics are no more based on a 'zero-sum' game than are international economics. This latter comparison is of some significance. In 1919 the makers of the new world order, unlike their successors in 1945, did not feel it necessary to set up regulatory international economic institutions, largely because they believed that economic relationships would look after themselves. They rejected comprehensively the view that war in 1914 had been brought on by economic rivalries that required management and regulation; instead, their main objective was to get back to rather than transform the world economy of the pre-war years.

Liberal internationalism has been described here as a coherent set of ideas that dominated thought in this period, but in fact its dominance was very insecurely based, and, for that matter, its coherence is easy to exaggerate. Of world leaders, only the US President Woodrow Wilson could be described as a whole-hearted liberal internationalist, and his influence even in the US was short-lived. The peace treaties of 1919 only partially reflected liberal principles, and, as is too well known to require retelling, the peace settlement itself was comprehensively overthrown within less than a generation. Liberal internationalist ideas were compellingly critiqued in the 1930s and 1940s by 'realist' writers, and the latter dominated the discipline of International Relations for at least thirty to forty years, and arguably still do. In short, liberal internationalism looks pretty much like a failed doctrine. First appearances are, however, misleading. In fact, liberal internationalist ideas remained potent throughout the twentieth century, and still have resonance into the twenty-first. In part, this is because realism has been itself, in certain key respects, a liberal doctrine – a point to be examined at greater length below – but the direct influence of liberal internationalism has also been important.

First, the institutional structure of international relations remains today more or less what it was in 1919. The United Nations is, in effect, a rebranded League of Nations – the decision to set up a new body in 1944 was more or less inevitable given the association of the League with failure, and the non-membership of the US in that body (not to mention the fact that the USSR was expelled from the League in 1940 in response to its invasion of Finland), but the essential structure of the UN is a revised version of its forerunner. The principles that lie behind the present vastly expanded set of international institutions in the world today are still essentially liberal. Perhaps more to the point, the wider 'settled norms' of contemporary international relations are, more or less, those of 1919. 'Settled norms' is a useful term developed by Mervyn Frost, drawing on legal reasoning associated with Ronald Dworkin and H. L. A. Hart; a norm is 'settled' if states endorse it even when their behaviour is apparently in contradiction to it (Frost, 1996). In such circumstances they will argue that appearances are deceptive, or that exceptional circumstances obtain – the fact that they are not willing overtly to break a norm is evidence that they regard it as settled.

Some of the settled norms of the current international order can be traced back to the origins of the Westphalia System, but in most cases the ideas of 1919 can be seen to have shifted the meaning of the norm in question, sometimes quite significantly. Thus, for example, it is a settled norm of the international order, and has been for several hundred years, that states claim to be sovereign, but, post-1919, sovereignty is no longer thought to convey the right to make war at will, which it was for much of the nineteenth century. Rather more controversially, Frost argues that the 1919 principles of 'democracy' and 'national self-determination' are also settled norms within the current international order. This is, perhaps, stretching a point, although it is clearly the case that most members of the UN do describe themselves as 'democratic'. The role of democracy in contemporary IR, however, goes beyond issues of self-description. The so-called 'democratic peace' thesis – which asserts that constitutionally secure liberal democracies do not go to war with each other – is highly controversial, but the core proposition appears to be well founded, and this again suggests links with the principles of 1919. It is also striking that many of the various notions of the emerging shape of international politics in the aftermath of the Cold War have involved versions of a return to 1919. Such was certainly true of George Bush's ill-fated 'New World Order' (Bush, 1990). His notion of a world in which all existing states would be guaranteed by the UN regardless of their internal constitutions was somewhat at variance with the theme of universal democratic government that was part of the original liberal internationalist package, but, as noted above, this was a feature of liberal internationalism that went by the board early on.

The reference to the Cold War in the above discussion points towards one reason why liberal internationalist ideas have been so long-lasting, namely their actual *lack* of radicalism. Students of International Relations who have been schooled to accept the realist position that liberal internationalists were starry-eyed utopians, idealistically engaging in wish-fulfilment and mistaking their vision of the world for reality, may find this a strange judgement, but what is striking about the version of liberal internationalism that has provided the settled norms of the current order is how much of the older Westphalia System is endorsed thereby. At the heart of this is the liberal acceptance of the sovereign state as the central actor in international relations – however much liberal internationalists have wanted to orient the behaviour of states in a particular peaceful direction, they have not attempted to undermine the state form as such. The contrast here with the Bolshevik ideology that also emerged at the end of the First World War is striking. It might well be argued that Leninist thinking was pretty soon submerged by the need to survive on the part of the new Soviet state, but at least in principle the Bolsheviks were genuinely globalist in their thinking rather than internationalist – that is to say, they saw the real components of world politics to be classes rather than states. Their account of the causes of war in 1914 stressed economic rivalry between states, a rivalry they believed to be basic to 'late capitalism' as a social formation, and their recipe for peace was, unsurprisingly, world revolution. In short, they looked to the transformation of the Westphalian political order rather than to its reform (Lenin, 1968).

Leninist thinking on international relations barely survived six months of the actual international experiences of the new Soviet state, and like so many other superficially attractive features of communism soon became simply one more intellectual weapon to be employed to preserve the power of the new Russian autocrats, Nonetheless, it and its successors – such as the 'dependency', 'centre–periphery' thinking of Third World and other critics in the 1960s and 1970s – have been, until the recent rise of neo-Gramscian thought, the real, albeit submerged, opposition to liberal internationalist ideas in the discipline of International Relations (Frank, 1971; Frank and Gills, 1993; Gill, 1993). However, because these ideas of the left have indeed been submerged – especially in the US, the post-1945 home of the discipline – it has often seemed that IR has been a battleground for a debate between liberals and realists, and to this rather less fundamental debate we now turn.

Realism

As noted above, the ideas of 1919 were never given a full field trial, and events in the 1930s – the rise of the dictators, the coming of the

Second World War – seemed simultaneously to undermine their explanatory capacity and to make irrelevant their normative thrust. In some circumstances it might have been possible to argue that it was the failure to implement liberal internationalism in 1919 that was at fault, but this hardly seemed to be the case in the 1930s; rather, it seemed that some of the root assumptions of liberal internationalism must be challenged. For example, the assumption that 'the people' are naturally peaceful was undermined by the rise of Hitler's Germany and Mussolini's Italy, which were not traditional military autocracies, but rather regimes which had come to power by quasi-democratic means and remained in power by the mobilization of popular support. Moreover, these regimes, although popularly supported, actually glorified war. The rhetoric of fascism and national socialism stressed the virtues of armed struggle and its importance in building the nation. And, of course, the stated foreign policy aims of these regimes could not be achieved by any means other than war. The fact that Nazism remained a popular force in spite of this posture dealt a terrible blow to liberal thinking.

The consequences of this blow were felt in particular with respect to support for the League of Nations and the rule of law. The basic premise of liberal internationalism was that the force of world opinion would buttress the League of Nations and that no state would be able to act against this force. The point of collective security under the League was to prevent wars, not to fight them. The League's cumbersome procedures would act as a brake to prevent a nation that had, as it were, temporarily taken leave of its senses from acting rashly – international disputes would be solved peacefully because that was what the people *really* wanted. The behaviour of Hitler and Mussolini made it clear that, in this context at least, these ideas were simply wrong. The liberal internationalist slogan was 'law not war', but it became clear as the 1930s progressed that the only way in which 'law' could be maintained was by 'war'. An inability to understand this basic point bedevilled liberal thought in the 1930s.

Gradually, in the 1930s, a critique of liberal internationalism emerged. In terms of his later influence, a key figure here is the American radical theologian (and, at that time, pacifist) Reinhold Niebuhr. Niebuhr's message is conveyed in shorthand in the title of his 1932 book, *Moral Man and Immoral Society*; his point was that liberals wildly exaggerated the capacity of collectivities of humans to behave in ways that were truly moral (Niebuhr, 1932). Niebuhr held that 'men' had the capacity to be good, but that this capacity was always in conflict with the sinful acquisitive and aggressive drives that are also present in human nature. These drives are given full scope in society and it is unrealistic to think that they can be harnessed to the goal of international peace and understanding in bodies such as the League of Nations. This essentially Augustinian position later became the basis for post-1945 American realism in the hands of the US diplomat George Kennan and the German-Jewish refugee Hans J. Morgenthau; the latter's text *Politics Among Nations*, first published in 1948, became the single most important source for realist thinking about international relations for the next generation, and was at the heart of most university syllabi in the subject in the US until at least the 1970s (Morgenthau, 1948; Smith, 1986; Murray, 1996a and 1996b; Rosenthal, 1991).

The equivalent figure to Morgenthau in the UK was E. H. Carr, the quasi-Marxist historian, journalist and, in the late 1930s, Woodrow Wilson Professor of International Politics at Aberystwyth. Carr produced a number of studies in the 1930s, the most famous of which was *The Twenty Years Crisis* (Carr, 1939). This book performed the crucial task of providing a new vocabulary for international relations theory. Liberal internationalism is renamed 'utopianism' and contrasted with Carr's approach, which is termed 'realism'. Carr's central point is that the liberal doctrine of the harmony of interests glosses over the real conflict that is to be found in international relations, which is between the 'haves' and the 'have-nots'. A central feature of the world is scarcity – there are not enough of the good things of life to go around. Those who have them want to keep them, and therefore promote 'law and order' policies, attempting to outlaw the use of violence. The 'have-nots', on the other hand, have no such respect for the law, nor is it reasonable that they should, because it is the law that keeps them where they are, which is under the thumb of the 'haves'. Politics has to be based on an understanding of this situation. While it is utopian to suggest that the have-nots can be brought to realize that they ought to behave legally and morally, it is realistic to recognize that the essential conflict between haves and have-nots must be managed rather than wished away. It is utopian to imagine that international bodies such as the League of Nations can have real power. Realists work with the world as it really is, utopians as they wish it to be. In fact, as Ken Booth has demonstrated, Carr wished to preserve some element of utopian thought, but, nonetheless, realism was his dominant mode (Booth, 1991).

Carr's position reveals its quasi-Marxist origins, and its debt to Mannheim's sociology of knowledge, in its stress on material scarcity and its insistence that law and morality serve the interests of dominant groups (Mannheim, 1960). On the other hand, the fact that the 'have-nots' of the 1930s were, on his account, Hitler's Germany and Mussolini's Italy suggests that Carr's Marxism was laced with a degree of power-worship, although this is contested by his modern followers (Cox, 2000). Nonetheless, Carr made a number of effective points. It was indeed the case that the League of Nations and the idea of collective security was tied up with the peace settlement of 1919 and therefore could be seen as defending the status quo. Equally, the leading status-quo nations, Britain and France, had not built up their empires by strict adherence to the rule of law. In any event, his critique of the international relations of the period became the key text for post-1945 British international thought, playing the same role in the syllabi of UK university courses in the subject that Morgenthau's *Politics Among Nations* played in the US – although it should be said that there were far fewer such courses in the UK than in the US.

To what extent is the realist position a restatement of pre-1914 international thought? Realists of this generation explicitly saw themselves as drawing upon the wisdom of the old European states-system, and indeed of earlier forerunners. The names of Thucydides, the historian of the Peloponnesian War of the fifth century BC, and of Machiavelli, Hobbes, Grotius and Vattel feature in the genealogies the realists provided for themselves, and the sense that they were drawing on a European tradition of statecraft was widely shared (Gilpin, 1984; Buzan, 1996). In fact, as Hedley Bull pointed out some time later, a guide to this tradition was particularly necessary in the US, because the latter's relative isolation from European international politics meant that its political elite did not have the grounding in the subject that came naturally to their European counterparts, and therefore a 'crib' to the tradition was required which Morgenthau and others provided (Bull, in Porter, 1972, p. 39). There is some truth to this, although US politicians, such as the very well-read autodidact Harry Truman, might retort that the supposed sophistication of European statesmen was not much in evidence in the 1930s.

On the other hand, the realists' use of the European tradition of statecraft was actually much more selective than they themselves seem to have acknowledged, or even, possibly, appreciated. Machiavelli was appropriated as a technician of power, but the humanist, republican side of Machiavelli did not fit with the realist picture of the world – indeed, none of the American or British realists of this period adopted a theory of the state that was republican or, in any other way, portrayed the state as a positive force in people's lives (Pocock, 1975). Hegelian theories of the state are either simply ignored or contemptuously dismissed out of hand – the only reference to Hegel in Morgenthau's *Politics Among Nations* equates his work with Fichte and describes him, in an absurd oversimplification, as a German nationalist philosopher (Morgenthau, 1948, p. 154). Although 'English School' writers such as Bull and Martin Wight were in touch with one part of the European tradition – the writings of the lawyers from Grotius to Vattel – they were much less familiar with Enlightenment and post-Enlightenment thought. Wight, for example, refers to the Nazis and communists as the children of Hegel and Kant, and, in order to prove that this is not an accidental aberration, produced a classification of thought in which Kant and Lenin are in the same category; this 'Kantian' category is characterized by an ethic that the end justifies the means, surely a unique reading of Kant's moral teachings (Wight, 1966, p. 28, and 1991).

Moreover, the realists of this period, for all their stress on these themes, do not draw upon the work of those thinkers who, unlike Machiavelli, could genuinely be said to be technicians of power politics. Treitschke, whose *Politics* was a major text of Wilhelmine Germany and who, unlike Hegel, could actually be seen as a forerunner of the Nazis, is ignored (Treitschke, 1916). Carl Schmitt, whose elaboration of the friend–enemy distinction in *The Concept of the Political* constitutes one of the most impressive intellectual assaults on liberal thinking about politics of the twentieth century, was actually a teacher of Morgenthau in the 1920s; Morgenthau regarded his work as deplorable and Schmitt himself as evil, influenced in this judgement, no doubt, by the latter's flirtation with Nazism (Schmitt, 1996). The characteristic realist virtue is 'prudence', which certainly played a part in the European tradition of statecraft, but the notion that glory and prestige are also important is largely missing from these thinkers; tellingly, 'prestige' is treated by Morgenthau essentially as an instrument of foreign policy rather than as something to be valued in its own terms.

The point that needs to be made here is that although the realists were much more aware of the importance of tribalism than most liberals, and although they place more emphasis on conflict than liberals usually do, nonetheless they are essentially working within the same broad, and essentially (Anglo-American) liberal, framework of ideas. The realist theory of the state, in so far as they express one, clearly relates back to the cluster of ideas developed by the proto-liberals Thomas Hobbes and John Locke – the state is a problem-solving mechanism coping with problems of domestic order. This position becomes even clearer later in the life of realist thought in international relations when rational choice models of political behaviour come to dominate.

Rational choice theory and the contemporary discourse of International Relations

Most of the key figures in the early and middle period of the discipline of IR treated the subject as *sui generis* – that is, the working assumption was that in order to understand international relations it is necessary to develop concepts and theories that are specific to the field. Notions of power and interest might well have domestic counterparts and implications, but international relations were still regarded as substantially different from domestic politics. The selective use of past authorities, noted above, was partly a product of this determination to keep IR in a separate category from domestic politics; the republican, humanist, side of Machiavelli was seen as applicable to his thought about the nature of politics internally, rather than to the external relations of states, and figures such as Hegel and Kant were regarded as political philosophers, the relevance of whose work is restricted to the internal affairs of states. It is not really clear why this *sui generis* assumption was so prevalent, especially in the UK – most likely, academics in the new discourse of IR saw themselves as more closely connected to the diplomatic culture and arcane skills of foreign offices and chancelleries, via bodies such as the Royal Institute of International Affairs (Chatham House) or the US Council on Foreign Relations, than to their colleagues in Political Science, a tendency amplified by the fact that, in the UK as opposed to the US, the biggest university departments of International Relations were often separate from departments of Government or Politics.

In any event, while British International Relations is still somewhat distant from wider trends in Political Science, from the 1970s onward the American study of the subject has been dominated by the same broad body of theory employed by US political scientists, namely rational choice (or social choice) theory. The presupposition of rational choice thinking is that politics can be understood in terms of the goal-directed behaviour of individuals, who can be conceptualized as acting rationally in the minimal sense that they make ends-means calculations designed to maximize the benefits they expect to accrue from particular situations (or, of course, minimize the losses). This perspective – sometimes termed 'neo-utilitarian' – draws much of its strength from the discipline of Economics, where rational choice assumptions are fundamental, and was widely applied in the study of American government from the 1960s onwards, with electoral, interest group and congressional politics in the forefront. It encourages the application of tools such as game theory to the study of politics, and opens up the possibility of quantitative studies employing regression analysis (and other statistical techniques largely developed by econometricians). In the late 1970s it came to American International Relations via, in particular, the work of Kenneth Waltz and the neo-realist school, although it should be acknowledged that Waltz is not content to have his work labelled as rational choice (Waltz, 1979, 1997 and 1998; Keohane, 1985).

Waltz's version of realism focuses on the structure of the international system (and thus, confusingly, is sometimes termed 'structural realism'); his root idea is that there is a basic distinction to be made between 'hierarchical' systems and 'anarchical' systems – the latter are made up of 'like' units, units which are differentiated in terms of capabilities but not in terms of functions, while the former are composed of functionally differentiated institutions. The members of an anarchical ('self-help') system are assumed to be unitary actors; they are egoists who are assumed, at a minimum, to seek to preserve themselves. In so far as they do so successfully – and there is no guarantee that they will – their actions will result in the creation of balances of power, and the balance of power is the 'theory of international politics' to which the title of Waltz's book refers. Waltz thus draws a sharp distinction between international and domestic politics (following classical realism in this) but he does so via the use of a form of reasoning which is common to both spheres, and indeed to other areas of social life – Waltz himself explicitly develops the analogy between states in the international system and firms in a market. Moreover, the same kind of reasoning can be employed to produce a rather different result. Thus, it is possible to argue that egoists can actually co-operate under conditions of anarchy – albeit at sub-optimal levels – and game theoretic models can be employed to show how this can be done; from out of this emerges the 'neo-liberal' alternative to neo-realism. The contest between neo-realists and neo-liberals has been a feature of US International Relations for the last twenty years, and most empirical work done by American IR scholars is informed by one or other of these meta-theories (R. Powell, 1991 and 1994; Baldwin, 1993).

For the purposes of this discussion two features of this rational choice dominance are particularly noteworthy. First, although neo-realism is usually seen as in opposition to neo-liberalism, both bodies of thought are, in a deeper sense, liberal. Both work on the assumption that states are entities that exist in order to solve problems of collective action; each assumes that states are egoistic – as Joseph Grieco has suggested, there is a clear difference between neo-liberals who assume that states seek absolute gains and neo-realists who assume they seek relative gains, but this difference, although real, is relatively unimportant in the wider scale of things (Grieco, 1988; R. Powell, 1991). In effect, neo-realists and neo-liberals are replaying a classical debate between Hobbesian and Lockean forms of reasoning – but both Hobbes and Locke are, of course, central figures in the Anglo-American tradition of liberalism. In this sense, the dominance of rational choice thinking in the modern discipline of international relations represents a continuation of the dominance of liberal thought in the discipline noted in the previous two sections of this chapter.

The second important feature of the dominance of rational choice thinking is the way in which a number of important questions about international relations, questions which featured in the classical international thought of the Westphalia System, and even in some classical realist thought, have been marginalized. Since the origins of West-phalia, a key question for international thought has concerned the nature of the obligations that individual human beings have towards their fellow citizens, as opposed to the obligations they have towards the rest of humanity – the question with which this book opened. This question of inclusion and exclusion was central to the thought of the international lawyers and philosophers of the seventeenth, eighteenth and nineteenth centuries; it was still being asked by many of the liber-als and realists of the mid-twentieth century, and, moreover, as will be demonstrated in the rest of this book, this question is still very much at the heart of contemporary international relations. It receives elabo-ration and specification in the discourses of the international human rights regime, of borders and refugees, of global economic inequality and so on. But it is a question which is very difficult to ask from the perspectives of neo-realist or neo-liberal thought, because the first premise of both these approaches is that states are rational *egoists*. Rational choice IR cannot deny the existence of the questions that cluster around matters of exclusion and inclusion, but the tendency has been for these questions to be relegated to a separate, marginalized and inferior discourse – perhaps 'normative international relations theory' or 'ethics and international relations'. The real cutting edge of theory is taken to be explanatory in nature, and questions that cannot be seen as conducive to the development of explanatory theory are put to one side.

Predictably, the dominance of neo-realism and neo-liberalism has produced counter-movements which are more sensitive to non-explanatory theory; they will not be discussed here in detail, because many of them will feature in the substantive chapters that follow. However, in spite of the blooming of a great body of unorthodox thought over the last decade or so, the strength of rational choice ortho-doxy ought not to be underestimated. The fate of 'constructivism', the most popular of the avowedly anti-establishment theories, is instruc-tive in this regard. In the late 1980s and early 1990s, constructivism was a radical doctrine that challenged in a fundamental way both the onto-logy and the epistemology of rational choice approaches. Drawing variously (and somewhat uneasily) on Wittgenstein's notion of a lan-guage game, Anthony Giddens' concept of 'structuration', and the social-psychological constructivism of Berger and Luckmann, early constructivists such as Friedrich Kratochwil and Nicholas Onuf pro-duced accounts of the world which were radically at odds with the ahistorical studies of Waltz, Keohane and the other neo-neo writers (Kratochwil, 1989; Onuf, 1989; Ruggie, 1998). These writers are still fighting the good fight, but constructivism as such has become to all

intents and purposes part of the mainstream which it originally criticized (Kubalkova et al., 1998). The most important recent book in the
area, Alexander Wendt's *Social Theory of International Politics*, pays
tribute in its very title to Waltz's seminal volume of 1979, and is content
to stake out a particular area of the field as its own rather than to
challenge the dominance of rational choice theory as such – whence
Kratochwil's accusation that this variant of constructivism is becoming
part of a new orthodoxy (Wendt, 1999; Kratochwil, 2000). In short,
although the rest of this book will demonstrate that there is a great deal
of high-quality work in the field today that does not fall within the
neo-liberal/neo-realist duopoly, this should not be mistaken for the
optimistic assumption that the latter is about to lose its dominance in
the field. On the contrary, international political theory is a minority
discourse and is likely to remain so for the foreseeable future.

Conclusion: an eighty years' detour?

Steve Smith in 1992 referred to a 'forty years detour' dated from, and
echoing the title of, Carr's *Twenty Years' Crisis* (Smith, S., 1992). Perhaps
eighty years would be more accurate, and the post-1919 establishment
of International Relations as a distinct academic discourse could be
seen as the key mistake? It may not be sensible to think of the foundation of a discipline as a 'mistake' given all the factors that are
involved in such an act, but, turning to the present, it is notable that
the distinction between the contributions made to international political theory by scholars of international relations, political science, political theory or political philosophy owes more to personal history than
it does to any other demarcation. Writers such as Brian Barry, Onora
O'Neill and Michael Walzer are by origin and current location political theorists and philosophers, while, say, Terry Nardin, Mervyn Frost
and Molly Cochran come from out of the discipline of International
Relations, but the impact of these personal biographies on the substance of their thought (as opposed to some of its more idiosyncratic
manifestations) is questionable. Moreover, the existence of a discrete
area of study named International Relations which is supposed to cover
all things international, but which in fact has a quite limited frame of
reference, has been positively disadvantageous to the development of
international political theory.

It would be difficult to argue outright that the notion of a separate
discourse of International Relations was a mistake, because the specific
problem to which this discourse was a response was, in all conscience,
serious enough; and, for what it is worth, the motivations of those who

gave the discipline its foundations in the 1920s and 1930s were thoroughly honourable. The need for education about international relations was as great then as it is now. At the same time there is reason to regret that discourse about international relations should have been disciplined in *quite* the way that it has been. Simply in educational terms, although International Relations contains much that is worthy of study, it may be doubted whether the disciplined study of 'International Relations' is possible – certainly any attempt to study IR separately from Political Science is doomed to produce a rather undisciplined body of knowledge and perhaps to stand in the way of the emergence of a more compelling focus. In any event, the remaining chapters of this book part company somewhat with conventional accounts of the discipline, and draw eclectically on the work of IR theorists, political theorists and political philosophers, as seems appropriate to the topics in question. It is for the reader to judge whether the result is to forge a coherent account of contemporary international political theory, but that, at least, is the intention.

5

Self-determination and Non-intervention

Introduction

The last three chapters provide a context for the contemporary discourse of international political theory, a launch pad for the rest of this book, which will focus on current problems and current theories. What are these current problems and theories? It could quite plausibly be argued that there is actually only one problem – although many theories – namely, the problem of finding the right relationship between the universal and the particular in international relations. The current international order poses this problem in a number of ways. Most fundamental is the clash between, on the one hand, the inherited norms of the Westphalia System, most of which privilege the particularistic values associated with the state, or nation-state, and, on the other, the more recently established norms which appear to promote universal values, most obviously in the area of human rights, but also, putatively, in the areas of global environmental politics and global justice. In the remaining chapters of this book these various manifestations of the central problematic of international political theory will be examined. In this chapter, the focus will be directly on the state and the Westphalian norms of 'self-determination' and 'non-intervention'. The aim will be to explore the justifications for these norms which are current today, and which might be employed to counter the arguments put forward by proponents of the competing post-1945 norms – hence, alternative titles for this chapter might be 'the justification of the state' or the justification of sovereignty. The structure of the chapter will be as follows. First, the meaning of 'self-determination' and 'non-intervention' will be established; next two common general defences of these sovereignty norms will be examined – that sovereign states are local agents of the common good, and that they allow different conceptions of the good to flourish. Finally, the chapter will focus on the international thought of Michael Walzer, whose influential, liberal defence of the rights of political communities is one of the most interesting achievements of contemporary international political theory, and whose work paves the way for the discussion of violence and war in the following chapter.

Sovereignty, self-determination and non-intervention

Strictly speaking, 'self-determination' is not a Westphalian norm and the key arguments in defence of sovereignty could, quite reasonably, be focused solely on the notion of non-intervention. However, over the last hundred years the two notions have become so closely intertwined that it makes sense to treat them together and, as will become apparent, some of the most influential defences of one notion rely on the other for their force. Although more recent in origin, it makes sense to begin with self-determination, because the root idea here is quite easy to grasp, even though, predictably, the elaboration of this idea poses difficulties. The basic idea behind self-determination was set out 150 years ago by J. S. Mill in his *Considerations on Representative Government*:

> Where the sentiment of nationality exists in any force, there is a prima facie case for uniting all the members of a nationality under the same government, and a government to themselves apart. This is merely saying that the question of government ought to be decided by the governed. One hardly knows what any division of the human race should be free to do if not to determine with which of the various collective bodies of human beings they choose to associate themselves. (Mill, 1972, p. 361)

A number of different ideas are, in fact, tied up in these three sentences – indeed most of the difficulties associated with self-determination are prefigured here. It should be noted that Mill initially associates self-determination with nationalism, but then makes it clear that this is a contingent association; there is no necessary connection between the two notions. In practice, it actually usually has been nationalists of one stripe or another who have promoted the idea of self-determination, but the proposition that 'the question of government ought to be decided by the governed' can be accepted even by those who are not nationalists. It is presented as simple common sense; any 'division' of the human race should be free to determine their own fate. However, for all the veneer of common sense with which these ideas are presented, there are numerous problems that are glossed over here but which have recurred with some frequency over the last century and a half, problems to which Mill has a solution, but a solution that has never been widely accepted.

First, can it really be possible that *any* division of the human race could have the right to self-determination? It is not to difficult to apply *reductio ad absurdum* arguments here. Second, what of the, surely very real, possibility that one division may wish to associate with another which, however, does not wish to associate with it? Third, it seems that, implicitly, self-determination involves the right to a particular territory, but what if two different divisions of the human race claim the same territory? These three, connected, problems would not have impressed Mill because it is clear from elsewhere in his work (for example in his important essay 'A Few Words on Non-Intervention') that he does not actually believe that *any* division of the human race is entitled to self-determination (Mill, 1984). Only progressive, historic nations have this right, 'barbarians' and the less developed require the tutelage of their betters. Needless to say, this has not been a popular solution to this set of problems in the second half of the twentieth century (Jackson, 1990). On the other hand, no better solution is immediately available. In practice the right of self-determination has been attributed to all colonies, but the principle of *uti possidetis juris* has been applied, the effect of which has been to ensure that self-determination takes place within the boundaries determined by the colonial powers, or within pre-existing boundaries of federal systems in the case of the break-up of composite states such as the old Soviet Union or the former Socialist Federal Republic of Yugoslavia. The problems this principle presents in those cases – the overwhelming majority – where these borders do not enclose communities who necessarily want to live together will be familiar to anyone with a cursory knowledge of recent world politics.

Setting these point to one side, another set of problems concerns democracy and self-determination. Mill rightly associates the idea of self-determination with popular government, and the idea that 'the question of government ought to be decided by the governed' is one of the reasons why self-determination is *not* properly speaking to be understood as a norm of the Westphalia System, where, originally at least, the property rights of the prince rather than the will of the people determined legitimacy. Two questions arise immediately: *how* do the people decide the question of government? And, can they decide *against* a system of popular government? These questions raise paradoxes associated with a notion of legitimacy based on popular choice. First, before the people can choose, the people have to be chosen, that is to say that popular choice presumes the existence of a defined electorate – but, of course, in practice, it is frequently precisely the matter of definition that is in dispute. Who ought to decide the future of

Northern Ireland – the people who live in the province, the population of Ireland as a whole, or of the UK, or of the EU, or wherever? There is no *democratic* answer to this question because democracy can only come into play once it has been answered. Second, Mill assumes that the people will choose 'free institutions' – indeed, self-determination for Mill is valued because only then can free institutions be established. But can it be assumed that this is the only choice the people will make, or is their choice only to be accepted as legitimate if this actually is the choice they make? As we will see later in this chapter, and at different points throughout the book, it cannot be taken for granted that 'the people' if given a choice will choose free institutions; is self-determination to be valued if it does not lead to free institutions?

Enough has been said here to establish that the notion of self-determination is highly problematic, but it is clear that self-determination is a norm of the current international order, and that one of the justifications of the state is that its sovereignty reflects the will of the people. What of non-intervention? Here the case is clearer in legal terms. Since the beginning of the Westphalia System the assumption has been that sovereign status implies non-intervention, that is to say that external bodies (including other states) have no right to intervene in the affairs of a sovereign state. Sovereignty, as we have seen, involves internal attributes and an international legal status, and the latter is summarized by the notion of non-intervention. This legal status is confirmed by the UN Charter, Article 2(4) of which forbids the use of force by states unless in self-defence or with the authority of the Security Council, and Article 2(7) of which confirms that the domestic jurisdiction of states is to be respected. As we have also seen, the norm of non-intervention has been repeatedly violated over the last 350 years, to the point that Stephen Krasner is prepared to use the term 'organized hypocrisy'; but that is another matter – the aim here, as with self-determination, is to try to pin down the meaning of the term (Krasner, 1999).

The most important difficulty in this respect is distinguishing between *intervention* (illegitimate) and *influence* (legitimate). Clearly states attempt to influence each other all the time and it would be absurd to suggest that this most basic of political and diplomatic activities is somehow improper. The problem is that the means by which states attempt to influence each other are not confined to simple persuasion and reasoned arguments. Sticks and carrots are frequently involved – or positive and negative sanctions, if you prefer – and the exercise of influence frequently (perhaps always) involves the exercise of political power directed against the civil society of another state. At what point does the exercise of influence shade over into intervention? When one state, or a group of states, organizes a boycott of products from another because of the domestic regime of the latter, does this constitute intervention? Is the refusal to sell arms intervention? And so on. One possible answer establishes a very firm distinction between influence and intervention; intervention takes place if and only if the power of decision is taken away from the state intervened against – which means, in practice, if physical force is used and actual control established. This is clear-cut, but it may be too restrictive; there are many cases where superior power is exercised without actual control and where one would wish to say that the exercise of influence has become illegitimate. There seems no obvious way in which a clear distinction can be drawn here.

This discussion has established that neither self-determination nor non-intervention are straightforward terms; both are difficult to define in operational terms. However, taken together they pose the basic question for the rest of this chapter. What justifications are available for a global political order the component parts of which are deemed to be sovereign in the sense that they have the right to arrange their own affairs without external intervention? Can the norm of self-determination legitimate this arrangement? In the sixteenth and seventeenth centuries these questions hardly arose; in essence, sovereignty flowed from the property rights of the sovereign, which included the right to manage and dispose of his/her property as an exercise of will. It seems clear that this is no longer a morally acceptable line of argument – but what can take its place?

The sovereign state as the local agent of the common good

The phrase 'local agent of the common good' is Hedley Bull's, and very useful it is (Bull, 1984a, p. 14). The basic idea here is very simple. There is a common good for all mankind – in that both medieval natural lawyers and modern cosmopolitans are essentially correct – but this common good is best realized by vesting political authority in local agents, viz. sovereign states. There are several modern versions of this basic position; the simplest will be examined first, then a rather more complicated argument will be presented before the obvious drawbacks are outlined.

The simple version is essentially a consequentialist argument – although interestingly it also appears in the work of Kant, the strongest opponent of consequentialism. The central thought here is that laws lose their force at a distance; the world is too big a place to be governed as one unit, therefore it is legitimate that there be separate jurisdictions. From a Kantian perspective – and from the perspective of modern

Kantian cosmopolitans such as Charles Beitz – the basic form of government that is conducive to the common good is 'republican' and there is no reason, in principle, why there should not be a world republic (Reiss, 1970; Beitz, 1979/2000). On the other hand, there are good practical reasons why a world republic may be unattainable, relating to problems of scale (and perhaps to the 'lock-in' effect identified in chapter 3, but that is a slightly different argument). So it makes sense to have a series of separate 'republics' through which the common good of a republican world can be realized. The utilitarian argument starts from a different point but ends up at the same place. All human beings count as one, and no more than one, their suffering has an equal demand on our attentions and there is no principled reason to privilege the utility of any particular sub-set of humanity. On the other hand, practice suggests that the general welfare is improved if delegation to lower levels than the whole takes place. Just as for each family to concentrate on its own children may be the best way of delivering child-care, so for each state to concentrate on the welfare of its own citizens may be the best way of delivering the common good on a world scale (Bentham, 1962). Each of these different arguments starts from a universalist 'moral cosmopolitan' viewpoint – on the difference between moral and institutional cosmopolitanism, see Beitz (1994) – but ends up giving qualified approval to a particularist political arrangement.

Arguably, both the Kantian and the utilitarian defences of the state as the local agent of a common good replicate a more general 'natural law' argument inherited from the medieval scholastic tradition (Finnis, 1980). Human beings are essentially alike, they have the same needs and wants, the state – or, indeed, any other political arrangement – exists in order to meet these needs and wants and whether there should be one state or many is a pragmatic issue which is determined by the effectiveness with which the political arrangements in question perform their task. Kantians and utilitarians fill out the implications of this basic position in slightly different ways, but without changing the nature of the argument. A key question, though, is whether this simple position does actually provide a justification for the norms of self-determination and non-intervention; the answer seems to be no. In the first place, variation in the performance of actual states makes it clear that they cannot *all* be seen to be acting as local agents of the common good, or at least if this is the basis for their legitimacy then many are actually illegitimate. Pragmatism here cuts both ways, often, indeed usually, against the grain of the norms of self-determination and non-intervention – Beitz at least would acknowledge this, arguing that much of the time there is only a different kind of pragmatic case against intervention, namely the difficulties of actually doing more good than harm by intervening (Beitz, 1979/2000).

But, second, even in cases where states *are* attempting to meet the needs of their peoples in the desired way, it is not clear that on this basis they would be entitled to the protection of a norm of non-intervention, nor is it clear that self-determination is necessarily desirable. In terms of the common good, the simple case in favour of self-determination might be something along the lines of a putative common need that everyone has to be part of a community – but some would deny that such a need is real, and in any event how is the value of being governed by one's 'own' people to be compared with the general benefit that comes from being governed well? Again, non-intervention may be justified on the basis that in any legal system there needs to be an accessible final point of decision and the sovereignty norm clearly identifies such a point – but it is not clear why this point of decision has to be found within a territorial political unit, or what would be lost by allowing for the possibility of external supervision of that unit. It is, to understate the case, by no means clear that the common good of the peoples of Europe over the last fifty years has been harmed by the existence of the European Convention on Human Rights and the possibility of an appeal from national jurisdictions to a higher, European, level.

This argument could be extended, but the basic point is that the simple justification of the state as a local agent of the common good will not take us very far – in fact, this simple version can look more like the basis for a critique of the norms of self-determination and non-intervention than a defence. However, there is a rather more elaborate version of the same basic idea which deserves to be considered, and which delivers rather more in the way of substantive content, although it is still problematic; that is the neo-Hegelian, 'constitutive', theory of the state associated most recently with the work of Mervyn Frost (Frost, 1996, 1998 and 2000; Sutch, 2000).

The constitutive theory of the state

Unlike Beitz, the utilitarians and, perhaps, Kant, Frost begins by acknowledging that there is indeed the possibility of a genuine contradiction between the common good – which he expresses in terms of the notion of universal human rights – and the 'sovereignty' norm of non-intervention. Whereas those other writers privilege the former in all circumstances and refuse to acknowledge that sovereignty is to be valued in its own terms, Frost argues that both rights and sovereignty are settled norms of the current system neither of which should be privileged above the other. Rather, the task should be to find some

background theory which explains how these two apparently contradictory norms are, in fact, consistent with one another.

The answer, he suggests, can be found by reference to some of the
Hegelian ideas sketched in chapter 3 above. The key step is to understand that although human individuality is something universally to
be valued – a genuine common good and the basis for all rights – it is
not something that exists independently of the social institutions of
the family, civil society and, crucially, the state. The state is the forum
within which individuals are reconciled to one another via their shared
and equal status as citizens; the inequality that is characteristic of civil
society and the particularity that is the essence of the family are, in
the ethical state, overcome and transcended by a form of equality
and impartiality which guarantees the rights of all, and therefore
the common good. The independence of the state is required for it
to perform this role (hence the norm of non-intervention) and the
citizens need to think of the state as *their* state and not simply as an
administrative apparatus or centre of power (hence the norm of self-
determination). The sovereignty of the state, in other words, is a precondition of its acting as the local agent of the common good, and not
simply a contingent, pragmatic feature of its performance of this role.

What of the circumstances where the state appears not to be performing the functions allotted to it by Frost/Hegel, by, for example,
being a major violator of human rights? Here Frost comes up against
a feature of Hegel's thought that has divided his followers for nearly
200 years. Is Hegel's account of the state essentially a sanitized account
of the status quo, a defence of how things are, which is the 'Right-
Hegelian' view, or a clarion call to change, an account of how things
might be, which is the 'Left-Hegelian' standpoint? One of the weak-
nesses of Frost's position is that he is reluctant to choose between these
alternatives. It is quite obviously the case that many, perhaps most,
states do not come very close to performing the integrative function
assigned to them by Hegel/Frost, but Frost is unwilling to draw from
this the radical conclusion that these states are illegitimate, and thus
that they are not entitled to the protection of the sovereignty norms.
Rather, his argument is that even the rulers of delinquent states
acknowledge the force of 'common good' arguments and the value of
equal citizenship; they must be encouraged to reform themselves
without external intervention – or at least whatever external intervention does take place ought to be oriented towards the promotion of civil
society and rights, and should not attempt to coerce states into developing in the desired way.

It could well be argued that this gives too much credit to rulers who
often have no one's interests except their own at heart, and the only

thing that prevents this from being a straightforward defence of the status quo is the belief at the heart of Frost's position that the power of rights thinking is such as to be able to overcome all opposition in the long run. On the other hand, it is difficult to see what alternative position is available to Frost, in so far as he wishes to defend the sovereignty norms and is not prepared to regard them as violatable on pragmatic grounds, which would be, for example, Beitz's response to this dilemma. Frost's refusal to privilege either sovereignty or human rights requires him to regard them as ultimately compatible, whatever the evidence against this position might be.

International society as a practical association

Although Frost focuses on the state, his is a universalist position, in the sense that the role of the state is to realize the common good – which in Frost's case is defined in terms of human rights and, in particular, the rights of citizenship. This position firmly locates him within one line of thought about international society and the value of sovereignty, that identified above as the idea that states are local agents of the common good. There is, however, another, opposite, line of thought associated with the notion of international society; on this account the justification of the state rests upon its role in allowing different conceptions of the good to flourish. The premise here is that it can by no means be taken for granted that every society will have the same conception of the 'good', and the role of the norms of non-intervention and self-determination is to avoid a situation in which any one conception of the good is privileged. There is a certain symmetry here in terms of the authors considered in the last two sections of this chapter. Whereas Kantians and utilitarians privilege the common good and are willing to support sovereignty norms on a purely pragmatic basis, and Frost refuses to privilege either the common good or sovereignty, this position privileges sovereignty not in opposition to the common good, but because the existence of a common good for all humanity – or at least one with political bite – is denied.

This conception of international society can be found within the work of the 'English School', most of whose members were (and are) torn between this defence of an international society of sovereign states and the one outlined in the previous two sections, but the most impressive modern defence of this position can be found in the work of Terry Nardin in *Law, Morality and the Relations of States*, although it should perhaps be noted that Nardin's own thinking has moved somewhat away from the ideas set out in that volume (Nardin, 1983 and 1989).

The feature of Nardin's 1983 work that distinguishes it from much of the rest of the international society literature is his desire to make contact with the wider world of political philosophy, and, in keeping with this ambition, Nardin's approach is based on a distinction elaborated by Michael Oakeshott in the latter's masterwork, *On Human Conduct* (Oakeshott, 1975). In this work Oakeshott draws a distinction between 'enterprise' and 'civil' associations. The former are voluntary associations in which people come together in pursuit of some specific goal; in Oakeshott's account of the world these features make this form of association non-political. Civil association, on the other hand, occurs when citizens (*cives*) come together to decide upon authoritative rules concerning the general arrangements of a society, and, because these rules are authoritative, civil association is non-voluntary. For Oakeshott, these features mean that it is the only true form of a *political* association, and in his hands this becomes the basis for a general critique of those accounts of politics which assume that the role of the state is to promote some conception of the common good. The properly constituted state allows its citizens to pursue their own conceptions of the good; they may combine one with another in this pursuit, forming enterprise associations, but, to reiterate, such associations are voluntary and non-political. The only common goal that is properly political is the goal of allowing citizens to pursue their own sense of the good under whatever general arrangements they decide are necessary to allow them to go about their business in this way.

These ideas have been moderately influential amongst libertarian critics of the welfare state, and were occasionally called in aid by Thatcherite publicists in the 1980s – although the Thatcher government's commitment to restructuring the British economy in the interests of efficiency could well serve as an example of a non-political enterprise usurping the proper role of the state. In any event, Nardin takes from the Oakeshottian position the idea that civil association is the only form of association compatible with freedom of the individual, and translates this into an account of an international society in which the individuality of the *states* of which it is composed is guaranteed. Since 'civil' is not quite right in this context, he renames civil association *practical association*, because authoritative practices come out of this form of association. Less helpfully, and unnecessarily, he renames enterprise associations *purposive associations*, which is a little confusing because practical association has a purpose too, albeit the purpose of allowing states to co-exist under conditions of peace and justice. International society he conceptualizes as a practical association; it is based on a set of authoritative practices at the heart of which are the formal principles of international law – non-aggression, self-determination, non-intervention – and the rules governing diplomacy.

These principles are formal in the sense that they are purely procedural; they do not commit the members of international society to any project based around the realization of a common conception of the good; the terms of practical association simply require that states behave towards each other in ways that are consistent with peace and a formal, procedural conception of justice.

This latter point is important to Nardin, whose understanding of 'justice' is encapsulated in the formula of the impartial application of rules that are themselves impartial 'in the sense that they do not discriminate arbitrarily against particular persons or ends' (Nardin, 1983, p. 258). Justice in this procedural sense contrasts with 'substantive' or distributive justice (Nardin, 1981). The latter notion has no role to play in international society because states have nothing to distribute in their roles as members of international society – this is, of course, hardly a surprising conclusion because Oakeshott makes the same argument with respect to the domestic political order. To behave justly in international relations means to act in accordance with the rules and authoritative practices of the society of states. Attempts to expand this notion via, for example, the demand in the 1970s for a New International Economic Order (NIEO), which will be considered later in this book, misunderstand the nature of international society, taking it to be purposive rather than practical. The only basis for complaint about the existing order from the Third World would be if it could be demonstrated that the existing rules are not in themselves impartial or are not impartially applied. Not so, Nardin argues, somewhat controversially – the rules of practical association in the area of international economic relations are indeed impartial and impartially applied. Lest this may seem to be an obviously false position, it should be noted that Nardin's argument does not commit him to the view that the same could be said for the rules of some of the purposive associations which deal with international economic relations. Thus, for example, the rules of the World Trade Organization may well not be impartial, but the WTO is a voluntary, purposive association whose members have signed up for it knowing what they are letting themselves in for. There is an element of unreality to this last point, given the difficulty of surviving in the world without being a member of bodies such as the WTO, but the point of principle holds. Some states do indeed hold aloof from such bodies and there is nothing inherently self-contradictory in such a stance, whereas to deny the force of, for example, such a practical rule of international society as the idea of diplomatic immunity is self-contradicting, because without such practical rules a state cannot be a state. The reasoning here is not dissimilar to the argument for the force of Westphalian norms presented at the end of chapter 3 (Kratochwil, 1989 and 1995).

States are entitled to the protection of the sovereignty norms because these norms summarize impartial rules and practices which give to *all* states the same capacity to develop their own conceptions of the good. However, an interesting question arises at this point: how do particular practices come to be seen as impartial in this sense of not forcing states to accept binding principles in areas that they think ought to be covered by purposive associations only? We might agree that demands for a NIEO fall outside the scope of practical association, but what of the international human rights regime that has sprung up over the last fifty years? On the face of it, this appears to commit states to a particular conception of the good that is by no means required in order to allow them to live together in peace and justice. Some states that do not respect human rights have been (and are) quite good international citizens who mind their own business and obey international law – why should they be required to sign up to the international human rights regime? Nardin is obviously reluctant to come to the conclusion that the human rights regime is not part of international society understood as a practical association; his argument seems to be that respect for human rights is now so firmly established in international law that this has to be regarded as a practice which defines membership of international society. Just as one cannot be a member of international society while denying the practice of diplomatic immunity, so it is now impossible to be a member of international society while denying the force of claims for universal rights. The fact that this is not a very convincing argument may explain why Nardin has moved in a more universalist direction in later work, moving away from the idea that international society simply provides an ethics of co-existence, and attributing to it more moral substance (Nardin, 1989; Mapel and Nardin, 1998).

The root problem with Nardin's earlier position is that it seems to overrule the basic distinction between practical and purposive association upon which his work is constructed. If simply being generally accepted as part of international law were to be a sufficient basis for being considered part of the rules of practical association, then the latter would lose its distinctive character. There is, in any event, a wider problem with Nardin's position, which is connected to the relationship between the state and 'conceptions of the good'. The justification offered for the sovereignty norms of the contemporary international order is that they allow different conceptions of the good to flourish – but it is by no means clear that states are necessarily the best carriers of such conceptions of the good. This takes us back to the starting point of Nardin's analysis – his analogy between states and citizens. Is it really the individuality of states that is important internationally? Or perhaps some other entity would be more appropriate here – political communities, for example?

The rights of political communities

This last point raises an important issue, which is partly connected to the origin of particular positions in international political theory. Terry Nardin may be particularly interested in international law and international ethics but his starting point remains the discourses of International Relations. A salient feature of these discourses is the centrality of the state, and it is safe to generalize that when IR scholars look to contribute to international political theory they tend to start from a state-centric position. International political theorists who come to the discourse via conventional political theory are less inclined to assume that this is a necessary starting point, and, perhaps for that reason, are more inclined to adopt cosmopolitan positions which do not attempt to justify the state or the norms of self-determination and non-intervention. However, one of the most impressive defences of these norms in contemporary international political theory comes from a scholar whose roots are not in international relations, and whose primary focus – although this is not always apparent – is the political community rather than the state as such; this is the American social theorist Michael Walzer. Walzer's work will be the focus of the rest of this chapter, and will feature in later chapters as well; he is one of the two or three most important contemporary international political theorists.

For most of the scholars discussed in this book, biographical details are not of great significance, but in Walzer's case some minimal details of his life are necessary to grasp the pattern of his thought. The key point here is his connection with American radicalism, and in particular the non-communist American left; he is in a line of American-Jewish social critics, a younger successor (b. 1935) to figures such as Sidney Hook and Norman Podhoretz, but with the key difference that he has not moved to the right, in the way that many figures out of this tradition did in the 1960s and 1970s. As editor of the left-leaning journal *Dissent* as well as one of the few holders of a permanent chair at the Institute for Advanced Studies in Princeton, he is a 'public intellectual' of some significance in both the US and Israel, and although hardly a radical firebrand, he remains committed to classical social democratic causes such as the provision of universal health-care and an effective welfare state.

Walzer's early work as a political theorist was on the political thought of the seventeenth-century English Revolution but he developed an interest in issues of direct concern to international political theory from a number of different angles and for different reasons, although the nature of political community is a common factor in each case (Walzer, 1965). It should be said that 'issues of concern to international political theory' is the right formulation here, because from his perspective he is doing political theory and acting as a social critic rather than explicitly contributing to the discourse of international political theory. In the 1980s and 1990s his *Spheres of Justice* was a major contribution to debates on the theory of justice stimulated by John Rawls's book of that title in 1971, and his *Thick and Thin: Moral Argument at Home and Abroad* and other writings contributed to debates about cultural relativism and universal human rights (Walzer, 1983 and 1994b). His general contribution to political philosophy can be traced most effectively via the essays by Walzer and his critics in *Pluralism, Justice and Equality* edited by Walzer and his British follower and associate, David Miller (Miller and Walzer, 1995). However, his first contribution to international political theory, and the best known to students of International Relations, was to the notion of the Just War. In the 1960s and early 1970s, Walzer was an active opponent of America's involvement in the Vietnam War, taking part in the various campaigns against the war on American university campuses, but he was not a pacifist; like the vast majority of Americans he was a strong supporter of Israel's war effort in 1967 and 1973. The desire to reconcile these two positions, to distinguish between just and unjust wars, led him to produce one of the best books ever written on the subject, and certainly the best of the last quarter century, *Just and Unjust Wars: A Moral Argument with Historical Illustrations* (JUJW) (Walzer, 1977/ 1992). This book remains a central text of international political theory (*Ethics and International Affairs*, 1997).

JUJW is a very rich and – if the word is not inappropriate in this context – entertaining volume, which will be referred to extensively in the next chapter. What is of particular interest here is the 'Theory of Aggression' set out in part 2 of JUJW, and helpfully anthologized as 'The Rights of Political Communities', with responses, in a useful collection on international ethics of 1985 (Beitz et al., 1985). This is the point at which Walzer sets out the circumstances which allow us to decide whether a particular resort to force is justified. The answer he suggests is that states are entitled to resort to force when the norms of self-determination and non-intervention are violated, and so the argument becomes, in effect, a defence of these latter norms – actually the best defence currently available. The argument encompasses an account of the rights of states in a world of states, and an account of *why* the rights of states ought to be defended.

The best way to set out the argument is to begin with what Walzer terms the *Legalist Paradigm*, which summarizes the contemporary international law on these matters. The legalist paradigm on his account is explicitly based on an analogy with domestic politics, and composes six elements (Walzer, 1977/1992, pp. 58ff): first, that there exists an international society of independent states, which, second, has a law that establishes the rights of its members, above all the rights to territorial integrity and political sovereignty (this establishes the centrality of the norm of self-determination); third, any use of force or imminent threat of force by one state against the territorial integrity or political sovereignty of another constitutes aggression and is a criminal act (which establishes the norm of non-intervention, and criminalizes breaches of the norm); fourth, aggression justifies two kinds of violent response, wars of self-defence and wars of law-enforcement; fifth, only acts of aggression can justify war; sixth, given the criminalization of acts of aggression, the punishment of an aggressor is justified.

The use of a domestic analogy here is controversial – English School theorists of international society such as Bull and Wight reject this move – but the content of the Legalist Paradigm is designed by Walzer to reflect current international law as established by the UN Charter, the Pact of Paris 1928 (the Kellogg-Briand Pact to outlaw war) and the London Charter of 1945 (which set up the Nuremberg Tribunal and established that planning aggressive war was an international crime). Walzer wishes to amend this paradigm on the margins, but before we get to the amendments, it would be useful to look at the background account of the state which leads him to argue that, in general terms, the legalist paradigm is morally acceptable.

In essence, his position is that the Legalist Paradigm is morally acceptable because it preserves the rights of political communities, and those rights in turn are morally acceptable because they rest upon the rights of the individuals who make up political communities – when the rights of political communities are preserved, individuals have the capacity to shape their own lives and choose the form of government they desire, and that is why these rights are worthy of support. Since Walzer is sometimes caricatured as defending the rights of states in virtually all circumstances, it is worth quoting at length his rebuttal of this position:

> [T]he moral standing of any particular state depends on the reality of the common life it protects and the extent to which the sacrifices required by that protection are willingly accepted and thought worthwhile. If no common life exists, or if the state doesn't defend the common life that does exist, its own defence may have no moral justification. (Walzer, 1977/1992, p. 54)

Thus it is clear that it is the rights of *political communities* rather than states as such that Walzer believes the norms of self-determination and non-intervention are designed to defend.

There is, of course, a potential problem here, because the latter norms are actually defended via the Legalist Paradigm, which concerns states rather than political communities, and, partly in response to this problem, Walzer proposes some amendments to the Legalist Paradigm. First, and least relevant in this context, he suggests a doctrine of justified pre-emptive war, in circumstances where one state has good reason to think another is likely to attack in the near future. More to the point, he suggests three circumstances in which the doctrine of non-intervention is not performing the task it is supposed to and therefore intervention is permitted (although not necessarily required). First, a particular set of boundaries may contain two political communities one of which is already engaged in a large-scale struggle for independence, and in those circumstances outside intervention may be legitimate. Second, when a foreign power has already intervened, counter-intervention may be legitimate. Most interestingly, third,

> [w]hen the violation of human rights within a set of boundaries is so terrible that it makes talk of community or self-determination or 'arduous struggle' seem cynical and irrelevant, that is, *in cases of enslavement or massacre*. (Walzer, 1977/1992, p. 90; emphasis added)

This very revealing sentence packs a great deal into a few words. The essential point is that there is no assumption that the common life of a community will necessarily be democratic in form or involve personal freedom. Communal autonomy - which is what the norms of self-determination and non-intervention are designed to protect – is central, not the form of government chosen by the community. Personal freedom may be desirable – Walzer certainly thinks it is – but it is not something that can be established by outside intervention; Walzer follows Mill's defence of non-intervention at this point. Those who wish for personal freedom will almost certainly have to engage in a political struggle to achieve this goal, a struggle that may be long and arduous (hence the reference to 'arduous struggle'). Normally this should be allowed to take its course, but the third allowed violation of the norm of non-intervention establishes the circumstances in which outsiders are permitted to take a hand; these circumstances are, it will be seen, very restrictive. Violations of human rights must be 'terrible', such that any talk of a community determining its own fate is an obvious nonsense, and Walzer is precise about what he means by terrible in this context, namely massacre and enslavement.

This position brings Walzer very close to the mainstream of international thought over the last 350 years. As was established in chapter 2, the international lawyers who developed the theory of international society rarely argued for an absolute rule of non-intervention; to use Martin Wight's phrase, intervention has generally been seen to be permissible in cases of 'gross violations of human dignity', and the sort of examples Wight had in mind – the slave trade, genocide – correspond to Walzer's position (Wight, 'Western Values', 1966). The difference is that whereas ultimately Wight and others defend this position in terms of the functioning of international society, making the point that without severe restrictions on the circumstances in which the norm of non-intervention could be breached international order would break down, Walzer defends his position in terms of the rights of the political community. In effect, people have the right to be left to their own devices even if this right entails them being subjected to what appear to be human rights violations; the assumption must be that such violations are in accordance with the will of the community, an expression of its common life – unless, that is, they are taken to the kind of extremes that would make a mockery of such an argument. Short of the latter situation, the working assumption must be that states do represent their peoples and are thus legitimately entitled to the protection of the sovereignty norms.

Walzer is sometimes associated with 'communitarianism', an intellectual and political movement that has developed over the last two decades in response to liberal notions of politics and the individual – the term was coined by Michael Sandel, an influential critic of the liberal political theory of John Rawls (Sandel, 1982). The core communitarian position is that the liberal conception of the individual as a pre-social being, entering into relations with other individuals already more or less fully formed, is mistaken – individuals are always 'embedded selves' shaped by their social environment. In fact, Walzer's relationship to this position is ambiguous. In his writings since *Just and Unjust Wars* he has put a great deal of stress on the importance of 'shared understandings' about the political arrangements of a society, which would seem to align him with communitarianism, but he has refused the label (Walzer, 1990). Some of these later writings will be discussed in chapters 7 and 10 in the contexts of critiques of the universalism of the notion of human rights and the issue of cultural diversity and international political theory, but two texts ought to be considered briefly at this point in the argument because they are germane to the central position under discussion here.

Thick and Thin: Moral Argument at Home and Abroad (1994) returns to the position outlined in the extended quotes presented above. Political arrangements reflect the shared understandings, that is, the common life, of particular societies, and these understandings are likely to differ from one society to another – when Chinese dissidents, say, demonstrate in favour of 'democracy' or 'justice' it is unlikely that they mean exactly the same by these terms as people in the US would. At the same time, it is equally unlikely that they will mean something totally different by these terms; probably there will be some kind of family resemblance between 'justice' Beijing-style and 'justice' New York-style. For a full ('thick') understanding of the notion of justice it is necessary that the concept be embedded within the shared understandings of a particular place and time, but there may well be a more basic, minimalist ('thin') understanding of the concept that is able to do some work, albeit not as much as its thick equivalent. Trying to find the content of this moral minimalism is an important task, and in international politics, Walzer argues, the notion of self-determination expresses much of this moral minimalism – at a minimum, whatever else they might want, communities ought to have the right to decide upon their own form of government.

But this cannot be an absolute right; not all forms of government can be justified in terms of the shared understanding of a society – slavery and genocide are examples of practices which would be wrong even if they were part of the shared understandings or common life of a community, which, of course, at times they have been. In *Interpretation and Social Criticism* (1987) Walzer sets out the difference between those social critics who emerge from within society and criticize it in accordance with its own norms and those who stand apart from society and criticize it from the perspective of universal values. He favours the former, but this is not to say that there is no role for the latter; he sets out here an interesting analogy, between a 'home' and a 'hotel room'. We all wish to live in a home (a morally dense, 'thick' environment) rather than in the minimally decent accommodation provided by a hotel room, but the latter provides a kind of model of a 'thin' environment which can be used to judge the adequacy of the former – if a so-called home does not meet the minimally decent standards provided by a hotel room then something is wrong, and 'homes' that are based on slavery or massacre would fail this test.

As noted above, Walzer's arguments will feature quite frequently in this book and will be criticized when they arise. However, it would be appropriate to note one or two general points here. First, it might well be thought that Walzer's strategy of giving the state the benefit of any doubt over the legitimacy of its social and political arrangements is altogether too generous. It is worth remembering that J. S. Mill, the originator of Walzer's defence of a right of self-determination, did not believe that all societies were fit to exercise this right. Walzer's universalism here is more democratic and less patronizing, but also, perhaps, less realistic; the argument that particular social and political arrangements reflect the common life of the people may have some substance in some cases, but many states in the world today clearly do not correspond to 'social facts' in the way the argument requires. For example, the inhabitants of most of the states of post-colonial Africa do not share a common life; they are communities of fate, thrown together by arbitrary decision made by rulers based a continent away. The same might also be said of the established states of Europe, but at least in many of these cases the arbitrary decisions took place much longer ago, and the peoples in question have had the time to develop some elements of a common life.

This argument feeds into another, which concerns the capacity of resistance to tyranny. Walzer, following Mill again, argues that peoples wishing to be free should engage in 'arduous struggle' to achieve this goal – but the technologies of oppression are rather more effective in the twenty-first century than they were in the mid-nineteenth, and 'arduous struggle' is a higher-risk activity than it once was. The fall of the communist regimes in Eastern Europe and the former Soviet Union between 1989 and 1991 demonstrates that determined opposition can overcome tyranny in some circumstances – likewise the fall of Slobodan Milosevic in Serbia in 2000 – but to say that the events in Tiananmen Square in the summer of 1989 show that the Chinese people were not really prepared to engage in an arduous struggle for freedom would be a harsh judgement to make. On the other hand, it may not be wholly inaccurate; the willingness of the Chinese People's Liberation Army to employ force against the demonstrators, as opposed, say, to the unwillingness of the security forces to protect Milosevic in 2000, does convey some information about popular attitudes, although perhaps not enough to justify a favourable judgement on the legitimacy of the Chinese regime.

All told, Walzer is one of the most interesting of contemporary international political theorists, but also one of the most highly controversial. Perhaps part of the controversy stems from his mode of argumentation. Jon Elster refers to Walzer as providing a 'phenomenology of the moral life', the implication being that Walzer describes the surface of events but does not reach the philosophical depths (Elster, 1992, p. 14). Elster did not entirely intend this as a compliment, but Walzer might well take it as such – his approach is indeed to make 'moral arguments with historical illustrations' to quote the subtitle of *Just and Unjust Wars*, and this could be seen as engaging in phenomenology, dealing with the immanent and not the transcendent. It may be that this is indeed an appropriate form of moral reasoning for international political theory.

Walzer's first book concerned the ethics of violence, and this is certainly a key topic in international political theory, and a matter of considerable importance for those who would defend the sovereignty norms of self-determination and non-intervention. The preservation of a system of sovereign states makes war – organized violence between collectivities – a perennial possibility, and for this reason the study of the ethics of war has always been a major field within international political theory. General issues about the legitimacy of the norms of non-intervention and self-determination will recur throughout what follows, but for the time being it makes sense to focus upon the consequences of these norms, and the ethics of war and coercion is the subject of the next chapter.

6

Force, Violence and International Political Theory

Uncomfortable though this thought may be, force, coercion and violence are features of *all* political orders, domestic and international. Sometimes – not very often, it has to be said – it has proved possible to establish political orders in which these features are sufficiently far below the surface that their existence can, temporarily, be overlooked, but even these fortunate societies do not in reality rest on the kind of social consensus that can be relied upon to keep things going in all circumstances without the necessity of forceful intervention. More characteristic of human history have been political orders whose basic nature was caught by the political theorist of reaction in post-Revolutionary France, Joseph de Maistre, when he stressed the key role of the figure of the executioner as a symbol of political authority (de Maistre, 1965). To restate the point, and using a phrase of Ernest Gellner's, all societies rest upon a systematic prejudgement – that is, positions which are not open to debate – and this prejudgement must always be defended, by force if necessary, if society is to survive (Gellner, 1994, p. 32).

The reason why it is necessary to make this sombre point at the outset of this discussion is because a great deal of writing on the phenomenon of international force and violence either implicitly or explicitly rests on a distinction between domestic politics and international politics that characterizes the former as a realm of social peace, and the latter as a realm of war, or the threat of war. The result of this characterization is to treat the problem of international violence as something set apart from 'normal' political processes, and requiring a specialized conceptual vocabulary and grammar if it is to be understood. But, while there are indeed some distinctive features of inter-state violence, this attitude is, in general, mistaken.

In this chapter, the initial focus will be on conventional international political theory topics such as the notion of a 'just war', but it will be stressed that it is a mistake to think of such topics as distinctively 'international' in origins or scope; the origins of just war thinking, for example, lie in the notion of a 'just peace', which refers to political order in general and not simply to the international order. From this more limited starting point, focus will shift towards a wider picture of the role of war and force in human affairs in which issues such as the distinctive Western conception of war and its links to particular conceptions of citizenship will come into play; the gendered nature of this picture will also come into focus. However, before moving to this agenda, it may be helpful to devote some thought to whether useful distinctions can be drawn between the notions of coercion, force and violence.

Conventional scholarship on the Westphalia System agrees that the attempted exercise of power by states is a constant feature of their relationships – that is to say, states attempt to influence each other's behaviour by the employment of positive and negative sanctions, or, if you prefer, sticks and carrots. Usually, of course, the sticks and carrots are kept in the background, and diplomats deploy reasoned arguments in favour of the positions they are instructed to promote. However, this kind of diplomatic statecraft rests ultimately on the understanding that there will be potential rewards for agreement and possible penalties for failing to agree; it is generally agreed that states are unlikely to respond simply to the strength of a better argument – and even when they do, instrumental considerations about, for example, good will in future negotiations will be in the minds of the diplomats concerned.

What kinds of 'sticks' can states deploy in negotiations? Clearly much here will depend on the particular circumstances, but conventional thought draws a clear distinction between the employment of measures of persuasion that do, and those that do not, involve violence. It would be unusual, to say the least, if, for example, fellow members of NATO or the EU were to threaten each other with force, but it is by no means unusual for even such close associates to employ other kinds of, no doubt *sotto voce*, threats to strengthen their hands in negotiations. The latter are legitimate moves, the former is not. However, the norm of non-intervention discussed in chapter 5 rests on more or less the same basic distinction, and, as noted there, it is in practice difficult to be quite as clear on the matter as theory demands. 'Influence' is legitimate, 'intervention' is not, but when precisely attempts to exert influence become acts of intervention is difficult to tell. In the previous discussion it was suggested that the removal of the power of decision might be the key here, and some similar proposition may be relevant when it comes to the exercise of power more generally. *Influence* is about trying to change someone's mind, *coercion* is about removing their options so that the state of their mind is irrelevant. We might stipulate that coercion involves the exercise of *force* because only thus can options be removed – but does force necessarily involve *physical violence*?

The answer to this latter question must be 'no'. There are many social circumstances where it is possible to prevent someone from doing something – to coerce them, in other words – without actually employing physical force. In such cases, the aim is to pin responsibility for violent behaviour on those trying to break a stranglehold rather than those applying it. A picket-line, where it is the strike-breaker who has to take physical action in order to get to work, fits the bill here and there are many non-violent actions that are intended to coerce in this way, that is to say, where the intention is to take away the freedom of action of the target unless the latter is prepared to win back this freedom by an escalation to physical force. International equivalents of this phenomenon might include the blockade or quarantine, where movement in and out of a territory is physically prevented, the peacetime equivalent of a siege. And there may be less dramatic and tangible forms of coercion: in 1990 the Iraqi regime claimed that Kuwait's oil policy had the effect of denying Iraq the oil revenues it required for reconstruction and development and that this constituted a form of coercion that justified Iraq's resort to violence. We might not, in the particular circumstances of the case, accept this position, but the general principle that it is possible to be coercive without resorting to violence is quite correct.

A related point concerns the concept of 'structural violence'. The basic proposition here is that there are certain kinds of relationships of exploitation that, although not characterized by the exercise of physical force, can be seen to be (structurally) violent in so far as they involve depriving the disadvantaged party of life-chances to the advantage of the exploiter. Thus the master–slave relationship could be said to involve violence of a kind, even if the slaves accept their status and therefore the masters have no need to employ physical violence to preserve their position. Powerful rhetorical positions are, of course, involved here on both sides. The masters invoke law and order and condemn the violence of those slaves who resist, and part of the point of the notion of structural violence is to allow the latter to respond that their violence is, in fact, a response to the structural violence to which they are subjected. The problem with the notion of structural violence, however, is that it is not clear just how far something that seems plausible in the context of slavery can be extended to cases of exploitation which are not quite so clear-cut. Johan Galtung – from whose thinking the notion of structural violence emerges – suggests that *any* relationship where the parties are unequal must be based on exploitation and structural violence, even if it cannot be demonstrated that the disadvantage of the weaker is the result of action by the stronger (Galtung, 1971). This, perhaps, pushes the notion of structural violence a little too far. If a relationship creates a situation where one party is severely disadvantaged then there may be circumstances where the use of the term violence is not inappropriate – but if this is to be used to legitimate counter-violence, then, on the face of it, it would seem quite important that a causal chain of some kind be first established.

The burden of this discussion is to suggest that conventional approaches to the ethics of force which draw a clear distinction between situations where physical violence is employed and those where it is not may be missing a large part of the game. Perhaps the emphasis ought to be on *coercion* rather than on violence, on the principle that violence is often a response to other forms of coercion and, moreover, an important point, that it is often the response of the *weak* rather than the strong. On the other hand, it may be that there is something to be said for holding on to the view that there is something distinctive about violence. Violence hurts, maims and kills – it is a way of taking away the autonomy of individuals and perhaps societies that is rather more permanent than most others, and it may be sensible to treat it somewhat differently as a result. Just as the concept of structural violence, although not implausible in itself, may have the effect of actually legitimating physical violence in circumstances where this may not be an appropriate response, so blurring the distinction between coercion and violence may also have the unfortunate effect of lowering the defences against the latter which most people would like to see maintained.

Pacifism, realism and just war thinking: an overview

Setting aside these considerations on the nature of force and violence for the moment, and returning to the conventional assumption that what needs to be examined is the use of military force by one state against another, what can be said in general terms about the ethics of such action? A key issue here is whether or not it is appropriate to discriminate between different circumstances and if so, on what basis; there are three distinct positions here, which might be termed, for the sake of convenience, pacifism, realism and the just war tradition.

The *pacifist* position is that discrimination is unnecessary because there are no circumstances where the use of military force could be justified. The moral absolute here is that the use of physical force against another human being is unconditionally wrong, and cannot be made right by any other principle, such as, for example, a right to self-defence. By way of contrast, the *just war* position argues that there are potentially at least some circumstances in which the use of military force could be morally justified, although, of course, exactly what those circumstances are is a matter for debate. There is, thus, a wide gulf between pacifist positions and just war positions, a gulf that is sometimes obscured by the misdescription as pacifist of positions that actually recognize that in some circumstances force may be justified. Thus, for example, Richard Norman's recent study is for the most part a very strong defence of pacifism, the best currently available, but it is, nonetheless, clear that Norman does not actually wish to argue that there are *no* circumstances in which military violence could be morally justified – rather, he wants to suggest that those circumstances are much more limited than those usually envisaged by just war thinking, which, although true of his position, does not alter the fact that he is engaging in discrimination (Norman, 1995). Martin Ceadal has invented the term 'pacifistic' for those people who are not actually pacifist but want to be very restrictive when it comes to the circumstances in which they would be prepared to see force used (Ceadal, 1987). This at least acknowledges that to discriminate is not a pacifist position, but it might be doubted whether it is a necessary coinage, because the sentiment it represents can be coped with within the context of just war thinking, so long as the latter is not defined too narrowly.

Realist thinking also discriminates, but not in moral terms. From the realist perspective the use of force is simply one option available to states. Because it is a costly option it should not be employed lightly – realists are critical of crusaders who resort to force too readily – but there are no particular moral objections to its use. Realism and pacifism here have some similarities in so far as neither position sees a moral problem associated with the use of military force; force is either unproblematically wrong (pacifism) or simply morally unproblematic (realism). In practice, in the twenty-first century there seem to be relatively few genuine pacifists or realists, and the rest of this section will be devoted to examining the logics of their positions before moving in the next section to a closer look at just war thinking, which, one way or another, consciously or not, is adhered to by most people who think about these matters.

The pacifist position holds that there are no circumstances in which the use of military force is justified, because to use military force involves the infliction of harm, and the damage this does (to the perpetrator as well as the victim) cannot be justified by reference to any supposed good that might result. This position is held categorically, that is to say that it does not rely upon some contingent calculation of probable outcomes. The obvious question is, what reason is there to hold such an absolute position? A list of the most famous pacifists would include Tolstoy, Gandhi and, possibly, Jesus Christ – although in the latter case the record is a little ambiguous – and organized pacifist groups include the Quakers and Jehovah's Witnesses; the religious dimension to this list suggests one possible answer to the above question. Pacifists are confident that force is never the right response because they hold to an account of the moral universe in which ultimate outcomes rest on non-human actions. An anecdote may help to illuminate this point; at a conference on just war theory attended by the author, a prominent Protestant pacifist was asked if he held to the maxim, 'let justice be done though the heavens fall'. He replied no, because 'the heavens' could not fall, a loving God would ensure that things came out right in the end, even if humankind were to be destroyed. Or, to put the matter in different terms, some kind of cosmic justice is always available even when human justice is not.

This position is not held by any of the main branches of the Christian church but its basic logic is unassailable, given the initial premises. Nor is it necessarily associated with inactivity: Gandhi's use of non-violent resistance ('soul-force') testifies to the commitment that many pacifists have to the righting of injustice – their position is simply that this cannot be achieved by the use of violence (Gandhi, 1996). Can this position be reached without some kind of cosmic guarantee? It is interesting that Conscientious Objection Tribunals in Britain in the two World Wars were generally disposed to accept pacifist objections to military service on religious grounds – especially if the individual in question was an established member of a group such as the Quakers – but very sceptical of secular pacifists. The latter were suspected of malingering or of objecting to the particular war in question rather than to war in general, and, of course, the state did not accept such a specific reservation as a ground for conscientious objection. The tribunals seem to have felt that, without the backing of some kind of religious belief, a pacifist position could not be sustained, and it does seem that many of those pacifists who were not religious in the conventional sense of the term had some sense of being in touch with cosmic forces – one thinks here, perhaps, of the mystical beliefs of the composer Michael Tippett, who suffered imprisonment for his pacifism in the Second World War (Tippett, 1991). One suspects that many secular 'pacifists' are actually Ceadal's 'pacifisticists' in disguise, although it ought to be said that the reverse is sometimes true; hence the perhaps apocryphal story of the Roman Catholic conscientious objector who, when asked whether he accepted his church's doctrine of the just war, replied that while he accepted that, in principle, there could be such a thing, he believed that there never actually had been.

Just as there are not that many true pacifists around today, so too, if realism is taken to imply the absence of any moral scruple about the use of force, the belief that decisions on the use of force ought to be taken simply with reference to calculations of utility, then very few modern realists actually fit the bill. A nineteenth-century figure like Clausewitz does; his account of war makes it clear that this is not a step lightly to be undertaken, but it also makes it clear that the calculation as to whether to take it rests simply on a materialist account of the interests of the state (Clausewitz, 1976). Most modern realists would demur somewhat from this position, on the principle that the costs involved in a resort to force are not quite like the costs involved in the employment of other policy tools. Taking life and putting one's own military personnel in harm's way is, generally and rightly, regarded as raising at least some kind of moral issue; thus, for example, when modern realists criticize just war thinking, it is not usually because the latter is morally discriminatory, but rather because it is seen as encouraging a crusading mentality and, thus, not taking the consequences of violence seriously enough (Gray, 2000).

What this suggests is that, with realists as with pacifists, the removal of moral discrimination from the consideration of force is not as easy as it seems to be. Most people who we think of, and who think of themselves, as pacifists are not actually absolutist on the matter; they are in some, albeit remote, circumstances prepared to envisage the use of force. Similarly, most realists are not amoral when it comes to force – they are prepared to acknowledge that military force is to some degree morally different from other foreign policy tools. In other words, most realists and pacifists are at opposite ends of a continuum when it comes to discrimination over the use of force, rather than occupants of absolute positions which lie beyond the reach of this continuum. This makes examination of the continuum itself an important task.

Just war thinking

One of the reasons why many pacifistically inclined thinkers reject the just war tradition is because they associate that tradition with too great a readiness to justify violence – realists, interestingly, make the same point. Politicians who are rather too ready to declare some particular use of force to be 'just', and the clerics who sometimes back them, have indeed devalued the term somewhat; in Nick Rengger's felicitous phrase, in an unpublished paper, far too often, 'Just War is just war'. Moreover, ironically, the most influential modern formulation of just war thinking, that of Michael Walzer in his important book *Just and Unjust Wars*, does not altogether help the case for the defence of the notion (Walzer, 1977/1992). Although his 'Legalist Paradigm' is a reasonably accurate account of the current legal regime on war, it is, as a result, clearly statist, that is to say, the basic requirement of a just war on this account is that the state in question is engaging in self-defence, or helping another to defend itself. Critics feel, with some justification, that this statism does not provide an appropriate basis for moral judgement. Further, in the Westphalia tradition, reflected in Walzer, a distinction is drawn between *ius ad bellum* and *ius in bello*, that is to say, the justice of a decision to go to war and the just conduct of a war (Walzer's 'war convention'), and some critics are also unhappy that such a distinction should be drawn. The final element of the case for the prosecution is that just war thinking is clearly tied into one particular moral outlook; modern versions descend directly from the medieval Christian thought of Saints Augustine and Thomas Aquinas (Johnson, 1975 and 1981). As the essays in a recent volume, which attempts an examination of *The Ethics of War and Peace* from a range of different ethical traditions, demonstrate, it is actually very difficult to find the equivalent of the doctrine of the just war elsewhere in the world (Nardin, 1996).

The case for the defence begins with the fact that most of these doubtful features of contemporary discourses on the just war are contingent, not essential, parts of the doctrine. The distinction between *ius ad bellum* and *ius in bello*, for example, was not drawn in the thought of the medieval natural lawyers who first set out a systematic account of the basis of discrimination that might be applied to decisions to use force, and the statism that is a feature of contemporary international law is also a later, Westphalian, addition. Properly understood, the just war tradition provides a vocabulary and a grammar for examining issues of force that is the best currently available, even if some elements of the tradition certainly require revision, and just war thinking can certainly be applied to contemporary conflicts (Ramsey, 1968; Paskins and Dockrill, 1979; Elshtain, 1991; DeCosse, 1992; C. Brown, 2000d).

Part of the reason for the widespread rejection of the tradition lies in the very term 'just war', which seems to imply that, in the right circumstances, war could be a 'good thing'. This is most definitely not at the heart of the tradition, which is rather that, in certain circumstances, the resort to force might be *justified*; force is always an evil, but it may be the lesser of two evils. 'Just peace' would be a more accurate summary of the doctrine, because the underlying assumption is that it is right that human beings should live together in communities in peace and justice; everything else flows from this basic proposition (Finnis, 1996). If peace and justice are the norm, then acts which violently disrupt peace and justice are wrong, and the key question is what ought to be done about such acts – in what circumstances is it proper to respond to such acts of violence with acts of violence? The answer to this question is complex, but always centres on the contribution that particular acts might, or might not, make to the restoration of this initial state of peace and justice. This means, for one obvious example, that on this count there is no automatic right of self-defence, and, *a fortiori*, states cannot claim such a right simply by virtue of being members in good standing of international society. Self-defence is legitimate if exercised in order to preserve peace and justice, but not otherwise.

Under what circumstances is a violent response to a prior act of violence legitimate? In the tradition this is discussed under several headings, all of which are important; just cause, right intention, proper authority, last resort, effectiveness, proportionality, discrimination. Taken together these notions provide the resources for a discussion on the ethics of violence in international relations (and, for that matter in other areas of social life) and they by no means have the statist implications with which the just war tradition is often associated. Taken individually, each notion is problematic, but the problems they pose reflect the real-life moral dilemmas that are involved with action – they are not problems simply associated with a scholastic frame of mind, as is sometimes asserted by critics.

Just cause is, in principle, the easiest of these notions to describe; the restoration of conditions of peace and justice is the paradigmatic just cause – the basic proposition of the tradition is that violence can only be justified if it is directed towards the re-establishment of conditions under which violence does not take place. Such a restoration might involve the right to self-defence of a victim of aggression, but not the unqualified right that the statist notions of non-intervention and non-aggression mandate – other factors, outlined below, qualify this right. One problem with this basic definition of a just cause is that it seems to assume that a disruption of normality has recently taken place; what happens when an injustice is long-standing? This is the kind of situation that arises with some frequency when humanitarian intervention is under consideration. Often here the issue is not the re-establishment of peace and justice but their establishment for the first time. This in turn raises the issue of whether *any* social arrangements can actually be characterized as peaceful and just in any unqualified way. As noted at the beginning of this chapter, all social arrangements involve some kind of prejudgement and ultimately rest upon coercion. This does not suggest that the ideal of peaceful and just social arrangements ought to be scrapped, but it does suggest that it ought to be recognized as just that, an ideal. There is no getting away from the need to make judgements about the *relative* peace and justice of particular arrangements.

Right intention is a more difficult notion. Anyone who uses violence ought to intend to restore/establish peace and justice, but is it necessary that this intention be the *sole* intention? Or is it sufficient if it is the

primary intention, or simply *one among many* intentions? What the tradition is saying here is that the motive for action is important, but it is
usually the case that when people/states act they do so for more than
one reason – is this necessarily illegitimate? This is an issue that comes
up with great regularity in international relations; for example, the
Coalition's motives in the Gulf War of 1990/91 were closely probed,
and it was suggested, quite plausibly, that restoring the territorial
integrity and sovereignty of Kuwait was only one among many
motives, and that preserving the West's oil supplies was rather more
in the minds of the decision-makers involved. Similarly, in the Kosovo
campaign of 1999, it was argued by critics, rather less plausibly in
this case, that the intentions of NATO were directed towards its own
aggrandizement rather than the relief of suffering in Kosovo itself
(Chomsky, 1999). Taking the issue a little further back in time, the
Catholic philosopher G. E. M. Anscombe refused to support the Anglo-
French cause in 1939, believing that the motives of the British and
French governments were compromised by power politics; her essay,
'The justice of the present war examined', is an interestingly extreme
statement of the importance of right intention (Anscombe, 1981).

Assuming that in each case the critics have a point, does the presence
of mixed motives necessarily detract from the justice of the act? Since
the motives of individuals are always mixed, if the answer to this question is positive, then it is very difficult to imagine that there will ever be
circumstances in which the criterion of right intention will be met and
in that case the discrimination that the just war tradition attempts to
enact will be defeated. It seems more sensible to argue that the righting
of a wrong should be a major motive for action but need not be the only
motive; Nicholas Wheeler, in his recent study of humanitarian intervention, adds the helpful proviso that other motives should, at the very
least, not be incompatible with right intention (Wheeler, 2000).

Proper authority is a notion that arises out of the concern of medieval
theologians to stamp out the then prevalent menace of so-called private wars, where particular local magnates would resort to force in
their quarrels with their neighbours; right authority in this context is
meant to indicate the legitimate secular rulers whose general authority was underwritten by the church and Catholic doctrine, in contrast
to the power held by these wealthy hooligans. Is the equivalent of
right authority in the current international order vested in the United
Nations? This would certainly be a legal answer to this question; the
UN Charter binds its signatories not to employ force as a means of pursuing their interests; states are entitled to employ force in self-defence
but only until the UN Security Council can be seized of the situation
(Article 2(4)). On the other hand, the UN Security Council is a political body which is often unable to reach any decision on important

matters because of the existence of the 'Veto' provision in the Charter, which allows the 'Permanent Five' to block action, and it would be strange if the *only* source of proper authority in contemporary international relations were to be subject to such blocking tactics. It seems more sensible to leave open the notion of proper authority – the UN is part of the story here, but not all of it.

Last resort is a relatively simple notion, but one that is often misunderstood. The basic point is that violence should only be employed when it is clear that no non-violent method of suasion would be effective. This might actually be clear immediately, and the last resort could well also be the first or only resort. Last resort does *not* require that all other strategies be tried first, so long as it is reasonably clear that they would have no realistic prospects of success – in other words, the criterion of the last resort ought not to be used as a delaying tactic. One feature of the last resort which it shares with the next criterion – a reasonable prospect of success – is that determining when the last resort has been achieved is not actually a matter for ethicists, moral philosophers and theologians. The latter group may insist that violence is only acceptable if it is the last resort, but they usually do not possess the information that would allow them to make a judgement as to whether some particular use of violence meets this criterion. Thus, to return to the Gulf War in 1990/91, ethicists would not be in a position to say whether the resort to war by the Coalition was actually the last resort, because to make this judgement it would be necessary to have some considerable grasp of the political psychology of the Iraqi leadership, their capacity to maintain control in Iraq, the ability of the Iraqi economy to resist sanctions, and a number of other areas of expertise which there is no reason to believe that moral theorists or theologians are actually likely to possess. All the latter can do is to argue that those who do possess this expertise should employ it to determine whether force is actually necessary.

Effectiveness – the notion that any resort to violence must have a reasonable prospect of success – is required because the purpose of violence is to right a wrong and if a particular wrong cannot be righted then violence serves no purpose, and the general injunction to do no harm takes over. As noted in the previous paragraph, whether or not violence is likely to be effective is a technical issue, and this again is a situation where the ethical theorist is in the hands of other specialists. Another interesting issue concerning effectiveness is that of 'exemplary' effects. Might it be right to respond forcibly in some situation even if success is unlikely if it can be shown that by so responding a message has been sent to other potential transgressors?

Proportionality says that a sledgehammer should not be used to crush a nut; violence in response to wrongdoing ought to be proportional to that wrongdoing. This is a difficult notion because it seems to require that we be as concerned with the damage done to wrongdoers as we are with the damage done to those acting justifiably, which seems somewhat counter-intuitive. Thus, the Coalition was criticized in 1991 for putting together an overwhelming force to retake Kuwait, and for inflicting tens of thousands of casualties on Iraq and only suffering hundreds itself; this, it was said, is disproportionate – but it is difficult to see the attraction of the alternative policy of making a 'fair' fight of it and accepting equal casualties with those of the wrongdoer. Assuming that the liberation of Kuwait was a just cause – and, of course, this actually needs to be argued rather than assumed – it seems to make sense to ensure that it was carried out with a minimum loss of life on the part of the liberators. However, this treats the casualties of Iraqi troops as irrelevant, and the just war tradition refuses to take this step. The harm done to the latter has to be factored into the equation, and it might well be held that if Kuwait could only be liberated by inflicting tens of thousands of deaths then the requirement of proportionality could not be met, and the action was wrong.

This leads into the last notion, that violence should be *discriminatory* if it is to be just. This is often nowadays translated into the notion of 'non-combatant immunity' but this is not what was originally intended by this requirement. The original notion was that the 'innocent' ought not to be subjected to violence, and it is clear that the moral notion of innocence cannot be equated with the technical status of being a non-combatant. Perhaps once this was a reasonable equation. When fighting took place between regular armies composed of volunteers, and wearing a uniform indicated acceptance of status as a fighter, the equation of non-combatant and innocent made some sense. Nowadays with conscript armies and, potentially, whole societies at war it is much less clear that this is so. A pay clerk in uniform but behind a desk a long way from the conflict seems rather more 'innocent' than a civilian munitions worker, or a politician who has supported a war of aggression – even though the pay clerk could be required to pick up a weapon and join the fight if necessary. Were the Iraqi dead in 1991 'innocents'? It seems plausible that in any moral sense many of them were, although the vast majority were combatants in the technical sense (Mapel, 1992). Clearly under modern conditions it is very difficult to make the kind of distinctions the tradition requires, although that is no reason for not making the effort, because without some such effort there is no distinction to be drawn between 'war and massacre' or 'war and murder', to quote two very useful discussions of this subject (Nagel, 1985; Anscombe, 1981). The issue of innocence is, to understate the case, particularly troublesome in the case of a potential nuclear war; for this reason some of the leading Catholic moral philosophers in the just war tradition have argued that even the threat to use nuclear weapons, let alone their actual use, is clearly wrong (Finnis et al., 1987).

The death of innocents is obviously not always necessarily a sign that there has been no attempt to discriminate. Such deaths may be accidental, but, according to one particularly troubling notion, they may also be anticipated. The doctrine of 'double effect' holds that the death of innocents may be acceptable, subject to considerations of proportionality, if such was not the intent of the action, even if it is a likely consequence. Thus, to take the kind of Second World War example often given in this case, it might be legitimate to attack a Gestapo headquarters where awful things are taking place, even though it can be anticipated that innocent civilians living alongside will be killed – such was not the intention of the act, even though it is an anticipated effect. This doctrine is, as might be expected, highly controversial (Woodward, 2001).

A number of features of the tradition set out above are worth noting, because they contrast with much modern thinking. Westphalian thinking divides 'ius in bello' from 'ius ad bellum', a distinction reflected in Walzer's separate treatment of the 'Legalist Paradigm' and the 'War Convention'; the tradition does not. The tradition holds that if a war cannot be fought justly it ought not to be fought at all, which explicitly disallows the notion of 'supreme emergency' as a reason for disregarding constrains on action – thus, Walzer famously argues that if saturation bombing of German cities had been the only way to prevent a Nazi victory in the Second World War it would have been right to adopt this non-discriminatory policy, but the tradition dismisses such consequentialist reasoning (Walzer, 1977/1992, p. 251). On the other hand, other aspects of the tradition, such as the requirement that there be a reasonable prospect of success, do rely upon the calculation of consequences. This makes the point that to think in just war terms requires the exercise of political judgement and not simply a knowledge of the moral principles that ought to underlie such judgements; just war thinking requires practical reasoning, and while the ethicist/theologian may have a lot to say about the principles that are to be applied, he or she does not necessarily have any standing vis-à-vis their actual application.

Perhaps the biggest gap between the tradition and much modern thinking lies in the importance attributed to intentions by the tradition, not simply under the heading of 'right intention' but also via the doctrine of 'double effect'. A more legalistic approach to war and aggression is less concerned with intention. If aggressive war is a crime then the motives of those who respond to this crime are not of great significance; thus, for example, if attacked on the street we expect the police to protect us, and if they do so we are not immediately concerned if the motives of the police officers concerned included factors such as the desire for promotion, or even the enjoyment of fighting for its own sake (although, reflecting at leisure afterwards, such motivations might give legitimate cause for concern). The act of giving assistance itself is sufficient irrespective of the motive for the act. Again, the innocent victims of an action legitimated by 'double effect' are unlikely to be much consoled by the thought that their suffering, though anticipated, was not intended. These features of the tradition reveal its theological roots – the ultimate focus of Augustine and Aquinas was on the fate of the souls of the individuals concerned, and for this reason the intentions behind action take on a significance that a non-theological account of the world would not support.

For all that, the just war tradition still provides a way of thinking that is relevant in all circumstances where force is used, and indeed can be extended beyond physical force to coercion more generally. Thus, for example, the ethics of the employment of economic sanctions can, and should, be judged in terms of the same basic set of criteria set out above. Notions such as proportionality, discrimination, effectiveness apply in these cases as they do in cases of the employment of physical force; indeed, sanctions are often much less discriminatory in practice than acts of physical force. Sanctions may be intended to cripple a regime but they usually have this effect, when they do, by bringing down suffering upon civilians. Far more innocent Iraqis have died since the Gulf War ended, as a result of lack of medical supplies and foodstuffs, than were killed in the campaign – although the responsibility for these deaths is contested since it is argued by their defenders that the UN sanctions do not apply to civilian goods of this sort. Still, what actually counts as a civilian good is decided outside of Iraq, and some potential medicines may be being ruled out because of their alleged alternative uses; as against this, it is clear that the Iraqi regime has used the sanctions campaign to buttress its internal support by directing anger against the US and its allies. The important point is that the criteria for legitimate action set out above can, and should, be applied in this kind of case. The same also applies to 'terrorism' – whether of the state or informal non-state variety. The oft-heard proposition that one man's terrorist is another's freedom fighter should be rejected; just as there are things that states ought not to do because they are non-discriminatory and disproportionate even in pursuit of a just cause, so some terrorist acts can be condemned in the same terms.

Contrary somewhat to the tradition, the statism of the modern approach to just war (seen at its best in the work of Walzer) should not be dismissed as morally reprehensible. As argued in chapter 5, there are good reasons why the autonomy of political communities should be respected and a set of positions such as the Legalist Paradigm which reflect that respect are valuable in their own terms. Part of the problem in thinking about the ethics of violence in modern conditions is the need to reconcile the legitimate interests of political communities with the existence of a code that transcends individual communities. This is a very general problem for international political theory and will be returned to later in the context of humanitarianism and humanitarian intervention.

War and the states-system: a re-examination

For most of the last four centuries the decision to go to war has been seen as one which states are entitled to take on their own terms; in the second half of the twentieth century this position came to be seen as unacceptable and the Legalist Paradigm came to dominate the *theory* of inter-state violence – but what of the practice? Is it actually the case that states have changed their behaviour in this respect in response to the changing norms? The answer seems to be that the nature of inter-state violence has indeed changed dramatically over the last fifty years, but not necessarily in response to changing norms; some other factors may be more important than the rise of a legal regime restricting war in changing the pattern of violence worldwide.

To understand what has happened it may be helpful to go back to the beginning of what Victor Davis Hanson calls *The Western Way of War* (1989), in the infantry battles of the pre-classical Greek city-states. These battles were highly structured, formal occasions. An army from one city would invade the countryside around another, symbolically attacking olive trees – symbolically, Hanson observes, because the roots of olive trees are deep and tough and damaging them is difficult – and then the citizens of the latter (all of them) would form up as heavy infantry in lines several deep, each line representing an age-cohort, and there would be a clash between the two forces. The winner, determined by who held the ground, would erect a trophy, the dead would be buried, and, victorious or defeated, the invading army would go away again since usually casualties were fairly light and, within their city walls, the defenders would be safe. This pattern persisted, at least in outline, up to the Peloponnesian War, where, as Thucydides' narrative illustrates, inter-city warfare became a grimmer business, often with no prisoners taken – Tom Holt's excellent historical novel *The Walled Orchard* vividly takes the failure of the Sicilian Expedition, and the killing of virtually all the Athenians who took part, as a key moment marking the end of the old ethics of war (Holt, 1997).

The Greek infantry battle was extraordinarily significant in terms of the social structure of the cities. The obligation of all free men who could afford the armour to stand in the line created a kind of democracy even in those cities where the form of government was oligarchic or tyrannical, and the idea that the free citizen is a bearer of arms becomes part of the republican tradition – still present in the notion of universal military service in Switzerland today. Even more significantly, women were excluded from the battle and, as Jean Bethke Elshtain has argued, the public–private divide so central to Western political thought dates back to the political practices this exclusion generates (Elshtain, 1981 and 1987). The free man/soldier dominates the 'public thing' (*res publica* in Latin), the public sphere, war, the Agora (market-place), while women's sphere is private, in the home. This distinction feeds into such topics as human rights and cultural diversity in international relations in a very direct way; the contemporary international human rights regime privileges rights in the public sphere, and is rightly criticized by feminist writers for so doing, while non-Westerners, with equal justice, point to the way in which such a privileging discounts alternative notions of human dignity.

The Greek infantry battle provides a model for the Western way of war. War is a formal process, with rules and procedures, which culminates in a decisive battle – an encounter on the battlefield between two regular armies which, in principle, will decide the outcome of the war. It is striking how this model has been applied in circumstances where it seems inappropriate; in the First World War, for example, the armies in the West were in constant contact in the trenches for four years, yet the period is still broken down into battles – the Somme, Verdun, Passchendaele, and so on – because that is how staff officers have been trained to 'see' war, and they manipulated events to bring such decisive contests into being, without, of course, creating actual decisions. In the general wars of the twentieth century the supreme military talent was organizational; figures like Brooke, Marshall and Eisenhower were the successful Anglo-American commanders in the Second World War, yet their success has often been questioned by people who look instead to the alleged battlefield skills of a Patton or Montgomery.

Since 1945 there have been very few 'decisive' battles. The Korean War saw several attempts to decide the war with one move, none of which succeeded, and stalemate has persisted to date; the French contrived a decisive battle at Dien Bien Phu during the first Vietnam War, and lost, while the Coalition's Desert Storm achieved the limited result of the expulsion of Iraq from Kuwait in 1991, but, generally, wars have not been fought in this way. Instead, the characteristic war of the last fifty years has involved long campaigns between regular armies and irregular forces, or, occasionally, especially in the Middle East, encounters between regular forces that have been militarily but not politically decisive. More recently, and very bloodily, we have seen campaigns between different groups of irregulars as in the territories of Former Yugoslavia. The model of a decisive battle around which so much of our thinking on war is based seems in abeyance. What we have seen instead is the return to full significance of 'non-Western' ways of war. The kinds of warfare characteristic of the last decades would have been alien to the classical Greeks, but not to the Chinese Empire for most of its existence, or the Middle Eastern and Indian civilizations before European dominance. For these folk, and their modern descendants, war is not some kind of game where the losers surrender with a good grace and make peace after losing a battle.

Technology is part of the reason for this shift. The weaponry available to Western armies has become such that the possessors of such tools are careful not to fight each other in formal wars, while those who do not possess such instruments in the first place find different ways of fighting those who do. When, in the latter case, formal conflict cannot be avoided – as happened as a result of Iraqi strategy in 1991 – the disparity in resulting casualties is quite extraordinary. The Coalition of Western regular armies fought a decisive battle with barely more casualties than might have been expected in a training exercise involving half a million soldiers. Their Iraqi opponents were simply swept away, sometimes literally as in the case of Iraqi soldiers who were buried in trenches filled in by bulldozers.

However, technology is not the whole story. Part of the reason for the shift lies in the changing attitudes to war on the part of the public within the West. Serving in the army is no longer seen by many as a 'republican' or 'patriotic' act. Western armies recruit regular soldiers by stressing the career opportunities involved, education, travel and sport. Small numbers are undoubtedly attracted to special forces because of the danger and the opportunities for officially sanctioned violence, but they are a minority – and in any event this particular motivation played relatively little part in the formation of the military classes who used to form the officer corps of Western armies. The gendered basis of the Western way of war is also eroding as women join armies in increasing numbers. Fighting old-style decisive battles is not, for most recruits, part of what they joined up for; it is striking that the deaths of the small numbers of Western soldiers killed in the Gulf Campaign of 1990 have generated more law-suits than those of the two World Wars combined. Such a reluctance to die is not universal, and when modern Western armies are obliged to fight pre-modern mentalities, confusion reigns and disaster is never far away – Mark Bowden's detailed account of the loss of eighteen US Rangers in Somalia in 1993 is a brilliantly empathetic story of such an encounter (Bowden, 1999).

However, we still live in a world where violence is regularly used by states and by other groups for political ends, and armies cannot be dispensed with. The interesting question becomes, how do modern armies exercise force in decisive ways without fighting old-style battles? One answer is some kind of 'virtual war' where new technologies are used in place of human beings; the cruise missile and airborne bombardment are the key here, and the Kosovo Campaign of 1999 provides an account of the possibilities and limitations of such a form of war (Ignatieff, 2000). From NATO's point of view, this was a 'zero-casualty' war, in which bombing from high levels appears to have been decisive – although just why the war ended when it did is still somewhat shrouded in mystery. But the political results of the war are less clear-cut – there may have been a new-style decisive battle, but it did not result in the enemy accepting the result. Instead, NATO seems committed to a protectorate in Kosovo for the foreseeable future. The precise use of military force and new technologies may make it possible for modern armies to win military encounters against less well-equipped forces with minimum losses, but the political point of war is lost if, at the end of the battle, the loser refuses to concede defeat. Ultimately the Clausewitzian view of war – itself an expression of the Western way identified by Hanson – makes sense if both sides in a conflict accept its logic. When one does not, the other cannot force a result.

Is it still possible to use 'just war' considerations when considering informal war and 'virtual war'? Clearly, the immediate answer is 'yes' – Walzer's book spends a great deal of time on historical illustrations drawn from irregular campaigns – but the sense that one is imposing a model drawn from one era on to another remains. As already noted, issues of proportionality inevitably emerge when high-tech wars are fought against low-tech opponents. Modern versions of the inviolability of the innocent reflect the idea that it is possible to draw a clear distinction between soldiers and the rest, a view that is increasingly difficult to sustain. In so far as there is no exact equivalent to the just war in other cultures, this may be a reflection of different ways of war, rather than different ethical senses. In summary, force and violence have some claim to be the best-developed area of international political theory, the area that has the longest pedigree of thought devoted to it, but this is also an area that is currently in some disarray, because the categories that shape the international political theory of force and violence seem increasingly inappropriate to a world in which conventional forms of violence are less frequently employed – and the forms of violence that are employed seem not to be amenable to traditional categories.

Still, before moving on, it should be noted that this is not simply a problem for international political theory; it is striking that some of the

most up-to-date areas of so-called explanatory IR theory have failed to
take on board the significance of recent changes in the nature of war.
The very Clausewitzian approach of, for example, Steven Van Evera's
work, with its focus on the debate between 'offensive' and 'defensive'
realism, still takes it for granted that war is a viable option for states;
the implications of a world in which many of the major states are only
able to make war under very extreme provocation or with a guarantee
of 'zero casualties' that cannot usually be given have not been theorized by mainstream IR theory (Van Evera, 1999). In fact, most interesting work in this area is either coming from within military
establishments in the West (unsurprising when one considers that they
are the people who are most directly confronting the issue) or from
'post-modern' writers for whom the virtuality of war is simply one
aspect of the virtualization of all areas of social life (Der Derian, 1992;
Toffler and Toffler, 1993).

7

The Contemporary International Human Rights Regime

The Westphalia System is explicitly a system of states, but there is a long tradition of interpretation that argues that individuals are the *ultimate* members of international society, even if its immediate members are states. Such a position is to be found in the scholastic tradition that contested with republicanism for dominance in the early years of the system, and is supported by the 'solidarist' interpretation of international society identified by Hedley Bull, which sees states as 'local agents of the common good' (Wheeler, 1992; Tuck, 1999). International action on behalf of individuals and groups in distress have been by no means uncommon over the last few centuries. At the same time, the international legal status of the individual has been a rather different matter. For the most part, individuals were only recognized by conventional international law in exceptional circumstances – famously, pirates were the unfortunate bearers of international recognition in so far as it was a customary rule of international law that any state could take action against them, irrespective of their nationality, while, at the other end of the social scale, diplomats held personal immunities also recognized by customary international law. In each case the reasoning was similar; diplomats are representatives of their state, pirates are deemed to have no state – in almost every other case, individuals are considered to be represented in (public) international law via 'their' sovereign state, and it was held that to give them recognition as legal personalities in their own right would be to undermine state sovereignty.

Since 1945, all this has changed. There is now a very extensive international human rights regime, based on global and regional declarations, covenants and treaties, backed up by international governmental and non-governmental organizations (Steiner and Alston, 2000; Ghandhi, 2000; C. Brown, 2001b). This regime rests precisely on the

notion that all individuals have rights by virtue of their very humanity, and that, in principle, they ought to be able to enforce these rights
against their own government. Individuals are held to possess economic and social rights as well as political and civil rights, and the
rights regime is not restricted solely to individuals – groups and
'peoples' are also considered to possess rights which they can assert
against the state (Crawford, 1988). The growth of the discourse of rights
over the last fifty years has been one of the most striking changes in
both the theory and practice of international relations (Vincent, 1986;
Donnelly, 1993; Dunne and Wheeler, 1999). However, this growth has
not gone unchallenged, nor has it been regarded as unproblematic even
by many of those who are broadly supportive of the development
(Brown, C., 1999b). The ontological standing of rights is, and always
has been, an issue even within the Western tradition in which they
originated, as is the relationship between civil and political rights and
economic and social rights – this latter relationship having been
particularly fraught during the Cold War years. The universalist
assumptions of rights discourse have been challenged by feminists,
who have stressed the point that it is not by chance that the rights-
bearing individual has generally been taken to be male, while non-
Westerners have sometimes denied that the rights promoted by the
international human rights regime are genuinely universal. And, of
course, the issue of compliance with international norms in this area is
rarely off the agenda.

Each of these points will be examined in this and the following
chapters. Consideration of compliance will be deferred until the next
chapter, where it will be considered in the context of humanitarian
intervention, and chapter 11, where the forthcoming establishment of
an International Criminal Court will be discussed. An examination of
the critique of human rights as cultural imperialism, and the debate
over so-called 'Asian values', will be offered in chapter 10, in the
context of the wider issue of cultural diversity and international political theory, although some of the main lines of argument here will be
prefigured below. Examination of the specific politics of economic and
social rights will be divided between this chapter and chapter 9, which
examines the notion of global social justice. In this chapter, after a brief
overview of the current regime, its origins and development, the putatively universal nature of rights will be discussed, and, in particular,
the feminist critique of the patriarchal basis of conventional rights
thinking; finally, some consideration will be given to the 'human capabilities' approach as an alternative to rights thinking. The way in which
the single topic of 'human rights' sprawls over so many areas of contemporary international political theory is a sign of how important this
topic has become.

The origins of rights, and human rights

At one level of generality, rights are ways to restrain the unfettered power of rulers. Most complex cultures, most of the time, have had some such mode of restraint as part of their arsenal of practices, but the idea of restraining rulers via *rights* is the product of one particular culture at one particular time – Western Europe during the Middle Ages, where the notion developed as part of this world's inheritance from the classical world of Rome and Greece. There were two aspects to this inheritance: first, the merging of Roman legal notions with the customs of the Germanic tribes, whose descendants made up the mass of the population of medieval Europe, to create a *particularistic* account of rights, and, second, the Christian notion of 'natural law', which was rooted in Greek ideas of human flourishing and pointed towards *universalism*; each contributed in a different and, potentially, contradictory way to the later emergence of a political discourse of the West in which rights played a fundamental role (C. Brown, 2001b).

The tribal societies that conquered Rome were in no sense democracies, but their kings were generally, at least in principle, elected to that status – usually from the members of a particular family deemed to be of quasi-divine origin – and they ruled with the rough and ready consent of their (male) subjects; things could hardly be otherwise in a context where 'the people' were, in effect, a war-band. Cutting a long story short, during the Middle Ages these consensual elements of rule were, in some places, combined with the legal notion, central to Roman law, of a 'contract', with the result that political authority came to be understood as based on, and limited by, a bargain struck between the rulers and those of the ruled in possession of sufficient bargaining power to be able to get their interests across. For the English-speaking world the most important such bargain is the 'Great Charter' (Magna Carta) of 1215, but European history provides a number of similar examples.

'Charter rights', like any other right produced by a contract, involve reciprocity – rights are always accompanied by correlative duties; they are usually quite specific, and the parties who hold rights and owe duties are themselves specified. These features carry forward into the theory and practice of rights in modern times. Theories of political obligation based on a notional 'social contract' work in much the same way, and the rights established as part of the legal codes of modern Western liberal democracies share the same features. Indeed, some argue that these features are essential to the very notion of a right and that the only true rights are specific and correlative 'claim-rights' (Jones, 1994).

It is clear that if this is so, there cannot be genuine 'human rights', that is to say, rights that adhere to an individual simply on the basis of his or her humanity. If the only real rights are those created as part of a legal system by an explicit or implicit contract between the rulers and the ruled, then those who are not parties to such a contract cannot be rights-bearers, or bound by reciprocal duties. Along with the idea of a 'contract', there was, however, another basis for rights that emerged in the Middle Ages – the idea of 'natural law', which, as we have seen, was an important feature of medieval and early modern international thought. The natural law tradition holds that human beings have an essential nature which dictates that certain kinds of human goods are always and everywhere desired as necessary for human flourishing; because of this essential nature we can think of there being common moral standards that govern all human relations, standards which can be discerned by the application of practical reason to human affairs (Finnis, 1980). Practical reasoning tells us that these moral standards can generate rights and duties which, crucially, are not justified by reference to, or limited in application by, any particular legal system, community, state, race, creed or civilization. In principle, every human being is subject to, and capable of discerning the contents of, natural law.

Thus, we have two different accounts of rights emerging out of the Middle Ages into modern European theory and practice: a particularistic, contractual, legal account and a universal, moral account based on the requirements of human flourishing. The politics of these two positions are rather different. From the former point of view, individuals possess the rights they do because they are citizens of a particular state and the law of that state endows them with these rights. If they live in a state governed by the rule of law, they will be able to exercise these rights, and will have the support of the judicial system in so doing. This is all well and good, but the downside is that this state of affairs only pertains in those societies which are actually governed by the rule of law. This limitation does not exist when it comes to natural as opposed to positive law – the problem here, on the contrary, is precisely that, because rights in this sense are not associated with particular forms of society or government and therefore can be genuinely 'human', they are also not associated with any particular enforcement mechanism. Further, whereas within a system of positive law the content of rights can be described with some accuracy and precision, which rights are actually mandated by general universal moral standards is quite likely to be a matter of controversy.

The reason for stressing this point is that a great deal of modern, liberal thinking on human rights blurs the distinction between legal rights and rights seen as expressions of universal moral standards. Of course, within a bounded community based on the rule of law, the fact that rights are described as 'universal' when they are, in fact, local need not matter very much. The ontological status of this universality may be shaky, but the fiction that universal rights exist is not harmfully misleading. Where this disjunction becomes of far greater significance is when a shift takes place from the use of rights language in a local context, to the employment of the category of universal human rights on a world stage.

The Universal Declaration of Human Rights

This first became a potential issue as a result of the humanitarian international standard-setting of the nineteenth and twentieth centuries. Thus, for example, the Congress of Vienna of 1815 saw the Great Powers accept an obligation to end the slave trade, which was finally abolished by the Brussels Convention of 1890, with slavery itself formally outlawed by the Slavery Convention of 1926. However, although such standard-setting eventually became quite extensive and complex, it existed within a context in which notions of sovereignty and non-intervention are taken for granted and only to be overridden with great reluctance; thus, for example, abolishing the slave trade, which involves international transactions, was much easier than abolishing slavery itself, which concerns what states do to their own people – and, indeed, pockets of slavery survive to this day in parts of West Africa and the Middle East.

The UN General Assembly's Universal Declaration of Human Rights (UDHR) of 1948 represents a break with this limited notion of standard-setting, building on some explicit reference to universal human rights in the UN Charter of 1945. This shift was in response to the climate of thought generated by the horrors of the Second World War, and, in particular of the murder of millions of Jews, Gypsies and Slavs in the extermination camps of National Socialist Germany. Given this context, the need to assert a universal position was deeply felt, and a UN Committee, chaired by Eleanor Roosevelt and containing representatives of the world's major religions and ethical systems, was tasked with drafting what became the Universal Declaration. In spite of the presence of these representatives, the text that emerged produced a list of rights that were remarkably similar to those enshrined in Western constitutions. In the Western-dominated UN of the 1940s it was adopted by forty-eight votes with none against, although the eight abstentions put down a marker for future debates – only one abstainer, South Africa, abstained on the conventional grounds that it wished to protect its domestic right to discriminate on grounds of race; six others, led by the

USSR, protested that the document reflected a bourgeois emphasis on political and property rights, as opposed to the economic and social rights allegedly promoted by Soviet communism, while Saudi Arabia abstained on the grounds that it could not accept the provisions on freedom of religion. This latter, cultural-religious, objection to universalism will be considered in chapter 10, and the Soviet Bloc abstentions raised the issue of the compatibility of so-called first- and second-generation rights which will be the subject of the next section of this chapter, but first one or two more general comments on the Universal Declaration may be helpful.

The UDHR can be taken as representative of the international human rights regime as a whole in so far as it attempts to set standards in ways that have been filled out by a raft of human rights declarations, covenants and conventions, regional and global, such that it is no exaggeration to suggest that, fifty years later, virtually all areas of the domestic political, economic and social structure of states are covered by some kind of international standard-setting. On what is this standard-setting based? International human rights legislation purports to create positive law in the same way that, say, the US Bill of Rights creates positive law, but it is clear that, in practice, this is not the case. International legislation is not effective in the way that the US Constitution is unless the law-making parties make specific provisions for enforcement and compliance either by utilizing existing institutions, such as the International Court of Justice at The Hague, or by creating new, treaty-specific bodies, and, with the exception of the 1950 European Convention for the Protection of Human Rights and Fundamental Freedoms, this has not happened. International human rights legislation has not involved the creation of effective enforcement machinery, for the obvious reason that not enough of the states involved actually wished to see human rights law enforced; indeed, even some states with a record of general respect for human rights have been reluctant to accept international supervision and have hedged around their ratifications of international agreements with extensive formal reservations – true, for example, of the United States and the United Kingdom. Predictably, the absence of enforcement mechanisms leads to lower levels of compliance with the provisions of the regime. The enforcement of human rights by the international community has been determined, in practice, by the foreign policy imperatives of the major powers and political, commercial and financial considerations frequently get in the way of a high-priority, even-handed policy on human rights (K. E. Smith and Light, 2001). That this is so may be deplorable, but is not surprising; the UDHR and its successor declarations and covenants have been promulgated in an essentially statist context, where the norms of non-intervention and self-determination are as firmly asserted as the newer standards – indeed, more firmly, given that the UN Charter places far more emphasis on protecting the sovereignty of UN members than it does on regulating their behaviour towards their own citizens.

Although human rights advocates are sometimes unwilling to admit that this is so, once we move to the international level, the positive law, contractualist account of rights is obliged to take a back seat and, by default, the strongest support for the international human rights regime becomes the sense that its provisions reflect the general moral standards of humanity. The lack of an effective positive legal foundation for the international human rights regime throws the spotlight directly on the universal claims of the regime. Are there actually universal moral standards which ground the existing human rights regime? Perhaps, on the contrary, there are many ways of being human, some of which are actually precluded by the existing regime – a regime which privileges a particular, liberal, perhaps masculine, European sense of what it is to be human at the expense of valid alternatives. Although this question has always been present, it has been over-ridden for most of the last fifty years by other issues which arose out of the Cold War contest between East and West, which was frequently translated into a contest between advocates of political and civil versus economic and social rights.

Political vs. economic rights?

The Soviet Union in 1948, believing, quite plausibly, that the West was using human rights as a weapon in the Cold War, put forward the counter-argument that political and civil rights are ultimately of much less significance than economic and social rights. This position was obviously self-serving, but was well grounded in a long tradition of socialist and radical thought which regarded a 'bourgeois' emphasis on political rights and equal citizenship as a smokescreen to cover the lack of economic equality. As Marx saw a century before, political rights are difficult if not impossible to exercise in a context where the majority suffer grinding poverty, and formal legal equality is mocked by radical economic inequality – as the nineteenth-century Irish judge Sir James Mathew remarked, in a phrase that has become a cliché, 'in England, justice is open to all – like the Ritz Hotel'.

In fact, and partly in response to such arguments, the UDHR does actually contain quite a few references to economic and social rights, which is one of the reasons why the conventional division of rights into 'generations' is misleading in so far as it implies that second-generation, economic, rights were articulated later than first-generation, political, rights. However, it should be said that some of the economic rights contained in the Declaration could be interpreted as directed against trade unions, the right to work for example being a standard piece of anti-closed shop rhetoric. Still, in so far as these economic and social rights were expected to be of benefit to any specific group in 1948, it was the industrial working class of the Western world who were expected to be the beneficiaries (just as the various international economic organs designed to promote economic growth were oriented towards the problems of post-war reconstruction in the industrial world). This was the context in which the Soviet Union's opposition to the Declaration was situated – as part of a struggle for the soul of the Western working class. But in the course of the next few decades this context changed radically, as the process of decolonization created a majority of 'less-developed' (i.e. poor) countries at the UN, and as these countries pressed for assistance from the rich and, more radically, for changes in the economic system that they believed produced rich and poor in the first place.

In response to this new situation, many Western countries distributed quite large amounts of economic aid, but such aid was regarded by most of its donors as a matter of charity, or as an instrument of foreign policy, rather than a response to any kind of right possessed by the recipient. By the 1970s, the position of the by-then-ailing Soviet Bloc did not essentially challenge this judgement; indeed, the Soviet Union's advice to the poor was to solve their own problems and not to look to the capitalist world to help. Instead, the politics of poverty was dominated in the 1970s by demands for economic justice through the establishment of a New International Economic Order, and, at that time, this debate – which will be considered in chapter 9 – was not based on the language of rights. Instead, the idea that this language should be applied to economic and social issues was elaborated by political theorists; a key figure here was, and is, Henry Shue, whose *Basic Rights: Subsistence, Affluence and US Foreign Policy* recast the issue in new terms, those of 'basic rights' (Shue, 1983).

A basic right, argues Shue, can be seen as 'everyone's minimum reasonable demand upon the rest of humanity' (p. 19) and this can be broken down into two components: *security* rights, that is, the right not to be subjected to murder, torture, mayhem, rape or assault, and *subsistence* rights, that is, the right to minimal economic security 'unpolluted air, unpolluted water, adequate food, adequate clothing, adequate shelter and minimum preventive public health care' (p. 23). Shue's point is that all other rights rest on these basic rights. Without physical security and the wherewithal for subsistence, no one is in a position to exercise any other kind of right, and therefore any individual is entitled to demand of all other individuals ('the rest of humanity') that his or her needs in this respect be met. Moreover, this demand is legitimated by international legislation on human rights – see, for example, 'the right of everyone to an adequate standard of living for himself and his family, including adequate food, clothing and housing, and to the continuous improvement of living conditions' (*Covenant on Economic, Social and Cultural Rights*, Article 11.1), or the 'right of everyone to be free from hunger' (Article 11.2).

Are these basic rights 'rights' in the full sense of the term, as opposed to 'desiderata', things we would like to see happen? They are clearly rather different from the conventional political rights with which the UDHR was mostly concerned. The *Covenant on Economic, Social and Cultural Rights* makes the realization of the rights it sets out an obligation on its signatories, but this is, surely, a different kind of obligation to the obligation to refrain from, for example, 'cruel or degrading' punishments. In the latter case, as with other basically political rights, the right is accompanied by a clear correlative duty, and the remedy is in the hands of national governments. The way to end torture is for states to stop torturing. The right not to be tortured is associated with a duty not to torture. The right to be free from hunger, on the other hand, is not simply a matter of a duty on the part of one's own and other states not to pursue policies that lead to starvation, it also involves a positive duty to 'ensure an equitable distribution of world food supplies in relation to need' (*Covenant on Economic, Social and Cultural Rights*, Article 11.2(b)). This may be a worthwhile objective, but it is not clear that it is best expressed in terms of the language of rights. There are several reasons why such language is problematic.

First, it is by no means clear that, even assuming good will on all sides, even basic subsistence rights could always be met, and to think in terms of having a right to something that could not be achieved weakens the concept of a right in such a way as to undermine those more precise claims to rights which can, in fact, be achieved (such as the right not to be tortured). Second, some states may seek to use the idea of economic and social rights more directly to undermine political rights. Thus, dictatorial regimes in poor countries quite frequently justify the curtailment of political rights in the alleged name of promoting economic growth, or economic equality. In fact, there is no reason to accept the general validity of this argument – Sen's work, for example, makes it clear that, in fact, development and freedom go together and not simply by chance but because political rights are crucial to economic success (Sen, 2000a) – but the argument will still be made, and not always in bad faith.

Finally, and perhaps most fundamentally, if it is accepted that all states have a positive duty to promote economic well-being and freedom from hunger everywhere, then the consequences go well beyond the requirement of rich states to share with poor states, revolutionary though such a requirement would be. They also make virtually all *national* social and economic policies a matter for international regulation. Clearly, rich states would have a duty to make economic and social policy with a view to its consequences on the poor, but so would poor states. The poor's right to assistance creates a duty on the rich to assist, but this in turn creates a right of the rich to insist that the poor have a duty not to worsen their plight – for example, by failing to restrict population growth or by inappropriate economic policies. Aid programmes promoted by the Commonwealth and World Bank and the structural adjustment programmes of the IMF regularly include conditions of this kind. They are, however, widely resented because they contradict another widely supported economic and social right that 'All peoples have the right of self-determination. By virtue of that right they freely determine their political status and freely pursue their economic, social and cultural development' (*Covenant on Economic, Social and Cultural Rights*, Article 1.1). Even when applied in a well-meaning and consistent way – which, of course, cannot be guaranteed – external pressures to change policy are rarely popular, even with those they are intended to benefit.

All notions of human rights necessarily involve some restrictions in the exercise of state sovereignty, but whereas political conceptions of human rights may still be just about compatible with the underlying norms of the existing international order, economic and social rights, if taken seriously as *rights*, are not. This is why problems of enforcement and compliance are even more general in this area than they are with respect to political and social rights; some countries in some parts of the world, in particular Europe, have moved towards incorporating international standards of political rights into their domestic political arrangements, but no country has been prepared to accept the implications of incorporating economic and social rights in this full sense. If the notion of universal moral standards can be defended, economic rights could still be seen as part of an emerging global consensus, even if human rights law in this area is likely to be slow to develop. This is, however, rather a big if; at this point it becomes necessary to investigate rather more closely the claimed universal basis for human rights.

Human rights: universalism and the feminist critique

To recapitulate: one of the roots of human rights thinking lies in the notion that all human beings have a nature such that certain kinds of human goods are always and everywhere desired as necessary for human flourishing. Because of this essential nature, we can think of there being, at some level, common moral standards that govern all human relations, and these moral standards can generate rights and duties which are genuinely universal, that is to say, are not justified by reference to, or limited in application by, any particular legal system, community, state, race, creed or civilization. The notion of a basic right in Shue's sense of the term ('everyone's reasonable demand on the rest of humanity') can be defended on these lines – and perhaps with more plausibility than by reference to legal documents which, clearly, many states regarded as, at best, declaratory. But can the root idea of a universal human nature be defended? If so, what is the content of this universal nature? And, is the language of 'rights' the best way of expressing whatever universal nature there be?

There are clearly a number of different questions here, and the kinds of answers commonly given to these questions do not always fit together neatly to produce coherent packages of ideas. Thus, for example, the grounding of human rights thinking in an 'essentialist' account of human nature is often criticized as privileging a particularly Western view of what it is to be human, and yet, as will be seen in chapter 10, many of the advocates of so-called Asian values who express this view themselves hold equally essentialist (albeit different) views of human nature. Then again, some writers hold very firm views about the existence of human universals, and yet would resist expressing these universals in the language of rights; Alasdair McIntyre, for example, has famously described a belief in rights as akin to a belief in fairies and witchcraft, and yet his own Thomist/Aristotelian convictions commit him to a universalist account of what it is to be human (MacIntyre, 1981, p. 67) . Others are happy to acknowledge that human rights are fictitious entities, but defend the notion as valuable nonetheless: Richard Rorty, for example, takes human rights to be simply shorthand expressions of the widely held beliefs of particular Western societies, and yet is prepared to defend and promote the 'human rights culture' on pragmatic grounds (Rorty, 1993). These are complex issues; for purposes of exposition, the strategy adopted here will be to begin with a feminist critique of the notion of rights which is also a critique of the kind of universalism to which the human rights regime is, apparently, committed. Then, alternative notions of universalism which lead in a direction other than that of rights – towards 'human capabilities' – will be considered. This discussion will prepare the way for later consideration of both issues of economic justice, and cultural diversity.

Is the characteristic rights-bearer of Western political thought necessarily a man? It is a commonplace that the vast majority of Western political theorists, including virtually all of those who have employed the language of rights, have explicitly or implicitly assumed that rights-bearers would be masculine. Of all the great names in the canon of Western political thought only John Stuart Mill makes a serious effort to avoid patriarchal assumptions. Such paradigmatic statements of human rights as the French Declaration of the Rights of Man and of the Citizen and the US Bill of Rights do not simply use the masculine noun as a universal, they have also been considered compatible with an inferior legal status for women – for example, women did not achieve equal voting rights in France until 1945, over 150 years after the Declaration. It is also striking that the Universal Declaration of Human Rights of 1948 is still written in language that assumes masculinity to be the norm, even while declaring equal rights for women. Throughout the document the assumption is that the male will be head and bread-winner of a family; the only explicit references to women's rights, apart from a general commitment to equality, is in the context of child-rearing and motherhood.

It might be argued that this gendered language is simply a product of its age. Since the chair of the drafting commission for the UDHR was Eleanor Roosevelt, one of the most prominent and politically conscious feminists of her age, perhaps not too much should be read into its wording. The liberal response to such gendered language is to try to purge it from contemporary discourse, and move towards an account of human rights in which implicit or explicit discrimination against women is barred. Later UN Covenants have been drafted rather more carefully and there is now an International Convention on the Elimination of Discrimination against Women (1979), which addresses gender discrimination in a sensible and sensitive way; from a liberal feminist viewpoint this is all that is required – what is important is that women should genuinely have the same rights as men. A good practical case can be made for such a position, but, nonetheless, there is a deeper issue involved here than simply a matter of the elimination of politically incorrect language. Human rights discourse in general assumes that to be human is to be a rights-bearer, and that the context in which rights-bearing makes sense is the product of something universal about the human condition. It is this proposition that is contested by many contemporary feminist writers, and the way in which they contest it has relevance beyond the feminist critique itself (MacKinnon, 1989 and 1993; Peterson, V. S., 1990; Cook, 1994; Peters and Wolper, 1995; Charlesworth and Chinkin, 2000).

What kind of human being is the bearer of the classical political and civil rights? He/she is someone who might meet with others to consider political issues ('freedom of assembly') and sometimes joins with them to promote a particular point of view or to practise his or her religion ('freedom of association, religious freedom'). The ability to speak one's mind in public is important to this individual ('freedom of speech'). If these freedoms are to be exercised effectively he/she must be protected from arbitrary punishments from those in authority ('freedom from arbitrary arrest, right to a fair trial'). He/she is also a property-owner who wishes to exercise his/her property rights free from arbitrary interference from government ('no taxation without representation') and in order to ensure this – and the other freedoms noted above – is a stakeholder in a political system based, one way or another, on responsible and representative government. This form of government, in turn, is underwritten by the exercise of freedom of speech, assembly, association and so on. In short, the classic rights-bearer is a public figure, an active citizen, or at least someone who could become such if he or she wished. The rights that he or she bears are held against those who would interfere with this role, which may mean one's fellow rights-bearers – since the tyranny of the majority is to be resisted – but, at a more fundamental level, means the government, the powers-that-be.

It should be noted immediately that to be an effective rights-bearer it is necessary to be a citizen of a polity within which rights can be exercised – the idea that rights can be decontextualised and applied to all socio-political systems makes very little sense. The point of freedom of speech and association, for example, is that by speaking and associating freely one is capable, at least in principle, of having some impact on events by so doing. A (rather implausibly) benevolent autocracy that permitted these activities, but was wholly unwilling as a matter of principle to take notice of what resulted from them, would not actually be providing a context in which it would be possible to say that human rights existed in anything other than a nominal sense. In this respect, the international human rights regime involves not simply a set of rights but a full-scale template for the political organization of society – a point that will be re-examined later in this book. In a similar vein, the importance of activism in the above composite description should be noted – although, it should be said, the right to be left alone is also a reasonable extension from the various classical human rights.

Returning to the feminist critique, it will immediately be apparent that, for most of human history, the rather inelegant gender-neutral formulations employed above would be simply wrong. As even the strongest advocate of human rights as potentially gender-neutral would have to acknowledge, until comparatively recently, in none of the countries where active citizenship has been valued and rights language has been developed have women had the same capacity to be rights-bearers as men – or even, in many cases, to be rights-bearers at all. The crucial point – and the point at which controversy enters – is that many feminists would argue that this exclusion is not to be seen as something contingent and, in principle, corrigible, but as something built into the very notion of a right, indeed of the state, in the first place (MacKinnon, 1989 and 1993). The simplest version of this argument is that rights thinking rests upon the political conception of the division of life into public and private spheres; rights are particularly associated with the public sphere from which, historically, women have been systematically excluded, and not associated with the private sphere, which is where women have been most obviously oppressed and in need of protection. Rights have been protections from the dangers associated with activities engaged in by men, and generally offered little protection from the dangers characteristically faced by women.

As noted in chapter 6, the origins of the public–private divide can be found in the life of the *polis* of classical Greece. The citizen of the *polis* was expected to fight for the city (in Athens as cavalryman, infantryman or oarsman on the state galleys, depending on his economic status), take part in its specific religious ceremonies and, one way or another depending on the city in question, take part in its governance. These citizens did not think of themselves as rights-bearers – for that the legalism of Rome was necessary – but they effectively defined for later ages what it meant to be an active participant in the public life of the city, and, by extension, of any subsequent polity. The other side of this public sphere is the private sphere, the family and, by extension, the family farm or family business. Here the citizen rules over women, children and servants, most of whom will be slaves; male children of the head of the household are potential citizens, but the other inhabitants of this sphere are barred from citizenship and the active life.

Those who do take part in the active life, then and now, to some degree or another put themselves in harm's way. In the world of the Greece city-states, the Roman Republic and *a fortiori* the Roman Empire, the public sphere was potentially a dangerous place. Indeed, in the age of the Caesars, members of the political class, senators and magistrates, faced dangers not experienced by the generality of Roman citizens – even during the reign of a Caligula or a Commodus the provinces were relatively well governed, and while ordinary citizens and especially the rich might find themselves gouged by the imperial tax collector, they faced none of the dangers experienced by those attempting to conduct public life in the presence of the Emperor. For much of the Middle Ages the notion of a public sphere was somewhat in abeyance, but once republican ideas revived, the old vision of an active public life returned, and with it the dangers of such a life in a world of absolutist monarchies. Even in England, where absolutism was defeated, it was not until well into the eighteenth century that political defeat did not bring with it the probability of general ruin and possible loss of life via impeachment.

Given these dangers, it is not surprising that those desirous of a public life should have thought in terms of developing the political and civil rights noted above. These rights corresponded to the dangers faced by, for example, 'Freeborn Englishmen' (whether in seventeenth-century England or eighteenth-century America) who asserted themselves against royal authority. Moreover, as the power of the state increased, and its reach extended beyond the court to the country as a whole, so the idea of rights became of greater general relevance – the public sphere became larger (although also more insubstantial, because the possibility of genuine self-government diminishes) and as more and more people were pulled in so more and more people required protection from the exercise of arbitrary authority. Rights-bearing became of wider and wider significance.

What of the *private* sphere and the dangers faced by individuals inhabiting solely this world? Clearly, in both the classical world and early modern Europe, members of the private sphere are exposed by proxy to some of the same dangers faced by those pursuing the active political life; the effects of disgrace and financial ruin are felt here – and sometimes, although not always, the physical dangers faced by members of the political class are faced equally by their dependants. In this sense, the extension of rights acts as a protection to everyone and not simply the classical rights-bearers. But there is another range of dangers not experienced in the public sphere to which those in the private sphere are subjected, namely those dangers that stem from the exercise of power within the private sphere by 'public' figures. Such extreme manifestations of inequality as domestic violence, rape within marriage and child-abuse may have been uncharacteristic in much the same way that the right of life and death over the household was rarely actually exercised by the Roman head of the family, but dramatically unequal property rights and unequal access to education for women were, until very recently, commonplace, and it is striking that the classic account of human rights has little or nothing to say on such matters. These are seen as matters for the *domestic* jurisdiction of states, a revealing term.

Human rights classically relate to the public activities of citizens, not to what these citizens do when they go home in the evening. Their activities in the home are, of course, subject to domestic legal codes but these latter codes have been developed by the people whose activities they are meant to constrain and, unsurprisingly, until very recently, they have been for the most part ineffective. In most jurisdictions it was taken for granted that men had the right to chastise their wives and children physically (within reason, of course!), to manage their property and to assert their 'conjugal *rights*' (another revealing locution). Just as local codes did not interfere with such 'rights', so were early human rights declarations silent. And, as Catherine MacKinnon has pointed out very eloquently, rape by soldiers has not, traditionally, been seen as a war crime – rather as a reward for soldiers (as in the Red Army's descent on Eastern Europe and Germany in 1944/45) or even as a tactic directed against the real enemy, the opposing side's menfolk, who are reduced to impotence because of their inability to protect 'their' women (MacKinnon, 1993).

In short, the problem with the discourse of rights is not simply that for most of human history the bearers of rights have been men; rather it is that rights seem a particularly appropriate response to one kind of oppression – that directed against active citizens attempting to engage in a public life – but not particularly appropriate to the equally damaging forms of oppression characteristically found within the private sphere. One response to this may be to try to conflate the public and the private – the slogan 'the personal is the political' summarizes one such perspective – and extend the notion of rights accordingly, but what this seems to undervalue is the importance of preserving the possibility of living a 'private' life. The assumption that the only life worth living is the public life, the life of the active citizen, is one that rights thinking encourages us to make, but, as is signposted above and will be developed below in greater detail, this sets in place a particular account of what it is to be human, which, in itself, presents difficulties.

Rights, duties and capabilities

The burden of this discussion has been that it is not self-evidently the case that human flourishing depends on an understanding of human beings as rights-holders, and, more, that there are some circumstances in which the discourse of rights will be positively unhelpful as a tool to combat particular kinds of oppression. On the other hand, it is important not to allow these legitimate objections to the notion of human rights to cause us to abandon the concept altogether. To think of human beings as rights-bearers is a way of drawing attention to features of the human condition that are of intrinsic value. An emphasis on rights draws attention to the values of freedom and autonomy, and although we might want to insist that the active life of the citizen is not the only one worth living, we may still value the idea that people ought to have the opportunity to choose such a life. Rights thinking also, indirectly, encourages the notion that we have obligations towards each other and the discourse of *human* rights establishes that these obligations are not restricted to our fellow citizens – again this is a valuable contribution to international political theory. Finally, although the feminist critique of the notion of human rights is very powerful, it is best seen not as a root and branch condemnation of the idea but as an exposition of its limits; human rights may not be a very useful response to the oppressions of the private sphere, but the oppressions it attempts to deal with in the public realm are real and demand a response. Such liberal freedoms as freedom of speech and assembly may be a precondition for the wider notion of freedom critics of the human rights regime espouse.

For all these reasons, it would be unwise to underestimate the value of the international human rights regime that has been developed over the last half century – and in any event, this regime *has* been developed and is now a fact of international life, even if occasionally it is a source of global dissension. But, by the same token, the fact that this regime rests upon an unsound, or at least highly questionable, ontology also ought not to be ignored or swept under the carpet, because when questions of this nature are disposed of in this way, they have an irritating habit of reappearing later at inconvenient moments. It is clear, for example, that the 'cultural critique' of rights which will be examined in chapter 10 below is not likely to go away, even if its most obvious current manifestation in the form of the Asian values debate may have a relatively short shelf-life. For this reason it may be helpful here to outline very briefly one or two universalist approaches that are not directly supportive of the conventional understanding of rights, but which do some of the same work as that notion, albeit on a different basis. These approaches will also be encountered in later chapters.

One such approach is the Kantian notion of a shift of emphasis from 'rights' to 'duties'; Onora O'Neill is particularly associated with this position (O'Neill, 1986 and 2000). The central propositions here are drawn from the Kantian notion of the 'moral law'. On Kant's account, this moral law is 'wired' into each human being – indeed, all possible sentient beings – and as such is truly universal; moral behaviour involves the choice of 'maxims' upon which our lives should be based, and which provide us with the basis for a code governing our behaviour towards each other. We have a moral duty to deal honestly with one another, to act according to rules which can be universalized, to treat each other as ends and not solely as means. That there is a relationship between this kind of thinking and rights thinking is quite clear. In effect, what is going on here is a kind of reversal of the conventional legal notion that a right involves a correlative duty. Instead, from a Kantian perspective we begin with the duty and from this can derive something like a right – thus, for example, the duty to tell the truth which is so central to Kantianism can be seen as generating a right to have the truth told to one.

The value of placing the emphasis on the duty rather than the right in moral terms is that it stresses the obligations of the individual, who is seen, not as someone who is a rights-bearer making demands on others, but as someone who is internally motivated to behave properly to others. This is particularly valuable when it comes to, for example, discussing issues of global inequality, where the idea that there are obligations to give assistance may be more soundly based than the idea that individuals have a direct right to expect assistance; the notions of 'special' and 'general' duties may also be very useful. Further, the very generality of the notion of a duty may be valuable, since the tendency to make rights specific can be somewhat self-defeating in so far as it encourages the tendency to draw up long lists of rights which are insufficiently internally differentiated – thus, for example, the value of a right to paid holidays from work, as promoted by the UDHR, need not be doubted, but it can be doubted that it ought to be treated as of the same level of importance as, for example, the right not to be tortured.

The Kantian approach relies on a universal account of what it is to be a moral agent; the 'human capabilities' approach, developed in different ways by such writers as Armatya Sen and Martha Nussbaum, and drawing on Aristotelian and Marxist roots, rests on a much more elaborate, but equally universalist, account of what it is to be a human being (Nussbaum and Sen, 1993; Sen, 2000a; Nussbaum, 2000). The capabilities approach emerges from the same source as the natural law approach to rights, the idea that human beings have a nature which shapes their relationships with one another and with their environment. For Aristotle this was a matter of biology (and teleology), but although the modern discourse of evolutionary psychology may be in the process of re-establishing the idea of a biological account of human nature, modern neo-Aristotelians have not taken the argument in this direction. Instead, the emphasis, for Nussbaum in particular, has been to try to establish the necessary social basis for human beings to be able to have the opportunity to develop their capabilities – the conditions that people need to be able to function as human beings.

These ideas have been developed by Nussbaum specifically in response to feminist arguments about the inadequacy of rights thinking, and to the cultural relativist critique of rights, and, as with the Kantian approach to duties, some of the functional capabilities that Nussbaum describes as essential could be translated into rights language. Her point is that by approaching the subject via human capabilities it is possible to avoid the ethnocentric and patriarchal assumptions of the language of rights, and also to bring into the equation all sorts of things that rights language cannot, at least not without being severely strained. Thus, 'a right to play' seems a strange notion, but the idea that 'being able to laugh, to play, to enjoy recreational activities' (Nussbaum, 2000, p. 80) is part of what it is to be human seems much more intuitively appealing – and the fact that we are talking here of the *social basis of capabilities* makes it clear that this is not some kind of 'right to happiness' to be guaranteed by the state. It allows for the possibility that individuals may choose not to develop this capability; what is important is that they have the opportunity to do so. There are problems with this approach, and the extent to which it is possible to present an account of what it is to be human without resting on some fairly culturally specific assumptions is certainly open to question (Connolly, 2000; *Ethics*, 2000). Still, the notion of capabilities has been brought into play here in order to make the point that there may be ways of preserving some of the advantages of the notion that human beings have rights, without buying into the kind of ontological assumptions upon which that notion rests.

In any event, the doubtful nature of these assumptions has not, as yet, stopped or even hindered the development of the international human rights regime, in part because the language of rights has become the way in which humanitarian impulses are expressed in the modern international system. There is, however, a gap to be bridged between the expression of such impulses and the realities of contemporary world politics, the subject of the next chapter.

8

Humanitarianism and Humanitarian Intervention

With the important exception of the European Convention on Human Rights, very little of the extensive international legislation on human rights post-1945 has been accompanied by effective mechanisms for enforcement – the possibility that the International Criminal Court which will probably emerge from the Rome Statute of 1998 will change this situation will be discussed in chapter 11. Compliance with the standards set in the various Declarations and Covenants has been regarded as a matter for the states that signed them – the latter are, in some cases, required to report annually on the progress of implementation of the obligations they have accepted to UN Commissions set up for the purpose, but, of course, such a requirement can be met without actually doing anything, and often has been. This lack of formal enforcement mechanisms may not always nullify the commitments made; in those countries governed by the rule of law, the fact that international obligations have been entered into can be a powerful argument in favour of the adoption of particular positions, even if there is no way in which these obligations can be enforced. International standard-setting becomes part of the rhetoric of domestic debate, strengthening the hands of those pushing for change in the relevant direction. And even countries which have less respect for the rule of law may still find that the obligations they have taken on have unintended political impacts – when the Soviet Bloc countries signed up to the human rights provisions of the Helsinki Accords in 1976, it was almost certainly in bad faith, but the informal 'Helsinki Monitoring Groups' set up by dissidents in order to try to ensure that these regimes lived up to their commitments without doubt played a role in delegitimizing the states of 'really existing' socialism in the 1980s.

Nonetheless, the lack of enforcement mechanisms is widely seen as undermining the effectiveness of the international human rights regime; this is the point at which the competing norms of 'universal human rights' and 'state sovereignty' come face to face, and state sovereignty generally wins the confrontation. In order for this not to be the case it would be necessary for the 'international community' – setting aside for the moment what is meant by that term – to intervene in the domestic affairs of one of its members for *humanitarian* reasons, which can provisionally be defined as 'primarily in the interests of the local inhabitants', and it is usually believed that only very rarely in the history of the Westphalia System has such action been taken. The last decade or so, however, has seen a number of putatively 'humanitarian interventions', including one case – Kosovo, 1999 – where a war was actually fought ostensibly for humanitarian reasons, and, on the face of it, it seems that the contest between individual rights and state sovereignty may be about to take a new form. This shift is sometimes attributed to a change in general consciousness as individuals, especially in the affluent West, become less willing to see egregious breaches of civilized standards elsewhere than they once were, but also clearly it has something to do with the end of the Cold War. Whereas during the course of the latter interventions either were or were not made in response to the constraints or necessities of the conflict itself, in the post-1989 world it has become possible for issues such as the wholesale abuse of human rights to be treated in their own terms rather than as part of the great contest. In any event, it is often suggested that a new norm of humanitarian intervention is evolving, and that, as one of the best books on the subject suggests, a 'solidarist' rather than a 'pluralist' conception of international society is emerging (Wheeler, 2000).

Most of this chapter will be devoted to an examination of this claim but, first, some of the underlying assumptions involved in this story need to be challenged. It will be suggested that, far from being a major feature of the Westphalia System as such, a strong general norm forbidding intervention on humanitarian grounds was actually only established in the mid-twentieth century. In the nineteenth century and earlier such interventions had been commonplace, but always in the context of a world in which a sharp division was made between the core Westphalia System with its European members, and the rest of the world, where humanitarian concerns were certainly present, but tied up with ethnocentric, racist assumptions about non-Europeans and the justifications for empire. As these latter assumptions were delegitimated in the course of the first half of the twentieth century, so the non-interventionism normative for the core system became normative for the system as a whole, and thus humanitarian intervention had to be reinvented and relegitimated at the end of the century. This, then, is a rather different story from the one that has become lodged in some people's minds, but before telling it, it is necessary to address one preliminary issue – what makes a humanitarian intervention truly 'humanitarian' and why do we need a separate category of intervention to describe such cases?

Humanitarian intervention is generally seen as a non-realist, even anti-realist, notion, but the idea that there is, or might be, a separate category of state behaviour that can be characterized as 'humanitarian' owes its existence to the dominance of realist assumptions about international behaviour. According to realism, states are egoists and act in pursuit of their material interests; it follows that when they do something that, on the face of it, seems *not* to be egoistic and *not* to relate to a material interest, some kind of special explanation is required. Realists believe that this only rarely happens, and that behaviour that seems not to be self-seeking usually will turn out to be so once closely inspected, but, on the rare occasions when this turns out not to be the case, a term such as 'humanitarian' is required to mark the fact that something unusual and extraordinary is going on. The problem with this position is clear; even those who wish to argue for a predominantly materialist understanding of the taproots of state behaviour can hardly deny that material interests need to be conceptualized before they can influence policy, and, in any event, a more ideational account of interests seems inherently more plausible than a purely materialist notion. This is the burden of the constructivist turn in international relations theory, as exemplified by the work of Alexander Wendt, but is also reflected in mainstream thinking (Goldstein and Keohane, 1993; Wendt, 1999). If, however, we assume that foreign policy behaviour is at least in part ideas-driven – that is to say, using older language, if we assume that through their foreign policy states desire to project their sense of themselves on to the world stage – then the necessity for a separate category of specifically humanitarian action becomes much less clear. A recent example may bring the point home.

In the course of 2000/2001 the UK has become increasingly involved in the civil war in Sierra Leone, training the Sierra Leone army and police force and generally providing advice to the Sierra Leone government. The realist looks to explain this commitment in terms of material interests – Sierra Leone's diamond mines usually figure at this point – and discounts the 'humanitarian' motives expressed by British decision-makers. There is no need to deny that diamonds feature somewhere in the story, but, given the cost of British action, more inherently plausible is the notion that UK involvement in this particular case is actually more the product of a national self-image as the kind of country that is prepared, if it can, to act as a good international citizen, especially in a region of the world where, because of its imperialist past, it considers itself to have special, albeit ill-defined, responsibilities. For some time now Britain has provided aid to the legitimate, more or less democratically elected government of Sierra Leone, a former British colony which is facing a particularly vicious internal uprising supported by a neighbouring dictator (Charles Taylor of Liberia). The initial involvement of British forces was directed to an evacuation of British citizens made necessary because of the collapse of a deal brokered by the UN and because of the ineffectiveness (and corruption) of UN forces in the country, but when British forces arrived it became clear in the minds of British decision-makers that a relatively small longer-term commitment could make a big difference. This commitment has not been made to secure access to diamonds, but because Britain likes to think of itself as the kind of country that is prepared to help out in these circumstances (always assuming the costs are not too high). There seems no reason to think of this as a specifically 'humanitarian' act distinguishable from the rest of British foreign policy.

This discussion has revolved around the question of motive; it is an apparently widely held assumption that for an action to count as humanitarian it must be motivated unambiguously by altruism. This emphasis on motivation is a little puzzling; although we might be unwilling to describe as humanitarian an intervention that was *wholly* motivated by non-humanitarian motives and whose humanitarian results were *solely* a by-product of less noble impulses, it seems rather unnecessary to demand that action be entirely motivated by humanitarianism in order for it to count as humanitarian, especially since in this, as in other areas of human endeavour, motives are almost always mixed. The word 'count' here is important – one of the reasons for an emphasis on motive is a desire to assign praise and blame, and underlying this is the medieval notion of 'right intention' which, as noted in chapter 6, was so important in determining what effect the use of force by particular actors would have on their immortal souls. This is all very well, but the beneficiaries of putatively humanitarian action are less likely to be impressed by such an exclusive concern for the moral well-being of the actor. It would seem, on the face of it, that a concern for humanitarian *effects* is at least as justified as a concern with motive (Ramsbotham and Woodhouse, 1996). This is not simply an abstract point, because in the context of the history of the Westphalia System it has not infrequently been the case that more or less unambiguously humanitarian effects have followed from action motivated by very unhumanitarian concerns.

Humanitarian intervention and the Westphalia System

Martin Wight, one of the leading theorists of international society, argues that the norm of non-intervention is basic to the Westphalian order, but that, under the influence of 'Western Values in International Relations' that norm may be breached in response to 'gross violations of human dignity' (Wight, 1966). The sort of example he had in mind is the British-led suppression of the slave trade in the nineteenth century, on which more below. Here we return to the ground examined in chapter 5 above: sovereignty is the norm but there are some (extreme) circumstances in which this norm may, legitimately, be broken. As we saw then, a similar position has been advocated by Michael Walzer, although on a different basis – Walzer is much more oriented towards the here-and-now, and explicitly makes the kind of domestic analogy that English School writers usually reject. Wight, on the other hand, is trying to make a more general statement about the Westphalian order as a whole, and this may be a weakness, since it is by no means clear that notions of 'human dignity' have remained constant throughout the last four hundred years.

In an influential essay, in turn influenced by English School thinking, Martha Finnemore has described the ways in which what she takes to be a norm of humanitarian intervention has been constructed over the last two centuries (Finnemore, 1996). Her argument is that this period has seen a change in terms of who is considered to be 'human'; in the nineteenth century overtly humanitarian interventions were carried out by the Western powers primarily in order to 'rescue' Christian communities under threat from non-Christian rulers – for example, Greeks in the 1820s, the Maronite Christians of Lebanon in 1962/3. The (often more outrageous) oppression of non-European, non-Christian communities attracted much less attention, especially when actually conducted by Europeans. She argues that this situation has changed in the twentieth century – the category of 'human' is now genuinely universal, and the interventions of this period have been less overtly ethnocentrically based, although it should be noted that those states with the power to intervene are still disproportionately of European origin and inclined to regard the oppression of fellow Europeans more seriously than that of non-Europeans.

Finnemore's work represents a genuine advance on that of Wight, but does not quite capture the ambiguities in the way in which ideas of race and empire worked for the expansionist powers of the Westphalia System, in particular, the way in which ideas of racial inferiority and superiority actually proved compatible with a kind of humanitarian concern for the welfare of the so-called 'lesser' races. This was true from the beginnings of the system, when the Salamanca School of Spanish lawyers attempted to mitigate the effects of Spanish rule in the Indies, and remained true throughout the period of the European empires. Moreover, an emphasis on the *effects* of action will reveal that even interventions explicitly designed to serve the interests of the imperial powers could have highly desirable results. Two examples will serve to illustrate these points.

In the first half of the nineteenth century, the British government led a determined effort, spearheaded by the Royal Navy, to end the slave trade. This campaign is usually characterized as either a generous, unqualifiedly humanitarian act, or, more characteristically in our cynical age, as an attempt to undermine Britain's competitors who were still reliant on slave labour. Recent work by Chaim Kaufman and Robert Pape undermines both of these stereotypes (1999). To meet the second point first, they demonstrate that this was a genuinely costly action, whose economic consequences were clearly damaging to Britain to the extent of a yearly average cost of 1.78 per cent of the national product – even if this is regarded as a ballpark figure only, it is impressive, far higher, for example, than current aid budgets. Perhaps more interesting is their account of the motivation for this action; they argue convincingly that the campaign was adopted as a response to developments in British internal politics, and in particular the need on the part of the governing elite to generate support for the political order from increasingly important low-church and non-conformist sections of the community. The latter took the issue of slavery very seriously, not because of any great affection for the slaves, much less because of beliefs in racial equality, but rather because they held that to own and trade in another human being – even an 'inferior' – was inherently wrong, and would lead to divine punishment for the slave-owning nation. To be against the slave trade was quite compatible with racist and imperialist allegiances and a selfish concern for British interests, although the latter were not defined in the materialist way favoured by realists. At the same time, it would be difficult to argue that the suppression of the slave trade – and the later campaign against slavery more generally – was *not* a humanitarian action. It is only an excessive concern for motivation that could lead to this conclusion.

The second case is perhaps more interesting – the issue of the so-called 'standards of civilization' whereby the European powers imposed restrictions upon the sovereignty of 'uncivilized' non-European powers whose legal codes and general conduct of affairs did not meet European standards; in such a case a 'regime of capitulations' would be established whereby countries such as China and Japan were coerced into surrendering their jurisdiction over Europeans in their territory (Bull and Watson, 1984; Gong, 1984). The idea here is clear – full members of international society are entitled to exercise general jurisdiction because they have 'proper' legal systems (i.e. systems that meet European standards, deemed to be civilized). Foreigners are entitled to call upon consular assistance to ensure fair play, but that is all they are entitled to as foreigners. However, European traders, missionaries and travellers in countries which do not have proper legal systems cannot be expected to put up with being treated the same way as the natives; European (including American) power was employed to ensure that this was not the case by establishing special courts and extra-territorial jurisdiction for cases involving foreigners (either as plaintiffs or as defendants).

These arrangements were unambiguously racist, and deeply offensive to peoples every bit as entitled to be considered as civilized as the Europeans who plundered their wealth, sold them opium and wantonly destroyed their cultural artefacts, as in the destruction of the Chinese Imperial Summer Palace in 1860. On the other hand, by obliging the Chinese and the Japanese to adopt legal codes in which the arbitrary power of the ruling elites – and, for example in the case of the Japanese, the right of members of the military class, the Samurai, to dispense summary capital punishment at will – were curbed, it could well be argued that the results of this policy were highly beneficial for the ordinary people of the countries concerned. Such was certainly not the primary motivation for the establishment of the policy, but, whatever the motivation, the effect was largely humanitarian. It is often suggested – usually by opponents but sometimes by supporters such as Jack Donnelly – that the international human rights regime of the twenty-first century has involved the re-creation of the 'standards of civilization' under new clothing (Donnelly, 1998). If so, this need only be considered wholly undesirable if motivation is taken to be the most important defining characteristic of humanitarian action – and, as suggested above, this is an unwarranted proposition.

Similar considerations apply to imperialism more generally. For the most part imperialism was certainly motivated by the desire to exploit colonies economically, and where this was not the case the search for prestige was central; it was equally true that racial theories provided a context for European imperialism. Moreover, these propositions remained true even when the Europeans themselves came to employ language which suggested that they were ruling on behalf of the 'natives' – the ideas of a 'civilizing mission' and of holding colonies 'in trust' may well have been sincerely held, but this should not cause us to overlook the less worthy motives that remained central to imperialism. Nonetheless, even taking these points on board it is still possible to argue that in some, perhaps many, cases imperialism had humanitarian *effects* – although the importance of the mental scars left by imperialism and racism should not be underestimated.

To summarize, throughout the Westphalian period two sets of norms concerning intervention were in place. Amongst the (European) full members of international society, the norm was non-intervention and although, as Krasner and others have demonstrated, interventions often took place, they were rarely humanitarian in either motive or effect, with the possible exception of those specifically legitimated by treaty (for example, by the clauses concerning minority rights in the Peace of Westphalia itself) (Krasner, 1999). On the other hand, in their relations with peoples not deemed members of international society, that is – prior to the admission of the Ottoman Empire to this status in 1856 – non-European peoples, no such norm of non-intervention was held to apply. States considered themselves free to intervene in the affairs of the non-European world whenever it was in their interests to do so, and whenever the local balance of forces allowed them the option. Such interventions were only rarely motivated by explicitly humanitarian concerns, but, quite frequently, they had humanitarian effects. Such was the situation in the closing years of the nineteenth century. The story of the first half of the twentieth century is that of these two sets of norms turning gradually into one, with the former coming to be seen as applying to all international relations.

The emergence of a strong norm of non-intervention

In the late nineteenth and early twentieth centuries, the rhetoric of European imperialism underwent a change, with increasing emphasis on the idea that imperial rule was undertaken in the interests of the inhabitants of the colonies. The very high-profile campaign against the savage rule of King Leopold of the Belgians in the so-called Congo Free State was a symptom of this shift (Hochschild, 1998). The legitimacy of imperialism was not challenged by this campaign – indeed, the campaigners often explicitly referred to the allegedly enlightened nature of British rule in Africa in order to make a contrast with the slavery and mutilation associated with Leopold's greed – but the traditional justifications of imperialism were. The idea that colonies were held in trust for their inhabitants was given a boost by the adoption in 1919 of a system of Mandates held under the League of Nations as a way of disposing of former German colonies – these were no longer simply distributed to the victors as had been the case in 1815; instead, for example, Britain held Tanganyika and South Africa held South West Africa as Mandates of the League, with an obligation to report to the League at regular intervals.

The Mandate system was not extended to existing colonies – and in a more explicit endorsement of the double standard, the Versailles Conference explicitly rejected a Japanese proposal to condemn racial discrimination – but even so the new system had unforeseen long-term consequences. Mandates were divided into Class 'A', 'B' and 'C' Mandates, with the expectation that all of them would eventually qualify for self-government, quite quickly in the case of the Class A Mandates, which were those parts of the Ottoman Empire that broke away after the war, but in the very longest of long runs in the case of the Class C, predominantly African, colonies. This almost certainly had some effect in terms of changing the prevailing sentiments about colonies, and it is interesting that, more or less simultaneously, the British Raj in India declared that its ultimate intention was that India should become an independent member of what was then the British Commonwealth, with a similar status to Canada and Australia, a status that, after the Westminster Conference of 1931, equated in effect to full independence. As Robert Jackson has emphasized in a classic study, it was not anticipated that any colony would achieve independence before it reached a level of economic development and administrative competence that would allow it to exercise effective self-rule and qualify it for membership of international society, and, in many cases, the date at which such an achievement would be realistic was generally assumed to be many years in the future (Jackson, 1990). This latter assumption was made by figures on the left as well as by apologists for imperialism. When the issue was discussed in British radical circles in the 1900s, the prevailing view was that to grant immediate independence to the majority of colonies would be to throw them on to the tender mercies of global capitalism, and ensure that their exploitation would continue in another guise, a position the truth of which the post-independence history of Africa has done nothing but confirm (Porter, 1968). Still, in the inter-war period, British planning assumed an independent India (within the British Commonwealth) by the 1940s. After the actual independence of India in 1947, the post-war Labour Government in Britain set up a commission on the future of the colonies which recommended that her African colonies be also prepared for self-government; it assumed that the more advanced of them would be ready for self-rule by the end of the twentieth century.

By then, of course, the general situation had changed quite radically. The terms under which the Second World War was fought as a liberation from Nazism did much to undermine racial ideologies more generally, and to promote a strong norm of self-determination; such a norm was built into the UN system, and the Trusteeship Council that took over the Mandates of the League pushed much more enthusiastically for the independence of colonies, especially when some of the new nations actually joined the Council. The outcome of the war was to weaken the traditional European empires – British, French and Dutch – while strengthening the position in world affairs of the Soviet Union and the United States, both of which claimed to be resolutely opposed to imperialism. Anti-colonialism became the order of the day, and the imperial powers were placed under considerable pressure to divest themselves of their colonies as quickly as possible. The Dutch were not in a position, in any event, to retain control of the East Indies, French efforts to remain in Indochina failed, and once Britain's Indian Empire disappeared, the economic rationale of her African colonies more or less disappeared. Within less than a generation, the only remains of the great colonial empires were those colonies where a large European population had settled and was unwilling to give up their position without a fight (Algeria, Rhodesia, South Africa) and the colonies maintained by Portugal, unwilling, until the fall of the Salazar regime in 1974, to admit that its status as a European great power was in the distant past.

The result of these shifts was the establishment for the first time in 400 years of an international system with a single norm concerning non-intervention – the old rules that applied only to fellow members of the European states-system now applied to all states. The human rights norms contained in the UN Charter and the Universal Declaration on Human Rights in 1948 were always qualified as not interfering with the legitimate exercise of state sovereignty, and were weak beside the norm of self-determination which was now applied more or less irrespective of the capacity for self-government of the collectivity in question. The Cold War saw a great many interventions driven by the desire to maintain the boundaries of the two camps – in Guatemala, Hungary, the Dominican Republic, Czechoslovakia and so on – but these interventions were almost always described as counter-interventions to exclude the opposing ideology/superpower. Neither side in the Cold War claimed a right to intervene on humanitarian grounds; each explicitly endorsed the notion of non-intervention as a concomitant of self-determination, however much they might both break such norms in practice.

Non-intervention became the norm of a single international society – but conditions on the ground revealed that such a norm came with a high price tag attached. The first of the major crises in former colonies came with the descent of the former Belgian Congo into anarchy in 1960, immediately after the independence for which it was manifestly unprepared. In the vain hope of preventing the fate of the Congo becoming an issue in the Cold War, a UN army was despatched with no clear mandate, providing assistance to the civil power in the absence of a civil power being beyond the capacity of the most ingenious of UN officials. The UN forces became involved in the military politics of the Congo, eventually being used to end a secession in Katanga; the UN Secretary-General died in a plane crash while visiting the operation – probably as a murder victim – and, generally, the experience of trying to be helpful in this difficult case was so awful that UN forces have never again been used in such a role (O'Brien, 1962). The Nigerian Civil War of 1967–70, a product of the Biafra secession, had more mixed results. There was no question here of direct foreign intervention; the international aid agencies (governmental and non-governmental) provided assistance to both sides until the spring of 1968, at which point the federal authorities forbade assistance going to the rebels. The official agencies, including the International Committee of the Red Cross (ICRC), withdrew, but the unofficial agencies led by Oxfam continued with an airlift to Biafra, the result of which was to prolong the war by perhaps a year, with an additional 200,000 deaths – the fear had been that defeat of the Biafrans would result in genocide, which was not, in fact, the case.

The experience of the Nigerian Civil War was instructive in a number of ways. This was a humanitarian intervention but by non-state actors. The British aid agencies led by Oxfam came away from Biafra in penitent mood, their own investigations having confirmed the judgement made above, namely that their intervention had actually prolonged the war to no good purpose, leading to many unnecessary deaths. They resolved that in future they would adhere strictly to the non-intervention norm, acting in future humanitarian disasters with the official agencies and with the approval of the state in question. Others took a different view; a group of French doctors left the ICRC over its decision to suspend aid to Biafra, and formed Médecins sans Frontières (MsF) under the leadership of the charismatic and controversial Bernard Kouchner, who was later to break away from MsF to form yet another group (and later still to be a minister in the French government and, in 1999–2000, the head of the civilian administration in Kosovo). Kouchner articulated the doctrine, taken up by other French leaders, of 'le droit d'ingérence' – a phrase that could be translated as a right (or law) of intervention (or interference) (Allen and Styan, 2000). This doctrine asserts that in cases where there are violations of human rights, the international community has a right to intervene, the terminology used implying that this is a *legal* right – although, as noted, the term '*droit*' is ambiguous here. This doctrine, little known in the English-speaking world, has had considerable impact in France, especially when Kouchner's star has been in the ascendant, and also where French is spoken, this latter point being of some significance when the Francophone Egyptian Foreign Minister Boutros Boutros-Ghali became UN Secretary General in the late 1980s.

For most of the 1970s and 1980s, however, the doctrine of non-intervention reigned supreme. Nicholas Wheeler has shown in detail that on three occasions in the 1970s – India's war with Pakistan as a result of the West Bengal crisis of 1971, Vietnam's overthrow of the Pol Pot regime in Cambodia in 1979 and Tanzania's overthrow of Idi Amin in Uganda, also in 1979 – when states might plausibly have claimed justification on humanitarian grounds they, very explicitly and deliberately, did not do so, preferring to cite what they thought of as the more legitimate grounds that they were facing a threat to 'international peace and security' (Wheeler, 2000). To these examples one might add the US intervention in Grenada against the murderers of the elected prime minister, which was justified in terms of counter-intervention (against Cuban engineers) and the rescue of US citizens, but, judging by the positive reactions of the Grenadines, could equally well have been seen as a humanitarian act. Still, by the end of the 1980s some movement was visible in doctrinal terms; during the various humanitarian disasters of that decade international governmental and non-governmental organizations not infrequently found themselves acting in contexts where the formal approval of the host government either was difficult to obtain or was effectively meaningless. The use of force to protect aid workers gradually came to be seen as legitimate, and in 1988 UN General Assembly Resolution 43/131 summarized the new understanding by simultaneously restating the doctrine of non-intervention, but legitimating strictly humanitarian action in rebel-held areas, which, it will be recalled, had been a key issue in the Nigerian Civil War, twenty years earlier.

Thus, at the end of the 1980s, the stage was set for the dramatic developments of the 1990s, and the re-emergence, under radically different conditions, of the occasional willingness of the international community to intervene on humanitarian grounds. This is a re-emergence because, as we have seen, the idea of a strict norm of non-intervention *applied on equal terms to all members of international society* was itself of comparatively recent origin. This re-emergence was partly a function of contingent factors, but the ending of the Cold War was a necessary, if not a sufficient, condition for even the possibility of a new norm to emerge/re-emerge. Given the reluctance that, in any event, many states have shown to acknowledge that there has been any change in this area, it is clear that without the ending of East–West conflict no such development would have been possible. For the first time in decades, in the 1990s the major powers were faced with situations where a call for humanitarian action was made and where it was actually possible for this call to be met. The rest of this chapter will examine this new situation, first via an overview of events on the ground, then via a more extended discussion of the putative emergence of a new doctrine of humanitarian intervention.

Intervention in the 1990s: an overview

The decade began and ended with interventions that were explicitly justified on humanitarian grounds. The lack of success of the interventions of 1991–3 in Iraq and Somalia led directly to an unwillingness to act in the face of circumstances that called out for action in Rwanda and Bosnia in the mid-1990s; partly as a response to a sense of guilt over the consequences of inaction the end of the decade saw a return to a more active stance in Kosovo and East Timor in 1999. The ambiguous results of these latter interventions suggests that this action–reaction cycle may continue into the 2000s.*

The Gulf War of 1990–1 was, in normative terms, a wholly conventional affair, fought in accordance with the Legalist Paradigm outlined by Michael Walzer in *Just and Unjust Wars* (see chapter 5 above); fighting between the US-led Coalition and Iraq ceased after Iraqi forces withdrew from Kuwait. Internal opponents of the Iraqi regime, on the other hand, attempted to overthrow Saddam Hussein with the tacit – and at one point explicit – approval of the Coalition, but, partly because the war ended before the regime's most loyal troops suffered serious casualties, their rising failed, and the centres of revolt – in the Kurdish areas of North Iraq and the marshes in the south-east occupied by predominantly Shia Arabs – faced the prospect of deadly retribution. Under the terms of the Legalist Paradigm upon which the Coalition acted, this was an internal, domestic issue, but, as was frequently commented at the time, it would be difficult to explain to an intelligent child why it could be right to use force to throw the Iraqis out of Kuwait, but wrong to prevent them from carrying out mass murder in the Kurdish areas of Iraq. In response to this situation, and to pressure generated by the media, the Coalition established 'enclaves' in the Kurdish areas, on Iraqi soil but where access was forbidden to Iraqi troops, and a 'no-fly' zone in the south of Iraq to provide some protection for the Marsh Arabs.

This was a genuine innovation in the context of post-1945 norms, and the Kurdish safe areas were legitimated by a UN Security Council Resolution, 688, where humanitarian concerns were explicitly referred to by some of its sponsors, especially Britain and France – although the majority of members who voted in favour relied upon those parts of the resolution that referred more traditionally to the threat to peace and security in the region, a reasonable concern given the peculiar position of the Kurds, who are to be found in three neighbouring countries (Turkey, Iran and Syria) as well as Iraq (Wheeler, 2000, pp. 141ff). On

---

* The following survey is based on a number of general studies and collections, with additional references to specific cases added where appropriate. Wheeler (2000) is the best overview, with Shawcross (2000) and S. Peterson (2000) as alternative, journalist's accounts, and Weiss (1999) and Haass (2000) more oriented to technicalities; the best collections are Moore (1998) – which has useful contributions by key decision-makers as well as by academic commentators – and Mayall (1996).

the other hand, there was no substantial deployment of a UN force, and although the enclaves policy averted an immediate humanitarian disaster, it provided no long-run succour to the Kurds. The situation in the south was even worse; Iraqi forces may have been unable to use aircraft against the Marsh Arabs but they employed heavy artillery at will, and more subtly and dangerously, embarked on a longer-term policy of draining the marshes, thereby destroying a habitat that had supported a particular way of life for millennia.

Armed humanitarian action in Iraq was, at best, only a partial success; some would not claim even that for the various operations in Somalia in 1991–3 (Clarke and Herbst, 1997; Makinda, 1993; S. Peterson, 2000). With the ending of the Cold War, the loss of strategic significance of the Horn of Africa and the concomitant loss of US aid, the Somali dictator Mohammed Siyad Barre lost control, and Somalia descended into clan warfare, becoming a paradigm example of a 'failed' state (Zartman, 1994). As a result of the destruction of crops and the confiscation by warlords of what food remained, in 1991/2 Somalia faced the prospect of famine and a humanitarian disaster to equal that of the Ethiopian famine of the mid-1980s. Private aid agencies could only work with the approval of the warlords, which meant that their assistance added to the resources of the latter; a UN force (UNOSOM I) was established to provide protection for the agencies, but at too low a level to operate effectively in the Somali environment. In the summer of 1992 the UN Secretary-General's Special Representative, Mohamed Sahnoun, an Algerian diplomat respected by all sides, developed a policy of slowly undermining the warlords by building up the clan elders as an alternative source of power, but in the autumn of 1992 the Secretary-General, Boutros Boutros-Ghali, removed him and appealed to the international community for a more forceful policy. This appeal was met by the Bush administration in its closing days in the United States, and in December 1992 some 30,000 predominantly US, French and Italian troops, spearheaded by US marines, landed as UNITAF (unified task force). This was the first occasion when a UN force was deployed without the approval of the host government, for the obvious reason that there was no host government to give its approval. UN Resolution 794 explicitly authorizes the establishment of the force on humanitarian grounds and is the first such resolution to be passed by the Security Council.

UNITAF was initially successful in re-establishing the security of aid supplies (although some argue that by then the worst of the famine was effectively over), but the short-term nature of the commitment, and its unwillingness to disarm the clan armies, meant that little was done to address the underlying problem. In May 1993 UNITAF was replaced by UNOSOM II, a weaker, multinational force; most US troops were withdrawn, but a Quick Reaction Force remained, reinforced in August by Rangers and Delta Force commandos. UNOSOM II soon became embroiled in clan politics, and after the murder of twenty-four Pakistani peacekeepers in June 1993, the UN/US forces targeted the leader of the strongest militia in Mogadishu, General Aidid, as a war criminal. Ineffective attempts to capture Aidid led to escalating tension and the deaths of many Somali nationals, including, in one disastrous raid by US forces, those elders of Aidid's clan who had the best chance of ending the conflict. In October 1993 a full-scale battle in the centre of Mogadishu following a US raid and the downing of two helicopters led to the deaths of eighteen Rangers, with the body of one man paraded through the streets by the crowd – the deaths of hundreds, perhaps over a thousand, Somalis in the battle attracted less media attention (Bowden, 1999). Partly as a result of this action US and most other troops were withdrawn in 1994, and Somalia returned to anarchy – to date no government has been able to assert effective control over the country as a whole, although an effective, largely unrecognized Republic of Somaliland has been established in the northern part of the country (formerly British Somaliland).

Somalia was certainly perceived within the US as a disaster, and as a warning not to allow US troops to be involved in such operations in the future; this had severe consequences for the peoples of Rwanda. That country had been the location for violence between its two main peoples, the majority Hutu and the Tutsi, since the late 1950s (Prunier, 1995; Klinghoffer, 1998). In the early 1990s the French-supported Hutu-based regime of President Habyarimana was under pressure from the predominantly Tutsi Rwanda Patriotic Front (RPF), an armed movement supported by Uganda. UN-sponsored peace efforts were agreed by the Rwanda government, but when Habyarimana's aircraft was shot down over the capital Kigali in April 1994, almost certainly by Hutu extremists, the latter set in train the systematic killing of all Tutsi and many Hutu moderates. In the genocide that followed 800,000–1 million were killed between April and August 1994; the killing ended only with the military victory of the RPF (Gourevitch, 1998).

The international community had been given warning of what was planned. A small UN monitoring force (UNAMIR), predominantly of Belgian troops, headed by a Canadian general, Roméo Dallaire, had been in Rwanda since 1993 and in January and February of 1994 Dallaire warned the UN that a genocide was imminent and asked for permission to act to confiscate arms. His warnings never got out of the Secretary-General's department. When the genocide began, ten Belgian troops were killed while attempting to protect the Prime Minister; the response was to withdraw Belgian troops, although they, along with French paratroopers, returned to evacuate *European* nationals to safety.

Dallaire's requests for reinforcement were ignored, and no intervention took place until, in June, France established a 'safe area' in the west of the country, an action that had the effect, if not the intent, of protecting the *génocidaires*, who were also the recipients of international humanitarian aid when they fled the country after the RPF victory (Prunier, 1995).

It is now clear that the Secretariat and the leading UN members in the Security Council knew what was going on in Rwanda, although some of the smaller nations on the Council, lacking access to intelligence reports, did not (Melvern, 2000). The US, Britain and France consistently referred to the events as ethnic violence or civil war, refusing until late in the day to use the correct term 'genocide' for fear of bringing into play the Genocide Convention with the obligation to act it lays on the international community. The US not only refused to allow its troops to become involved, it also refused logistic support to those few, mainly African, countries that were prepared to act. French opposition to action was partly the product of long-standing support for the Hutu majority government, and fears for French influence should the English-speaking RPF win, but US opposition seems to have been very heavily influenced by the failure in Somalia. Whether intervention could have been effective once the genocide had begun is still contested, but action earlier could certainly have made a difference (Des Forges, 2000; Kuperman, 2000).

A similar unwillingness to commit troops on the ground underlay US policy towards the wars that followed the break-up of the Yugoslav Federation in the early 1990s. The story here is too complicated even for the kind of summary given above, but by 1994 the Serbian-dominated Yugoslav National Army was in possession of a substantial part of newly independent Croatia, while Bosnia-Herzegovina was divided into three parts: that controlled by the internationally recognized, Muslim-dominated government in Sarajevo, Croatian-controlled enclaves, and a large part of the country dominated by ethnic Serbs seeking either their own republic or union with Serbia (Gow, 1997; Rose, 1998; Campbell, 1998; Daadler, 2000). This situation was, at the very least, a humanitarian disaster, and the aid agencies, official and unofficial, attempted to provide assistance, protected not very effectively by a UN force, and European soldiers under the aegis of the EU, NATO and the OSCE. Although the EU had taken the lead in recognizing the independence of Bosnia, European leaders consistently refused to follow through the logic of that recognition by giving support to the legal government of that country. Instead, government forces and Serb and Croat forces were routinely referred to as the 'warring parties', an allegedly neutral designation that actually delegitimated the government by placing it on an equal standing with its foes. However, in defence of this apparent inconsistency, it should be said that the circumstances under which Bosnia-Herzegovina achieved independence, on the basis of a referendum in which most ethnic Serbs abstained and most ethnic Croats voted positively only on tactical grounds, did not inspire confidence.

Armed intervention under UN auspices eventually led to the establishment of 'safe areas' on the Kurdish model, but in July 1995 the fall of Srebrenica, one of these safe areas, led to a massacre of Muslims which the weak and ill-supported UN troops present were unable to prevent. This massacre set in train a series of events which in the summer of 1995 finally led to NATO intervention in the form of air and artillery support for a Croat-Bosnian government offensive which pushed back the Serbs in Bosnia, and led to the ethnic cleansing of the historic Serb community of the Krayina in Croatia. Under this pressure, the Serbian government agreed to come to terms with its opponents, and the Dayton Peace Accords in October 1995 established an uneasy peace based on a nominal federation in Bosnia, but in practice on the partition of the country (Daadler, 2000).

Unsurprisingly, there was in the West a widespread feeling that pusillanimous diplomacy on the part of its leaders had betrayed the peoples of former Yugoslavia. A War Crimes Tribunal was established in the Hague, but the person who in most people's minds was the leading criminal, the Serbian leader Slobodan Milosevic, was given a safe-conduct in order to allow him to attend the Dayton talks. Part of the deal struck with Milosevic at Dayton involved keeping the situation in Kosovo off the agenda. Kosovo had been an autonomous region in Serbia with a predominantly ethnically Albanian population; in 1989 Milosevic illegally suspended this autonomy; in response the majority population engaged in a very widely supported campaign of peaceful civil disobedience in the hope of garnering Western support for, at least, the restoration of their autonomy. The West's refusal to take up the issue at Dayton sent a clear message to Kosovo – only violence would attract attention. A Kosovo Liberation Front soon formed, carried out actions, provoked retaliation against the civilian population from the Yugoslav army, police and paramilitaries, and set in motion the next round of internecine war.

This time NATO and the West were unwilling simply to watch a humanitarian disaster unfold. As the Yugoslavs ratcheted up the oppression in 1998, ethnically cleansing villages and creating hundreds of thousand of internal refugees, the US and NATO issued threats; in the autumn a military campaign was averted by a last-minute deal involving unarmed OSCE observers in Kosovo, but in early 1999 it became clear that the KLA were using the respite to rearm and that the Yugoslavs were not to be deterred from committing atrocities by the presence of unarmed observers. A conference was sponsored at Rambouillet to broker a Dayton-style deal, but negotiations foundered, the Kosovars signing the original document with the Serbs refusing. Rambouillet failed for many reasons, but the unwillingness of the Serbs to accept armed NATO troops and NATO's conviction that nothing else would suffice were basic (Weller, 1999a). A six-week NATO military campaign followed, exclusively based on, largely US, air power, beginning with attacks on Serbian military institutions but rapidly leading to attacks on the infrastructure of Serbian society. This first so-called 'humanitarian war' took place without UN approval (although a resolution to condemn the action was heavily defeated) and provided cover for the Serbs to carry out a larger-scale ethnic cleansing than would otherwise have been possible (Roberts, 1993). Over a million Albanians were driven from their homes. This had the effect, counterproductive for the Serbs, of sufficiently outraging Western public opinion that the Alliance held together, in spite of some high-profile mistakes which led to civilian casualties in Yugoslavia. At the point at which it looked likely that a ground campaign might prove necessary, the Serbs capitulated, and what is, in effect, a NATO protectorate has been established in Kosovo. This first full-scale, armed humanitarian action can only be counted as, at best, a qualified success – although it has stimulated an unprecedented volume of academic, legal and quasi-official commentary (*American Journal of International Law*, 1999b; Roberts, 1999; Booth, 2000; Danish Institute for International Affairs, 1999; *Ethics and International Affairs*, 2000; Freedman, 2000; Independent International Commission on Kosovo, 2000; Judah, 2000).

The final humanitarian intervention of the 1990s took place on the other side of the world, in East Timor, a former Portuguese colony murderously annexed against its will by Indonesia in 1975 and the site of a simmering conflict ever since (Cotton, 2001; Dunne and Wheeler, 2001). In late 1999, partly because of the fall earlier that year on corruption charges of Indonesia's long-standing military leader Suharto and the emergence of a slightly more sympathetic government, the conflict came to a head, and Indonesia was prevailed upon to accept an Australian-led UN peacekeeping force. In the weeks leading up to the arrival of UN troops there were many atrocities committed and this was clearly another case where armed intervention was taking place in essence against the will of the host government – although actual fighting between the UN force and the Indonesian army was narrowly avoided.

Apart from the above cases of humanitarian action and inaction, there were a number of other 1990s cases which might be describable as 'humanitarian interventions', most especially the long-standing UN attempt to assist in the establishment of democracy in Cambodia, but the cases discussed above provide ample material for an examination of developments in the international political theory of humanitarian action. What conclusions can we draw from these events?

Reflections on humanitarian intervention in the 1990s

The first point that emerges from this experience is that, as suggested in the introduction to this chapter, the very notion that there is a distinction between 'humanitarian' and other interventions is open to question. All interventions involve the exercise of power, all involve, in one way or another, taking sides in local political conflicts, and the motives for all interventions are mixed. On a number of occasions in the 1990s, the UN or other groups of states attempted to disprove these propositions, but in the event, merely demonstrated their force.

Interventions involve the exercise of power, but in both Somalia and Bosnia the attempt was made to intervene with forces mainly, or at least significantly, drawn from countries without a tradition of exercising extensive political power and employing troops who were in no sense elite fighting forces. This was very much in the tradition of UN peacekeeping over past decades. In Somalia the initial commitment in UNOSOM I involved Pakistani peacekeepers, and again later in UNOSOM II, Pakistani, Bengali, Malaysian and other Muslim 'Southern' troops were placed in key roles as an explicit decision to rely as little as possible on the US troops who made up the bulk of UNITAF – it was thought that the Somalis would find it easier to relate to fellow Muslims, a rather orientalist assumption that proved inaccurate. 'Peacemaking' is different from 'peacekeeping'. These troops were largely outgunned by the forces of the Somali clan leaders – the course of the Cold War in the Horn of Africa had left lying around a great deal of modern ordnance which had fallen into the hands of local forces, and, without the involvement of US and other European forces, superior power on the ground could not be established. The situation was very unlike that of, say, UN forces in Cyprus, where the capacity of the UN to police the green line between the two communities does not rest on superior fire power, but on the consent of those two communities, and the moral force of the UN uniform. In Somalia the communities had not given their consent to be policed, and showed no respect for the blue helmets of the UN, as the Pakistanis found out to their cost in June 1993. Thereafter the superior fire power of US forces was brought to bear, but the relatively small size of the latter ensured that they became simply one more participant in a local power struggle – whereas the overwhelming strength of US forces earlier in the year, during the UNITAF period, created a window of opportunity when, in the view of many, intervention could have been successful and the clan armies largely disarmed.

In Bosnia, the use of troops from a large number of countries, many of whom had very little experience of the conditions they would face, was also the product of a deliberate desire for the intervention not to be seen as the exercise of brute force (Rose, 1998). The intention was that these forces would be involved in humanitarian activities and therefore would not need to overwhelm the forces with which they would have to deal – the aim was that they would act neutrally and therefore would be treated as neutrals, and in such circumstances reliance on such combat-hardened soldiers as the French Foreign Legion or British Parachute Regiment would be unnecessary, indeed, quite possibly counter-productive. In the event, what transpired demonstrated both that the idea of a neutral intervention is a chimera, and that, when neutrality is not respected, there is no substitute for fighting spirit on the part of the intervening troops. If privation of civilians is being used as a weapon of war, as was the case here, then to provide humanitarian aid will be seen as a political intervention whether the interveners want it to be or not – and even when the policy appears neutral a certain degree of strength on the part of the interveners may be necessary. The fate of the 'safe areas' for government-supporting Bosnians is exemplary here; the troops that were supposed to be protecting the safe areas had neither the strength nor the will either to prevent those inside from using them as bases to attack the Serbs, or to prevent the latter from overwhelming the safe areas and committing atrocities. The Dutch battalion at Srebrenica was badly let down by its superiors in Bosnia, but their own lack of willingness to assert themselves as soldiers certainly contributed to the atrocity that took place in this unsafest of safe areas. It is not too fanciful to suggest that a battalion of Legionnaires or Paratroopers might have been rather more willing to find out whether the Serbs were actually prepared to fight OSCE/UN troops; at the very least they might have been less willing to hand over their equipment undamaged to the Serbs – the use by the Serbs of UN uniforms and vehicles to lure their victims from hiding was particularly humiliating for the peacekeepers. It is also difficult to imagine a Legion commander emulating the Dutch commander who accepted a bottle of wine and flowers for his wife from a Serb commander who had just murdered between 5,000 and 10,000 unarmed prisoners – and allowed himself to be filmed by Serb propagandists to complete the humiliation.

In short, effective humanitarian intervention is an act of power; it involves taking sides, choosing which of the various parties to support and enforcing one's choice by superior strength. This may not be a pleasant sight – to put the matter bluntly, the aim must be to bully the bully, which means that the behaviour of the successful intervener may not be particularly attractive, and may indeed involve temporarily contributing to humanitarian distress. This will appear particularly unpleasant because, as anticipated at the start of this chapter, the motives for intervention are rarely likely to be purely altruistic. In the case of the interventions of the 1990s, critics such as Noam Chomsky and John Pilger have made a point of stressing this absence of purity to the point of denying that there are any occasions when action has taken place for unselfish, non-materialistic reasons, the finest example of this way of thinking being Pilger's condemnation of the intervention in East Timor as being designed to preserve the territory for global capitalism (Chomsky, 1999; Pilger, 1999). The local inhabitants seem not to have seen things that way, and this is, in any event, a particularly absurd exaggeration, but the general point has some force. Even if NATO's war in Kosovo was not part of some master plan for the US to control the Balkans it certainly was partly fought to preserve NATO's credibility, and while no material interest lay behind the US intervention in Somalia the desire on the part of the defeated Bush administration to 'go out' with a foreign policy success should not be ignored. Equally, the decision to attack Serbia's infrastructure undoubtedly imposed costs on innocent civilians – in addition, of course, to those who became victims of the inevitable mistakes that accompany any military campaign.

One answer to this point is, as suggested above, to put emphasis on effects not motives, in which case most of the interventions of the 1990s can still be seen as broadly unsuccessful, but for the rather more sensible reason that they generally did not produce the effects they were designed to produce. It may well be that this is a general characteristic of armed humanitarian action and that a more subtle approach will almost always bring better results. The Somali experience is instructive here; Mohamed Sahnoun's approach to the conflict, before he was fired by the UN, involved establishing contact with clan elders and persuading them to use their authority to undermine the more warlike clan leaders – this was the traditional way in which conflicts between the clans were restrained in Somalia and it may have been successful on this occasion, especially if backed by financial aid (Lewis and Mayall, in Mayall, 1996; Sahnoun, in Moore, 1998). We will never know whether such a strategy would have worked, but we can say that the alternative preferred by Boutros-Ghali and the US certainly did not, and that the killing of many clan elders in a US raid in July 1993 was the single biggest disaster of the affair. In Bosnia and Serbia, as in Eastern Europe more generally, it has been suggested quite cogently that financial and other assistance directed to civil society groups might have paid dividends in terms of constraining the warlords in that region (Kaldor and Vojevoda, 1998).

The work of critics such as Chomsky, Pilger and, in different keys, Kaldor and realists such as Mandelbaum, manages at times to convey the impression that armed 'humanitarian' action – or, rather, action purporting to be humanitarian – was a common event in the 1990s (Mandelbaum, 1999). In fact, of course, the most striking feature of the period was the relatively small number of occasions on which action replaced inaction. The biggest single disaster of the period – the Rwanda genocide – produced no helpful intervention, and in general the civil wars and massacres of Africa, especially in Angola and Zaire/Congo, were ignored by those who had the power to act. The selective nature of the interventions that did take place is a common criticism directed against them – if not Rwanda, why Kosovo, and so on. Apart from the fact that it is not clear whether those who make this criticism actually want more interventions or fewer, selectivity in itself is more or less inevitable and it is equally inevitable that the criteria for selection will not simply be humanitarian criteria. To take a fairly obvious example, armed intervention to stop the Russians doing to Chechnya what the Serbs wanted to do to Kosovo would be equivalent to a declaration of war on a power which is still in possession of large-scale armed forces and a nuclear capacity. Unsurprisingly, no one has seriously suggested such a course of action, but it is not clear why this reluctance should be taken to delegitimate intervention in Kosovo, where similar considerations do not apply. The search for a law-like rule that will determine when intervention should take place is likely to be unsuccessful.

The relative infrequency of humanitarian interventions as opposed to circumstances in which it might have been hoped that someone would intervene, but in fact no one did, provides the context for an assessment of Nicholas Wheeler's recent study of the emergence of a norm of humanitarian intervention (Wheeler, 2000). Wheeler approaches the subject from the perspective of a theorist of international society with constructivist leanings; his underlying premise is that the way in which states describe what they are doing when they act influences the actions they actually take, perhaps even determines what action it is possible for them to take. He examines the public utterances of states, in particular in the context of their votes on key resolutions in the UN Security Council, in order to find out whether they claim that a right of humanitarian intervention actually exists, or whether, when they act in ways that appear to involve such a claim, they actually invoke more conventional positions, such as the right to self-defence, or the argument that a particular position represents a

threat to international peace and security. He finds, first, that during
the 1990s there were genuine innovations in international law, in particular at the beginning of the decade, when the various UN forces
in Somalia were legitimated on specifically humanitarian lines, and,
second, that the language states employed did change significantly
during the decade. By the time of the Kosovo War a highly qualified
right of humanitarian intervention was being asserted by some states,
although, as he acknowledges, a number of important members of the
international community such as China, Russia and India remain more
or less implacably opposed.

This is a fascinating study, the best yet on the experiences of the
1990s, and the various case studies of UN law he presents are, and will
remain, invaluable, irrespective of the fate of his thesis as a whole. As
to the latter, much of its force will depend on the role one is prepared
to assign to norms in the explanation of state behaviour. It might well
be the case that there has been a shift in the normative foundations of
IR over the decade, and that the firm bar on intervention – which, it
will be recalled, is largely the product of the post-1945 world – has been
partially lifted, but whether this will actually affect in any substantial
way the behaviour of states is another matter. Nor is it clear that such
a general shift in state behaviour would be desirable.

In any event, the fate of the Kosovo intervention is instructive; the
official justifications employed to support the intervention certainly
claimed or implied a right to intervene, even in the absence of explicit
UN authorization (Blair, 1999). Moreover, one very influential philosophical voice went so far as to see the action as just possibly serving
as a precursor to the emergence of a more Kantian international system,
a Pacific Union of liberal-democratic states (Habermas, 1999). On the
other hand, the post-Kosovo War experience of the NATO/UN protectorate in Kosovo has been sufficiently depressing as to make it
highly unlikely that any state is likely to enter into such an action again
in the near future. It is clear that the only thing to be said in favour of
the current situation is that it is better than it was before the action took
place, and even this justification is likely to disappear if, as seems distinctly possible, NATO finds itself coercing the local ethnic Albanians
to come to terms with the newly democratic Serbs in Belgrade. Moreover, the effect on the UN of the justifications for the war could well
be quite serious. In the past it had been understood that a resolution
with the formula 'all necessary means' or something similar would be
needed before UN-authorized violent action would follow; on this
occasion it was argued by NATO that earlier UN resolutions con-
demning human rights violations in the region and calling on the
Federal Yugoslav authorities to end them could provide legitimation
for action; if such an argument came to be accepted the probable result

would be that in future resolutions with this latter wording will be vetoed by states that do not want to see this slippage occur.

The difficulty here is clear: the argument is that humanitarian intervention may be becoming a norm in the sense that it is part of customary international law, but norm-creating of this kind requires a broader base than that which has been present over the last few years. The claim of the powerful, affluent Western states of Europe and North America to be able to create such norms without the consent of the rest of the world is bound to be resisted, and rightly so. The norm of non-intervention has positive as well as negative sides, and it is no accident that it is defended by many weak states who know that they will never be interveners, but fear that they might be intervened against. It may be that the preservation of a firm norm of non-intervention along with a tacit agreement that sometimes it might be right to break this norm is the best solution here – although most lawyers are, understandably, resistant to a notion which appears to play fast and loose with the rule of law.

Two final points should be made before changing somewhat the terms of the discussion. Can it in fact be argued that human welfare would actually be promoted if no norm of humanitarian intervention should be established? This is an interesting point, because the usual assumption is that intervention to stop a violent conflict is in general a 'good thing'. Is this always so? Edward Luttwak has recently argued that in some cases the general welfare would be served better if military force were to be allowed to settle matters – this would, at least, prevent conflicts from dragging on unresolved, which, given the absence of authoritative conflict-resolution mechanisms in the current system, is likely usually to be their fate (Luttwak, 1999). This may seem a counsel of despair; still, it is not too difficult to call to mind past conflicts where it is by no means clear that an early imposed peace would have been desirable. Would a European-mediated conclusion to the American Civil War in 1862 that involved the recognition of the Confederacy and the continuation of slavery have been a good thing? Or an externally imposed peace between Britain and Germany in 1940? In both cases, the high human costs of war would thereby have been avoided, but could we really say that such a result would have been in the long-run interests of *any* of the participants? Hardly – but then do we make this judgement because we know that the alternative to a mediated peace was a Northern/Allied victory? Would we feel the same way if the South, or, much worse, the Nazis, had won?

The issue of counterfactuals is important and neglected. Consider, for example, the situation in Rwanda in early 1994. Suppose, for the sake of argument, that General Dallaire's request for authority to act had been granted and that he had had the resources to confiscate the weapons stockpiled by Hutu extremists. This might well have led to violence, and UNAMIR could have found itself engaging with Hutu militias and even part of the Rwandan army; the Rwandan government might well have been replaced by more extreme elements, and the Rwanda Patriotic Front might have gone on the offensive, effectively acting with UNAMIR. There is very little doubt that had this quite plausible chain of events come about, this chapter would have contained a discussion of what went wrong in Rwanda, seeing this as a case similar to that of Somalia, where an overactive UN stepped into a conflict it did not understand, and made things worse. What we would not now be doing is comparing this chain of events with what actually happened, because the genocide, on this account, was prevented – in our world we know that, but in the new world created by effective but messy UN action, this would be a matter for speculation only. Events in Kosovo also need to be seen in this light – we simply do not know what would have happened had NATO not intervened as it did, but there is at least some reason to think that things would have been worse than they actually are for the people most closely affected. The more general point is that the exercise of political judgement requires a recognition that there can be no guarantees that one is doing the right thing, and that the results of inaction can be as damaging as the results of action. The Hippocratic injunction 'do no harm' – proposed by Chomsky as the principle that ought to govern interventions (Chomsky, 1999, p. 156) – is hard to apply in an imperfect world.

Humanitarian intervention and especially armed intervention, as conventionally understood, is something that states do, or not, as the case more usually is. Non-state aid organizations are also involved heavily in actions that look very like interventions nowadays, and, of course, bodies such as Amnesty International are more widely involved in promoting human rights in ways that could well be seen as interventionary. There is a wider point here. If what we are actually seeing is a growth in *humanitarianism* then it would be a serious mistake to judge such a growth simply in the context of major human rights abuses, or the breakdown of societies, or their dissolution. The major source of human misery in the world today is poverty, the accompanying malnutrition and stunted life-chances. The international community may respond to, for example, actual famines, and when, as is usually the case, these famines take place in conditions of political oppression and unrest, this may raise wider issues, but the misery of constant but non-dramatic malnutrition attracts much less attention. In the case of actual or possible humanitarian interventions there is usually an identifiable enemy who can be held to account – but the global inequalities that generate such extremes of poverty are less easy to personalize. It is often asked whether it is right that members of one society be asked to make sacrifices for another by, for example, sending soldiers to assist the latter to achieve liberation from tyranny, but the issue of international obligation arises just as powerfully, although less dramatically, when the relief of poverty is at stake. What obligations do the rich owe to the poor, when the latter are not their fellow citizens?

9

Global Inequality and International Social Justice

As we have seen, it is now widely held that all individuals possess certain political and civil rights simply by virtue of their humanity, and some at least would extend this position to argue that, when these rights are violated, the international community ought to act to ensure that individuals are able to claim the rights to which they are entitled – although it is clear that this latter extension is contested and that a norm of humanitarian intervention is, at best, nascent rather than currently operative. Nonetheless, the notion of a 'rescue' by the international community has taken on some currency, and not simply in cases of human rights violations; it is also widely assumed that international action is called for in the event of humanitarian disasters such as earthquakes or famines. The latter action is, no doubt, partly a response to the widely held belief that individuals have economic and social rights as well as political and civil ones, although a more general belief in the importance of humanitarianism is probably a more potent motive for assistance when need is so dramatically demonstrated.

In the case of political and civil rights, it is generally held that international intervention is required only in extreme circumstances. The working assumption is that, while the normal state of the world may involve the existence of many governments that, to some degree, deny rights, oppression is generally at a level that does not call for international action, certainly not forceful international intervention. Given the dubious results of international humanitarian interventions, it is a reasonable supposition that, most of the time, it is better not to intervene even when minor violations are common – in other words, the background level of adherence to human rights standards in the absence of any concerted action from the outside is, most of the time, at least an acceptable, tolerable, level. The situation with respect to economic and social rights is rather different. Quite clearly the 'background conditions' in this case are far less satisfactory; famines are relatively unusual, but perhaps a third of the world's population is mal-nourished, not as a result of some exceptional set of circumstances, but on a regular basis. The present international economic order is charac-terized by a very high level of inequality, and this is not simply a ques-tion of inequality within a tolerable range as might be said to be the case when it comes to the observance of political rights; the most basic indicator of all, life expectancy at birth, shows dramatic variations: a citizen of the advanced industrial world can expect to live into his or her late seventies, whereas an inhabitant of, say, sub-Saharan Africa will be lucky to see fifty.

The idea that international humanitarianism constitutes an appro-priate response to disasters such as famines or genocides has little pur-chase in this context, where 'intervention', if it is to be effective, has to address a deep-seated problem, the nature of which – the cause of this inequality and poverty – is not immediately or intuitively obvious, although, in fact, as Sen has demonstrated, the same might also be said of famines (Sen, 1982). Moreover, this is not a set of problems that can be related easily to a tradition of international thought. As we have seen, the norms of the Westphalia System have always made some pro-vision for intervention in response to 'gross violations of human dignity' or some such formula, and it can be argued that the discourse of humanitarian intervention in the contemporary international human rights regime can be seen as a continuation of this earlier position. There is no such resource upon which thinking about the implications of global inequality can draw, if only because this inequality is, both practically and theoretically, a fairly recent phenomenon.

It may be helpful to consider this latter point at greater length; it has three components. First, it is only since the early nineteenth century that economic inequality within states/communities came to be seen as less significant than inequality between states/communities; elites within every society have been and continue to be substantially richer than the masses, but before the Industrial Revolution the living stan-dards of elites and masses did not systematically and regularly differ greatly across borders – thus, for example, the condition of the English working class and agricultural labourers may have been rather differ-ent from that of Indian artisans and peasants in, say, the 1770s, but this difference was less striking than the difference between either and their rulers, whether English or Indian. Industrial capitalism changed this by, initially at least, depressing the living standards of Indians, but also, and more significantly in the long run, raising the living standards of the industrial working class. Certainly, by the end of the nineteenth century a clear gap in terms of indicators such as life expectancy emerged, although class differences in the industrial West remained significant.

Second, for much of the period between the early nineteenth and the twenty-first centuries, the poorer parts of the world were governed by the richer. One of the features of imperialism was that it placed responsibility for the poor squarely on the shoulders of the imperial power – which, of course, only rarely lived up to this responsibility. Thus, the idea that the international community *as such* has a responsibility to promote the development of the poorer parts of the world was rejected in a system composed of empires; it is noteworthy that when the International Bank for Reconstruction and Development (a.k.a. the World Bank) was designed at Bretton Woods in 1944, it was the reconstruction and development of the economies shattered by the war in Europe and Asia that was envisaged – the World Bank's role as provider of development assistance to the 'South' came later, after the fall of the old empires.

By the 1950s, with decolonization in full flow, the UN's first Development Decade was declared and the problem of global poverty and inequality became internationalized and a potential issue in international political theory – but only a potential issue, partly because of the impact of the Cold War, but also because of the third component of the newness of the general issue, the role of the media, and communications/transport issues more generally. Certainly, in terms of famine, the importance of electronic news-gathering can hardly be underestimated – the great famines in, for example, Madras in the late nineteenth century or Bengal in the 1940s took place under the British Empire, but, equally important, in a pre-television age. The print media cannot compete with the raw power of images of death in one's living room. But this point does not just concern the media, it is also a question of the capacity of one society to assist another. The role of non-governmental and international aid agencies has been transformed by the coming of civilian jet aircraft, relatively cheap air freight, and the existence of satellite phones and the internet to enable instantaneous communication virtually everywhere in the world. There are things one can do today about international economic inequality and poverty that one could not do yesterday, always assuming the will to act is there. Ignorance of the conditions under which the rest of the world live is no longer possible, or at least no longer defensible.

All these points came together in the late 1960s and the 1970s when, on the one hand, a coalition of 'Third World' states placed on the international agenda a demand for a New International Economic Order, and, on the other, analytical political theorists, reinvigorated by the publication of Rawls's *A Theory of Justice*, came to realize that their discussions required an international dimension. It is noteworthy that these two sources of thought on the subject largely acted independently. The demand for a New International Economic Order was, of course, noted by theorists of international relations, but not responded to directly; the characteristic response of international relations theorists was to place the demand for a NIEO within the context of the sovereignty problematic. Terry Nardin, for example, whose work was discussed in chapter 5, saw the demand for international distributive justice as incompatible with his account of international society as a practical association (Nardin, 1981 and 1983). Hedley Bull, in *The Anarchical Society*, took international justice to be 'commutative', that is to say, 'based on the recognition of rights and duties by a process of exchange or bargaining', rather than distributive, and, in any event, privileged order over justice – although his later Hagey Lectures do indicate a shift in this position that might have been developed further, had he lived (Bull, 1977/1995, p. 80, and 1984a).

One conventional international relations theorist who did address directly and at some length the demand for a NIEO is Stanley Hoffmann, in the context of a response to attempts to import Rawlsian justice theory into international relations. He was very critical, as might be expected of a writer who, in the same text, paints a picture of Michael Walzer's *Just and Unjust Wars* as the work of a starry-eyed idealist, not, it must be said, the usual reaction to the latter's work (Hoffmann, 1981). Perhaps the most characteristic conceptualization of the NIEO in IR theory was that it represented a response by Third World states to their perceived *political* vulnerability, and that their underlying agenda was to create a new international political order – an interpretation that is not unreasonable, given the essential statism of the NIEO and, it should be said, the bad faith of many of the leaders of the South (Krasner, 1985; C. Thomas, 1987; C. Brown, 1997/2001).

Because of this abdication by conventional international political theorists, the discourse of global inequality and international social justice has been dominated by analytical political theorists, but before considering their work, a short detour to examine what is probably the single most influential article on global inequality of the last thirty years would be in order. Peter Singer's 'Famine, Affluence and Morality' still challenges the reader, and working out why, eventually, it is unsatisfactory is a good introduction to the problems that theorists of social justice address (Singer, 1985).

Famine, affluence and morality

Peter Singer is the most influential utilitarian philosopher of our age, best known now for his espousal of the cause of animal 'liberation', and his defence of a limited practice of euthanasia, the latter having stirred up controversy recently upon his appointment to a chair of Philosophy at Princeton University. Singer takes utilitarianism to be a critical theory, the purpose of which is to shake up conventional moral thinking by putting its maxims to the test of the greatest happiness principle, and from this background in 1972 (the original date of publication of his article) he addressed the problem of famine and world poverty – his article was occasioned by the world's inadequate reaction to the famine in Bengal in 1971, but the principles it sets out are intended to have much wider application. Singer's argument is of great simplicity, which adds to its power. It consists of an assumption and a deceptively simple principle (which comes in two versions), backed up by an illustration.

The assumption is that suffering and death from lack of food, shelter and so on are bad, and the principle is 'if it is in our power to prevent something bad from happening, without thereby sacrificing anything of comparable moral importance [in the weaker version, 'anything morally significant'], we ought, morally to do it' (Singer, 1985, p. 249). He goes on to illustrate this proposition by hypothesizing a child drowning in a shallow pond – the damage done to one's clothes in effecting a rescue in this case would not be of comparable moral importance, indeed of any moral significance, set against the potential death of a child. So far, most readers are with him, but he then reveals two features of the principle set out above that he regards as implicit; that distance is unimportant, and that the 'we' in the imperative 'we ought' refers to us as individuals as well as to our rulers. If we accept that these two features are, indeed, implicit in our earlier agreement, we find that we have endorsed a very radical account of the obligations we have to the global poor. A great many of the things we spend our money on in the advanced industrial world are of less moral significance than the relief of suffering in the rest of the world, and the 'we' in this case are not simply plutocrats or honest middle-class university teachers – anyone who spends more on food than he or she needs to or buys new clothes which are not strictly necessary is implicated, which means pretty well everyone in the West who is not actually sleeping rough. Moreover, if the requisite transfers are not made by collectivities, the responsibility remains with us as individuals.

Many people – perhaps most – when confronted with this argument are, initially at least, convinced, but rarely actually change their behaviour in the way that Singer suggests is obligatory; instead, a sense of guilt is instilled, but is usually put on the back-burner fairly quickly. This, incidentally, rather suggests that from a strictly utilitarian point of view a somewhat less demanding argument might be more effective in actually changing behaviour. Is this guilt justified? Before confronting two real problems with Singer's argument, it may be helpful to eliminate two important side-issues. First, Singer assumes that transfers of wealth are possible, that is, that some kind of aid programme which actually worked could be designed. Since much of the work there is on aid and development suggests it is actually rather difficult to transfer wealth in a meaningful way and, especially, to the right, that is poor, people, this may be a rather big assumption (Cassen, 1986). However, it is an assumption that most, if not all, theorists of global social justice make and, whatever the difficulties, it would be excessively defeatist to assume that aid is, in practice, impossible. Still, as a utilitarian, Singer does not believe in gesture politics, and if it were to be the case that aid is impossible then there is no reason to give it, and every reason not to – one would be reducing one's own welfare without benefiting others, which would be silly. The logic of this position is well expressed by neo-Malthusians such as Garrett Hardin, who have argued that famine-relief in Africa should be abandoned because, at best, it merely delays the onset of starvation; the premise here may be wrong, but the logic is impeccably utilitarian (Hardin, 1974).

A second, very important point, although still a side-issue in the context of the argument, is that Singer is committed to the ending of unnecessary suffering and death, and not to global equality as such. His requirement, in the strong version of his basic principle, is that transfers to relieve poverty should take place up to the point at which one would take one's own position below that of the recipient; this is intended to set an upper limit – in practice, he argues, plausibly enough, that a much lower level of transfer would actually prevent famine and raise the living standards of all above the level of malnourishment and life-threatening poverty. Beyond such a point inequalities remain, but need not necessarily be of concern. If everyone's basic needs were met (on which see Henry Shue's work, discussed in chapter 7), then while there might still be a case for further transfers, other issues would be allowed to come into play.

These points do not reach the heart of the argument, but others, more closely connected to Singer's utilitarian position, are more damaging to his case. Consider the proposition that unnecessary death and suffering are bad; few would disagree, and those who do, as Singer argues, take themselves out of the discourse. There are, however, other things that are bad, and it is by no means clear that these other things can be brought into the same calculus as death and suffering. Singer begins his article by pointing out that Australia gave less to famine relief in Bangladesh than it spent on the Sydney Opera House; this may well indicate misplaced priorities, but it is not clear that *all* expenditure on such cultural activities should be suspended all the while there are some people seriously in need. On this basis, none of the cultural artefacts that define and sustain most people's lives would exist – not

Opera Houses, nor Premiership football, neither poetry nor rap music. There clearly is a direct trade-off between the resources that a particular society puts into the alleviation of poverty on the one hand, and the promotion of popular or high culture on the other, but the belief that these two goals can be placed in the same calculus, each reduced to its contribution to the general happiness, is peculiar to utilitarianism (Barry, 1982/1989). Most non-utilitarians would say that it is important that both goals be pursued (along with many others) and that what is important is to get the balance between them right. Transferring this argument to the international arena, it is clear that Singer places famine-relief above, say, the preservation of state autonomy. It is a *child* who is saved from drowning in his thought experiment, which saves us from considering whether the individual concerned is paying the price for the value she places on her autonomy, or, in extremis, is entitled to take her own life. Singer would have no objection to a policy of benevolent imperialism if this were the best way to alleviate unnecessary suffering, but, of course, peoples have quite frequently preferred to govern themselves badly rather than to be well governed by others, and it might be argued that respect for their autonomy should allow them to make this choice.

Distance, says Singer, is irrelevant to the application of his simple principle. Why? If we take distance to be something that can be measured in miles or kilometres his position makes sense – distance in this sense is meaningful in accordance with the technology of the day, and it may well now be the case that we can, metaphorically speaking, rescue the drowning child on the other side of the world almost as easily as we can the drowning child in our own neighbourhood. But if 'distance' is understood in social terms it is by no means clear that distance is irrelevant. Common-sense morality suggests quite strongly that we have different kinds of duties towards those nearest and dearest to us than we have towards distant strangers, and the attitudes most people reveal by their behaviour in the advanced industrial world suggest that we also believe that our fellow countrymen and women deserve special consideration. It may be the case that many people believe they have some kind of duty of care to humanity as a whole but the overwhelming majority (in rich *and* poor countries) seem to feel that this duty of care is rather less compelling in practical terms than the duty they feel towards those closer to them. Singer thinks there is something wrong with this position – although many utilitarians have supported it on the grounds that the special duties we have towards our fellow citizens are simply practical instances of the general duties we have towards everyone – and he is, of course, entitled to argue that those of us who think this way are mistaken and should change our views. However, the simple assertion that distance is irrelevant when considering his basic principle does not constitute such an argument.

Putting these two points together, it might be said that individuals actually have projects for their lives, and senses of their obligations towards others, that do not conform to Singer's utilitarian expectations. Many of us may want to see a more equal world, with less pain and suffering, but we also want to develop our own projects and are not prepared to put these aside entirely in the interests of others. Most of us are willing to give some attention to the needs of distant strangers, but not necessarily to the same degree that we respond to the needs of those who are closer to us. What we require is not a single calculus that can be applied to compute our responsibilities, but a set of principles that can tell us how far we are justified in pursuing our own projects, and how we can reconcile the needs of those who are in a special relationship with us with those to whom we are more distant. In other words, what we need is a theory of justice in a wider sense than that offered by utilitarianism.

John Rawls and international justice

In one sense, most of the literature discussed in the first part of this book could be described as contributing to 'theories of international justice', if by the term justice we mean some such formulation as 'giving people/states/communities what they are entitled to', but most of these conventional theories assume that, as between states, justice is pretty much a *procedural* as opposed to a *distributive* or *social* notion (C. Brown, 1997 and 1998). The distinction between procedural and distributive notions of justice is perhaps not quite as clear-cut as might seem at first to be the case, but is of some importance nonetheless; in essence, proceduralist accounts of justice focus on impartial rules impartially applied, while distributive notions focus on outcomes rather than the rules which have generated those outcomes. The classic paradigm of proceduralist justice is the notion of a 'fair trial', but, in terms of outcomes, it should be noted that the fairness or otherwise of a trial does not guarantee a 'correct' verdict; an innocent person can be wrongly convicted after a fair trial, or rightly acquitted after a blatantly unfair trial. In general, conventional theorists of international justice have assumed that justice as between states is made manifest by principles of international law that are impartial and impartially applied, and that are not intended to have distributional implications. It is only in recent years that theories of international *distributive* justice have been promulgated, largely by analytical political theorists working in the shadow of John Rawls's magisterial *A Theory of Justice*, which has reinvigorated normative political theory in the last generation (1971/1999).* However, and somewhat ironically, Rawls himself agrees with the older tradition that regards distributive justice as inappropriate to international relations. In order to sort out this situation it will be necessary first to set out Rawls's general position, then to outline his international theory, before considering why many Rawlsians believe he has misunderstood the implications of his own work.

Rawls is predominantly concerned to determine the conditions under which the institutions of a society could be considered just; his aim is to write ideal theory, and to generate a realistic utopia, which can be defined as an account of the world which is *utopian* in so far as it does not reflect existing social arrangements, but *realistic* in so far as it does not contravene anything we know about human nature – and Rawls is conventionally liberal in so far as he does believe that humans have a nature, that they necessarily seek to meet their interests, but are capable of reciprocity in their dealings one with another. Unlike, say, many socialist utopias, his realistic utopia does not involve changing these characteristics by creating some kind of 'new' human being. His account of justice, 'justice as fairness' is constructivist in a sense different from IR theory's constructivism – the assumption is that what is just can only be determined by the device of a fictional 'social contract'; the basic institutions of a society are just if the principles upon which they are based would be agreed to, under ideal conditions, by those they concern, and there is no other way in which justice can be discovered.

Society is taken, for these purposes, to be a 'co-operative scheme for mutual advantage' – this definition is important in terms of his international thought – and we are invited, as a thought-experiment, to imagine the arrangements to which potential members of such a scheme would agree prior to its formation, in what is termed the 'original position'. These potential contractors make their choices under the 'veil of ignorance'; they know that there are certain 'primary goods' that all rational persons behind the veil can be assumed to want whatever else they want – in the revised version of *A Theory of Justice* it is, importantly, made clear that these primary goods include what people need in their status as free and equal citizens as well as what they need for their general welfare and survival – but they do not know certain key facts about themselves, such as their race, talents, gender, or intelligence, or even their 'conceptions of the good or their special psychological propensities' (p. 11). We are invited to consider what principles would be chosen under these conditions.

* References in the text are to the 1999 edition.

Rawls assumes contractors will be risk-averse, which rules out principles that dramatically disadvantage some to the gain of the rest; thus, for example, no one would choose a society based upon slavery unless they knew that they themselves would not be slaves, and this knowledge is denied them by the veil of ignorance. Accordingly, the first principle of justice that will be chosen by contractors is that 'each person is to have an equal right to the most extensive scheme of equal basic liberties compatible with a similar scheme of liberties for others' (p. 52). More controversially, Rawls suggests that the second principle concerning distribution of social and economic goods will have two parts; first, is what he calls 'fair equality of opportunity', that is, a system in which positions are, as far as possible, available to all under conditions where the influence of social circumstances is eliminated. Second, he argues, contractors will accept as just only those inequalities of outcome which can reasonably be expected to be to *everyone*'s advantage, which means those inequalities which work to the benefit of the least advantaged members of society; this is what he calls the 'difference principle' (because it concerns legitimate differences in responsibilities and authority). There is a lexical ordering here; providing the most extensive equal basic liberties takes priority over distributional principles – contractors will not trade freedom for increases in economic efficiency. This is why they will reject the principle of average utility which is one possible alternative to the 'difference principle' set out above: Peter Singer please note. On the other hand, the other possible principle of justice is strict egalitarianism, but this will be rejected because it could leave *everyone* worse off than under the difference principle.

Whether these principles are thought to be universal in application or are only appropriate to societies composed of people committed to liberal principles is an important issue. The original text of *A Theory of Justice* was confusing on this point. Rawls now argues that his theory was actually intended to provide principles for a liberal society; however, he argues, this theory was based on liberalism as a 'comprehensive doctrine' to which all were expected to adhere, and this was a mistake; this position is set out in *Political Liberalism*, where it is established that political liberalism is based on an overlapping consensus of reasonable comprehensive doctrines (Rawls, 1995). The second edition of *A Theory of Justice* has been revised partially to reflect this shift. This is a matter of some significance for Rawls's thought on relations between liberal and non-liberal societies, which will be discussed later – here another aspect of Rawls's theory is more central, his handling of the issue of international distributive justice.

Rawls simply assumes that there is more than one society, and that for the purposes of his theory each society can be treated as though it were self-sufficient. Justice as between societies (he later says 'peoples') is to be determined by a second contract forged in a second 'original position', in which the representatives of just societies meet under a new veil of ignorance – this time they do not know the size of the territory, population, resources or relative strength of the people whose fundamental interests they represent, but they do know that they represent just societies (and in the new version of the argument set out in the revised *Theory of Justice*, just liberal societies). What will emerge from this second contract, he suggests, is, in effect, the conventional principles and practices of international law and diplomacy – equality of peoples, self-determination, non-intervention, non-aggression and so on; in a later version of the argument he includes, in addition, respect for human rights and 'a duty to assist other peoples living under unfavourable conditions that prevent their having a just or decent political and social regime' (Rawls, 1999b, p. 37). These principles are explicitly taken to be analogous to the first principle of justice in society (the most extensive equal basic liberties), but there is to be no international equivalent to the second principle which concerns equality of opportunity and outcomes, that is, no principle of international *distributive* justice. This is because the 'society' composed of peoples who send representatives to the second contract is not a society in the sense that it constitutes a co-operative scheme for mutual advantage, and therefore it has no output to distribute. Just institutions in domestic society must cover issues of distribution because all the members of society contribute to its collective output and therefore should have an equal say in the principles which govern the distribution of that output, but this reasoning does not apply at the international level.

The critics of Rawls

It would be fair to say that virtually no one is happy with Rawls's reasoning on this issue. One of the very first full-length critiques of *A Theory of Justice*, Brian Barry's *The Liberal Theory of Justice* (1973), made the key point: the way Rawls refuses to allow for principles of international distributive justice produces results that are, on the face of it, perverse. For a theory of social justice to have nothing to say about the extraordinary inequalities that exist between societies is a bizarre state of affairs – in Rawlsian terms it would be possible for a world composed entirely of internally just states to contain great inequalities in terms of life-chances, with no principles available to address this situation, which seems intuitively wrong. For Barry this is symptomatic of wider problems with Rawls's project – international justice poses problems that are structurally similar to those posed by, for example, intergenerational justice and environmental justice; in each case the central notion of a contract based, at least in part, on the search for mutual advantage on the part of the contractors cannot easily respond to the interests of those who cannot be present as contractors, that is, foreigners, future generations, the mentally handicapped and 'nature'. Moreover, the requirement that arrangements be in some sense based on reciprocity is equally, if not more, limiting – if issues of international equality are to be addressed, then decidedly unequal obligations have to be laid on the rich as opposed to the poor (Barry, 1989).

Barry's own account of 'justice as impartiality' rests quite heavily on an alternative, non-contractarian, formulation of Thomas Scanlon's:

> [judgements] of right and wrong [are] judgements about what would be permitted by principles that could not reasonably be rejected, by people who were moved to find principles for the general regulation of behaviour that others, similarly motivated, could not reasonably reject. (Scanlon, 1999, p. 4, derived from Scanlon, 1982; Barry, 1994)

The full implications of this position have yet to be applied by him to international justices, but existing papers testify to the radicalism of this approach (Barry, 1998 and 1999). In his 1998 paper he argues that it is reasonable that the basic needs of all should be met before the non-basic needs of anyone are satisfied, and thus that people moved by Scanlonian considerations would be bound to regard the existing distribution of wealth – and the principles of political economy that underlie that distribution – as unreasonable; equally, the environmental degradation characteristic of contemporary capitalism would be regarded as unreasonable. The inescapable conclusion is that the advanced industrial world should slow down, or put into reverse, its growth and transfer resources to the poor; that is to say, a system of 'progressive' global taxation should be introduced.

Other critics of Rawls have been more Rawlsian, but reach not dissimilar conclusions. The most important text here is the first, Charles Beitz's pioneering study, *Political Theory and International Relations* (1979/2000), because many of the arguments that surface later first see the light of day here. Beitz offers two reasons why Rawls is wrong, but it should be noted that, unlike Barry, he accepts the basic premises of the Rawlsian approach (at least that of 1971), namely an account of justice as based on a contract made by liberal individuals under ideal conditions. His first point is that, even if we accept that states are separate self-contained societies, their representatives would insist on a more wide-ranging contract than Rawls envisages. His second point is that, since states are not self-contained there is no reason to look for a second contract between them – instead Rawls's full account of justice should be applied worldwide, including a global 'difference principle'. These are quite separate arguments.

Beitz's first argument concerns the treatment of 'natural' resources; he argues *contra* Rawls that the representatives of states meeting in the second original position would not agree to a rule that confirmed that natural resources belong to the states whose territory encompasses them. The existing distribution of natural resources is morally arbitrary in so far as there is no sense in which states could be said to deserve their resource endowment, and, he suggests, no representative would agree to a rule the effect of which might well be to leave her state bereft of any share of the world's resources. Instead, Beitz argues, not knowing whether their state was resource-rich or not, risk-averse representatives would introduce a rule that distributed the world's resources equally, via some kind of global wealth tax.

This is, on the face of it, a rather strong argument, and it is interesting that the same conclusion can be reached by a number of different routes. Thus, as noted above, Barry also argues for a global tax system without employing the veil of ignorance or a second original position, but simply as an 'impartial' rule, while Hillel Steiner derives a similar idea for a redistributive Global Fund from libertarian foundations (Steiner, 1994 and 1999). Moreover, the argument that international justice requires equal access to natural resources is not dependent on state-centric assumptions. As Barry acknowledges, there may be practical reasons why it would be convenient to redistribute to states but this is not a matter of principle, while Steiner's position, which is rather too complex to be summarized here, essentially involves the distribution to individuals of a sum that represents their share of the common inheritance of all human beings. The main problem with all these proposals is that, in so far as they are based on natural resources, they could produce unintended and counter-intuitive results; as Rawls points out in his later defence of his position, the wealth of a state is only very loosely correlated with its material resource base, if at all (1999b). If resources are defined in strictly material terms – coal, oil, copper and so on – some very poor countries might find themselves subsidizing some very rich ones (Namibia and Japan, say).

One way round this – elaborated by Steiner – would be to include land values in the definition of resources, so that, say, ground rents in Metropolitan Tokyo would factor into the calculation of Japan's wealth. The problem here is that one could reasonably argue that such values, which are essentially created by the industry of – in this example – the Japanese people, are in a different category from genuinely unearned resources such as mineral deposits. To counter *this* point it might be said that it is true of all natural resources that they have no value until there is a demand for them and someone is prepared to bear the cost of extraction – but this argument in turn undermines Beitz's point that the distribution of resources is morally arbitrary, and thus, also, his assumption that international contractors would adopt a norm of equality in this area. Perhaps Rawls was right to think that his approach would rule out a principle of international resource equality; however, it should be noted that neither Barry's nor Steiner's argument is damaged by this redefinition of a natural resource, because neither of them rely upon the idea of a contract at this stage of their arguments.

Beitz's second position is more controversial. He argues that, as a result of interdependence, the world must now be treated as a single society, which means that Rawls's full account of social justice applies, with no necessity for a second contract between state representatives. He explicitly addresses the idea of a 'morality of states' and rejects it, on the basis that states are not like individuals in a Hobbesian state of nature. Instead, they are interdependent and this interdependence means that the world has to be treated as though it were a single society (Beitz, 1979/2000, part 1). There are several problems with this position. First, as will be apparent from earlier chapters of this book, the notion that sovereign states are the moral subjects of international political theory does not necessarily rely on an analogy between individuals in the state of nature and states in an international system. Writers such as Nardin and Bull argue that it is the lack of common conceptions of the good that underlies the moral pluralism of international society. Second, even making allowances for subsequent deepening of interdependence since the late 1970s when Beitz wrote, it remains the case that the present world system cannot plausibly be defined as a co-operative venture for *mutual advantage* which, as we have seen, is the definition of society Rawls employs to get his schema under way. Possibly parts of the advanced industrial world could be seen in this way – the European Union for example – but it would be difficult to see relations between rich and poor countries as a whole in this light. The international economy certainly is based in liberal theory on the idea that everyone benefits from economic exchange, but it would be a particularly enthusiastic neo-liberal who argued that this applies across the board to all interactions between rich and poor. The alternative view that the rich are exploiting the poor makes it difficult to argue that the kind of reciprocity involved in Rawls's definition of a society can apply at the global level.

Beitz has now acknowledged the strength of this criticism and effectively abandoned much of the Rawlsian justification for his cosmopolitanism in a later article – but not the cosmopolitanism itself, which he now grounds in a Kantian account of the moral equality of persons (Beitz, 1983). To some extent, Beitz's original position is restated by Thomas Pogge in his *Realizing Rawls* and later papers

(Pogge, 1989, 1994a, 1994b and 1998). His argument is that Rawls is not justified in assuming that there will be two contracts, that is, in assuming the existence of separate societies; rather, Pogge suggests, we should hypothesize that it is legitimate to have separate societies only if they can be seen as the product of a decision that emerges from a kind of meta-original position in which all the inhabitants of the world are represented. The latter may well decide to create separate societies, bearing in mind the usual scale problems associated with a world government, but they are unlikely to endorse Westphalian-style sovereignty norms. Instead, the units created through this contract will acknowledge responsibilities towards one another. Pogge, like Barry, favours a scheme of global taxation (a Global Resources Dividend) and, like Beitz, sees it as best based on natural resources – but in order to meet environmental goals he suggests it should be based on the value of natural resources actually used, rather than on those left in the ground.

Rawls's response – the law of peoples

Rawls also was unsatisfied with his own arguments on international justice and has subsequently revised and extended his international theory – although not in the direction his critics would have wished – in 'The Law of Peoples', an Amnesty International lecture of 1993, subsequently published as a short monograph with the same title in 1999 (Rawls, 1993 and 1999b). The *Law of Peoples* is addressed mainly to the issue of relations between liberal and non-liberal peoples, and as such is highly relevant to the issue of cultural diversity and international political theory – the subject of the next chapter of this book – but since this also has clear implications for his account of global justice it is convenient to consider his argument here. In Part I of *The Law of Peoples* Rawls restates the argument from *A Theory of Justice*, with two main clarifications or elaborations. First, he explains why he refers to 'peoples' and not states. Liberal peoples, the subject of this part of his text, have three characteristics, all of which are important: 'a reasonably just constitutional democratic government that serves their fundamental interests; citizens united by what Mill called "common sympathies"; and finally, a moral nature'. This latter requirement, 'a firm attachment to a political (moral) conception of right and justice', is essential, because liberal peoples are both rational and reasonable (Rawls, 1999b, pp. 23–4). They are rational in so far as they engage in instrumental reasoning in order to pursue their interests, but this pursuit is constrained by their sense of what is reasonable, reasonableness entailing a concern for reciprocity and the interests of others; it is only because of this sense of what is reasonable that just societies are possible in the first place, and reasonableness is equally required for the establishment of justice *between* peoples. This is why the law of peoples is not quite the same as international law. States are generally inclined to act *rationally*, but even liberal states cannot be relied upon to act *reasonably*. Thus, the 'law of peoples' is the set of principles that the representatives of peoples would agree upon in the second original position – but, and this is where some confusion and blurring of the argument seems inevitable, the same set of principles are also the underlying principles of contemporary international law, which provides a framework for the relations of states. Perhaps the best way to understand this argument is that the law of nations is a shadow of the law of peoples; because it is a law governing states, and states tend to act rationally but not necessarily reasonably, the law of nations is vulnerable to contingency, which the law of peoples, which rests on the rational and reasonable will of peoples, is not.

A second innovation in his presentation of the argument in *The Law of Peoples* concerns the stability of the peaceful relations established by this law. For this he now relies on the so-called 'democratic peace' thesis of Michael Doyle, Bruce Russett and others (see chapter 4 above). This may not be a wholly wise move, given the controversial and contested nature of the 'democratic peace', but Rawls does provide one of the most compelling versions of the thesis, largely because he moves the notion from its usual context – the foreign policy orientation of existing liberal-democratic states – and situates it within the realm of ideal theory. Thus, on his account, a constitutional democratic society is not to be described simply in terms of purely formal guaranteed constitutional liberties; it also involves fair equality of opportunity in education and training, a distribution of income that guarantees to all the ability to take intelligent advantage of their basic freedoms, basic health-care for all citizens, society as an employer of last resort, and public financing of elections and for the provision of information on matters of public policy (Rawls, 1999b, p. 50). The fact that actually allegedly constitutional regimes do sometimes make war on each other (he instances US interventions in Chile, Guatemala and so on) merely highlights the extent to which these regimes fall short of the requirements of a just society.

In part II, Rawls asks whether the law of peoples can be extended to non-liberal peoples, and if so, which. Much of the first part of *The Law of Peoples* relies on Kant, and, as noted in chapter 3 above, the Kantian position here, summarized in the first definitive article of *Perpetual Peace*, is that only 'republics' – which is nowadays, perhaps mistakenly, translated as liberal democracies – can be members of the

Pacific Union. Rawls's cosmopolitan critics such as Beitz and, especially, Barry follow Kant in this, but Rawls does not; his argument is that provided

> a nonliberal society's basic institutions meet certain specified conditions of political right and justice and lead its people to honour a reasonable and just law for the Society of Peoples, a liberal people is to tolerate and accept that society. In the absence of a better name, I call societies that satisfy these conditions decent peoples. (Rawls, 1999b, p. 60)

There are, in principle, different kinds of decent peoples, but Rawls puts most of his efforts into describing one particular kind – 'decent hierarchical peoples'. These peoples respect a minimal set of basic human rights, including political freedoms and subsistence rights; they live under something like the rule of law; they are unaggressive with respect to the rest of the world; and, at a minimum, they have some form of mechanism for consultation. However, they are not liberal societies because they privilege a particular comprehensive doctrine – religious or political – and non-adherents to this doctrine are not accorded the same rights as adherents (although they possess the minimum rights, which include, for example, freedom of speech and religion). Crucially, were it to be represented in the second original position, a decent society would choose the same set of principles that liberal societies have established as the basis for the law of peoples – it should be noted that there is no question here of liberals inviting decent societies to join a liberal scheme; the law of peoples belongs equally to both groups because, it is supposed, it would be chosen independently by both groups.

Not all peoples are 'well-ordered', and the world contains much that is unjust and evil and so liberal and decent people need to know how to operate under non-ideal conditions. Rawls has interesting things to say about this; he suggests that as well as liberal and decent peoples, there are *outlaw states* (note, not peoples), *burdened societies* and other kinds of regimes. Outlaws are non-compliant with the law of peoples and oppress their own folk; liberal and decent peoples need to be able to defend themselves from outlaws, and may intervene against them, if internal violations of basic human rights are gross, and if they can do so successfully. There is nothing distinctive about Rawls's treatment of outlaws, but more interesting is his account of *burdened societies*, that is, societies 'whose historical, social and economic circumstances make their achieving a well-ordered regime, whether liberal or decent, difficult if not impossible' (Rawls, 1999b, p. 90). Well-ordered societies have an obligation to assist burdened societies to become members of the society of well-ordered peoples, but, he argues, this is essentially a matter of helping such societies to develop the appropriate political culture, and a rational and reasonable approach to their affairs. A well-ordered society need not be a wealthy society, and there is no reason to regard inequality in wealth as necessarily something that requires correction. The only obligation on well-ordered societies is to assist burdened societies to get to the point where they can make their own choices; once they have reached that point, whatever inequalities exist are a reflection of social choices which well-ordered societies have separately made, and which they are entitled to make without external criticism or interference.

Rawls believes that the socio-economic variations that exist in the world today are essentially the product of the political culture, the political and civic virtues of particular societies, and of the choices they make. *Contra* Beitz, Pogge et al., the level of resource endowment is, except in extreme cases, pretty much irrelevant. Basic human rights are of far greater significance, and development assistance that does not take into account the need to develop the appropriate political culture will be ineffective. Once societies become well-ordered (that is, liberal or decent) they may well make choices that dramatically affect their long-term wealth – by, for example, having a relatively high savings rate – and because they may, in fact almost certainly will, make different decisions, this will increase inequality, but the law of peoples has nothing to say on this, and there are no principles of international justice involved. This argument suggests a lack of interest in the actual functioning of the international economy, and it is unrealistic and naïve to think that internal factors are the only determinants of international economic success in the modern world – but it may be that this somewhat misses Rawls's point. Rawls here is walking a line between ideal and non-ideal theory; he is trying to determine what the appropriate duty of assistance of a Society of well-ordered Peoples would be towards burdened societies, and in a Society of well-ordered Peoples the kind of neo-liberal economic consensus that currently dominates the major organs of the international economy would no longer be in place.

Nonetheless, Rawls is explicitly not providing a cosmopolitan viewpoint and his argument in the law of peoples has been comprehensively rejected by cosmopolitan critics, as has been his category of decent (but not liberal) peoples (Beitz, 2000; Buchanan, 2000; Kuper, 2000). From a cosmopolitan perspective in which the well-being of individuals is paramount, the variations possible under the law of peoples would be unacceptable (Pogge, 1994b). Rawls proposes a final thought-experiment. Assume two just, liberal societies in each of which inequalities are arranged to the benefit of the least advantaged, but where the least advantaged in one is worse off than the least advantaged in another; suppose it were possible to redistribute from one society to another so that each continued to meet the criteria of justice, but the variation between them would be lessened. The cosmopolitan would prefer the redistribution to the distribution, but the law of peoples is indifferent between the two distributions. 'Basic fairness among peoples is given by their being represented equally in the second original position with its veil of ignorance and nothing more is required' (Rawls, 1999b, p. 115).

In short, Rawls remains committed to the view that societies have to be seen for the purposes of theory as self-contained co-operative schemes for mutual advantage, and that relations between societies must reflect this fact. In the most penetrating cosmopolitan critique of *The Law of Peoples*, Allen Buchanan argues that by making this assumption Rawls is providing 'Rules for a Vanished Westphalian World'; this gets to the heart of the matter (Buchanan, 2000). Following Beitz's earlier argument, it is suggested here that globalization has undermined the possibility that peoples can be seen as living in self-contained worlds – but does this necessarily undermine Rawls's argument? As noted above, Rawls sees liberal peoples as essentially defined in moral terms – they are defined by a reasonably constitutional government, common sympathies, and are capable of behaving reasonably as well as rationally in promoting their interests. Non-liberal but decent peoples may not share the first of these three categories but they possess the next two. His key point is, in effect, that neither complex interdependence nor globalization is likely to create the conditions for this trilogy to exist on anything like a *global* scale in the foreseeable future.

On the face of it, this is surely correct – it is difficult enough for particular peoples to come close to his account of what they could be, and to spend too much time thinking about the emergence of a global 'people' is wasted effort, especially since he believes that a justly constituted society of well-ordered peoples could provide everything that one could want to find from a global political order. Still, these issues will be returned to below in the penultimate chapter of this book – the next step here is to undertake a wider assessment of the cosmopolitan theories set out above, bearing in mind that, although Rawls's international thought leans in a communitarian direction, it still has substantial cosmopolitan elements, in particular through his advocacy of a package of basic universal human rights. A good way to carry out such an assessment – because it allows for the introduction of some intrinsically interesting new issues as well as assessing ideas we have already encountered – is by examining how liberal cosmopolitan ideas 'cash out' when they come up against the manifold problems associated with borders and international political theory. Borders do not simply raise practical issues, they also represent one physical manifestation of the distinction between 'insiders' and 'outsiders', so central to international political theory.

The limits of liberal theories of social justice: the case of 'borders'

The meaning of inter-state borders has changed quite radically over the centuries of the Westphalia System. Initially, borders simply enclosed the dynastic lands of the rulers who established the system, but with the rise of national states in the nineteenth century borders took on a new significance; it became thought desirable that borders should be drawn on national lines, and correspond to 'natural' features or historic frontiers – these criteria were, of course, not necessarily compatible. Borders which enclosed 'citizens' were more significant politically and morally than those which previously had enclosed 'subjects'; the result was an increasing number of bitter border conflicts in Europe, many of which, especially in the Balkans, persist to this day.

Modern thinking on borders, on the other hand, takes place within three key parameters. First, borders are of immense significance to the lives of ordinary people. Being one side of a border rather than another may involve dramatic changes in average standard of living and in life-chances; social and welfare services vary across frontiers as do job opportunities and, in some cases, access to the police and to physical security. Second, no borders are natural; the idea that particular geographical features dictate the siting of state borders is clearly false. In many parts of the world state borders have been drawn by foreigners in chancelleries continents away. Even the so-called natural frontiers of well-established European states such as France, Spain or the UK are the result of hundreds of years of war rather than geography – the Channel could have been a highway rather than a barrier; Occitania and Catalonia form as 'natural' a political unit as those shaped by the frontier on the Pyrenees. Where populations speak different languages across borders this is usually the result of state educational policy – dialects in, say, the Rhineland merge into each other, with no clean break between French and German. Third, borders cannot be democratically legitimated. Democracy in one form or another is the great legitimating principle of the last hundred years but before 'the people' can vote it has to be determined who the people are, which leads to an infinite regress when borders are at issue. Plebiscites can determine the fate of particular border areas, but they cannot determine which border areas should have their fate determined by plebiscites.

These three features of borders, taken together, make for a fascinating set of issues, both theoretical and practical – the politics of asylum-seekers, refugees and large-scale economic migration make up a good part of the real-world international political agenda today (Dowty, 1987; Loescher, 1993). Consider, for example, the notion of a political refugee, and what Sherlock Holmes might call 'the case of the bogus asylum-seeker'. The norms of the Westphalia System give states the right to police their own borders and refuse entry to foreigners. However, partly for humanitarian reasons, partly because of Cold War politics, states have created the status of political refugee, which entitles individuals to a right of asylum on the basis of a well-founded fear of persecution. Large numbers of individuals claim this status even though their primary (sometimes only) motive for migration is economic – the (equally) well-founded belief that their personal circumstances will improve if they are able to enter the host country. The advanced industrial states of Western Europe have felt obliged to establish quite elaborate, expensive and time-consuming procedures for distinguishing these 'bogus asylum-seekers' from the real thing, and large numbers of people at any one time exist in a kind of limbo in these societies as a result, unable to work, unsure of their future and dependent on state hand-outs for their sustenance.

How does cosmopolitan liberalism handle this issue? Some liberal opponents of the immigration rules that most Western European states currently operate argue that too restrictive a version of what counts as a well-founded fear of persecution is employed by those states; this may be so, but a more basic point is whether states ought to have the right to exclude foreigners, whether or not the latter are genuine asylum-seekers. From the perspective of Westphalian political theory such a right is implied by the sovereignty of the state. But from the perspective of liberal accounts of global social justice this cannot be accepted without further justification. Indeed, from a cosmopolitan perspective it might be thought that a 'borderless world' is mandated. What is interesting about a great deal of this thought is the extent to which it goes in order to *avoid* this conclusion.

Virtually no one endorses the immediate removal of frontier controls. The writer who comes nearest to this is Hillel Steiner; as a libertarian Steiner believes that 'national boundaries possess no less – and no more – moral significance than the boundary between my neighbour's land and my own' (Steiner, 1992, p. 93). It is all a matter of property rights, and anyone should be allowed to live anywhere they can afford to live – with, of course, no assistance from the state, direct or indirect. For most other cosmopolitans, the normal position is that, although the presumption is for free movement and the burden of proof rests with those who would impose restrictions, nonetheless 'restrictions may sometimes be justified because they will promote liberty and equality in the long run or because they are necessary to preserve a distinct culture or way of life' (Carens, 1992, p. 25).

This is an interesting formulation which captures nicely the dilemma for cosmopolitans; borders can be legitimated solely on pragmatic grounds, but these pragmatic grounds may actually be quite wide – 'promoting liberty and equality in the long run' and a 'distinct culture or way of life' between them cover quite a lot of space. In any event, neither clause is quite as straightforward as it seems. The cultural argument will feature in the next chapter of this book; here the focus is on the argument that borders might promote liberty and equality in the long run. Onora O'Neill provides a good summary of this argument in one of the best examinations of the political philosophical implications of boundaries in the literature (O'Neill, 1994). After examining the ways in which so much of political philosophy is dominated by an uncritical acceptance of boundaries and thus by unspoken assumptions about the limits of moral responsibility, she, nonetheless, specifically *rejects* the idea that

> only a world without state boundaries could be a just world. Such a world – a world state – might concentrate so much power that it risked or instituted much injustice. The common reasons given for fearing world government and its colossal concentrations of powers seem to me serious reasons. The reasons for thinking that justice is helped by bonds of sentiment between citizens, and can be destroyed by lack of all such bonds, are also strong. The evidence that those bonds are easier to forge when a sense of identity is shared is also considerable. (O'Neill, 1994, p. 85)

This seems clear, but, on the same page, O'Neill goes on to say that boundaries are not acceptable when they 'systematically inflict injustices on outsiders'; her acceptance that justice does not require the abolition of states is accompanied by the proviso that it does demand 'an interpretation of sovereignty that does not constitute an arbitrary limit to the scope of justice' (O'Neill, 1994, p. 86).

How does this argument work? Let us take a fictionalized real-world example, the implications for borders and frontiers of a somewhat idealized version of the social policies of the Scandinavian social democracies – or 'Norden', as the composite, not-quite-accurately portrayed Scandinavian country is sometimes known for the sake of convenience. In Norden there is a strong sense of identity among citizens, and from this sense of identity bonds of sentiment emerge and generate social policies that are generally thought of as effective attempts to create a just society. All this is compatible with O'Neill's first formulation. However, we can still ask whether Norden 'systematically inflicts injustice on outsiders'. Nordanes believe that although they defend their national sovereignty quite firmly and are sceptical of supranational schemes, they are good international citizens – loyal members of the UN, upholders of international law, with comparatively high aid budgets and generous policies on asylum-seekers and refugees. Nonetheless, the extensive system of social benefits they have developed are designed for citizens and invited guests. The Norden welfare state is socially inclusive but excludes those who are not Nordanes, employing the sovereign powers of Norden to do so. Does this policy set 'an arbitrary limit on the scope of justice'?

If the answer to this questions is 'yes' then it is difficult to see why O'Neill does not simply argue that state boundaries ought to be abolished. Here we have a society which is doing its best to create liberty and equality, and yet the equality it creates necessarily depends on preserving a greater inequality between its citizens and the rest of the world. In the world in which we live, *any* effective welfare state will have this effect, and *no* effective welfare state could exist which did not restrict its benefits to members/citizens. If one is serious about the moral irrelevance of boundaries and frontiers then one ought to be opposed to schemes of social welfare which are restrictive, and, as we have seen, cosmopolitans criticize Rawls on precisely these grounds. However, in practice, most liberals – apart from libertarians such as Steiner, but certainly including O'Neill – do not actually want to abolish welfare states, and so they will try to deny that Norden systematically inflicts justice on outsiders. However, it is difficult to see on what (liberal, cosmopolitan) basis they can do so.

Liberal nationalists such as Michael Walzer and David Miller are happy to argue that Rawls was essentially correct to assume that distributive justice can only be a feature of bounded communities (Miller and Walzer, 1995). A socially just society will involve redistribution of resources and the willingness of citizens to redistribute depends crucially on the existence of a sense of community (Miller, 1995). A community is not a random collection of individuals, but a mutual aid association, membership of which will confer benefits and duties; such benefits cannot be made global given the current state of the world, and it is reasonable that such an association should have the right to determine its own membership. It may be desirable that this right should be exercised liberally – and Walzer is clear that legal immigrants ought to have the same citizenship rights as others – but it still ought to remain within the capacity of communities to restrict entry (Walzer, 1983). It is noteworthy that this position is compatible with an acknowledgement of the essentially arbitrary nature of borders; it is not how a community came to be defined that is crucial for its legitimacy, but rather its conduct in the here and now, its commitment to social justice. Even so, from this perspective, a world of socially just communities might still be a radically unequal world. Can such a state of affairs truly be just?

There seems to be a genuine impasse here. It does indeed seem to be the case that those societies that come closest to the social-democratic ideal of a just community do have a clear sense of their own national identity, and are willing to protect this identity with immigration controls every bit as effective as those employed by societies whose commitment to social justice is less well developed. Thus, for example, the real 'Nordanes' – the Netherlands, Denmark, Sweden and Norway – are broadly social-democratic states, good international citizens, upholders of the UN and human rights – but they are at least as committed to policing their borders as those European states with less shining credentials on the world stage. Moreover, they have good reason for this position since their levels of welfare provision could hardly be made available to all-comers – as it is, these societies are having difficulty in sustaining their commitment to social justice even vis-à-vis their own citizens. On the other hand, the only justification these states can employ to defend this practical distinction between insiders and outsiders is that the former benefit substantially thereby, which, of course, would only begin to be part of a satisfactory justification if the distinction between insiders and outsiders were to be already established in a morally acceptable way. The dilemma here is clear: the requirements of international justice seem to be such as to destroy the limited but significant degree of internal social justice these states have struggled to achieve – perhaps understandably, their peoples take the view that this would be unacceptable. The result is that the argument is left in a kind of no man's land.

This impasse is not simply a product of the issue of borders; difficulties posed by the politics of borders are symptomatic of a wider set of problems for contemporary cosmopolitan liberalism. If it is no longer legitimate to take as given that there is a clear distinction between the political and the international, then the moral significance of the distinction between 'insiders' and 'outsiders' requires rational justification. If rational justification in this context means that international political arrangements and actions have to be judged in accordance with the criteria employed domestically – if, in other words, domestic politics comes to subsume international relations – then rational justification is simply not available within the terms of liberal political discourse, as the case of Norden demonstrated. But the implication of this seems to be that a politics *without* the distinction between insiders and outsiders, a politics without borders, is mandated, and, as we have seen, there are good reasons drawn from history and from current practice to suggest that this ideal is unattainable. Put in these terms, there seems to be no solution to this dilemma.

Perhaps it is the terms that are problematic. The feature of liberal, cosmopolitan, social theory which generates this difficulty is, arguably, its reduction of political theory to moral theory – the insistence that a *legitimate* account of the political is a *moralized* account of the political. Thus, politics becomes equated to a search for legitimacy in which all social arrangements are regarded as in need of rational justification – a position which is not simply characteristic of justice theorists such as Rawls, Beitz and Barry, but also of legal theorists such as Lea Brilmayer, and critical theorists such as David Held, Andrew Linklater and Jürgen Habermas (Habermas, 1973; Brilmayer, 1989; Held; 1995; Linklater, 1998). The point is that there is no reason to think that such a rational justification is always going to be available, and this becomes immediately apparent once the attempt is made to move from 'ideal' theory to practical politics, and, for that matter, whether one is dealing with domestic or international politics.

One way of illuminating this problem is provided by William Connolly; on his account liberal political thinking, broadly defined, has always attempted to prioritize both liberty and practicality, but this is an impossibility. In the domestic context, liberals have been able to square the circle only by assuming that the welfare state can be a practical potential vehicle of liberty and justice (Connolly, 1987, p. 83). He argues that changes in the nature of the economy are making this assumption increasingly difficult to hold – and, in any event, as we have seen, even a fully functioning welfare state can only come close to operating as a vehicle of justice and liberty by making exclusions which cannot be justified in terms of liberal principles. Connolly suggests that liberals characteristically react to the dilemma of legitimacy in one of two ways: they gradually retreat from practicality, articulating principles which are increasingly abstract and which they are unable to link to particular questions, or they retain the commitment to practicality by sliding into a technocratic conception of politics (Connolly, 1987, p. 84). Both tendencies can be seen in the case explored above. Whether an asylum-seeker is bogus or not is an eminently technocratic question, while a retreat from practicality is clearly visible in the unachievable liberal commitment to open borders.

There are other routes to Connolly's agonistic conception of politics. Thus, for Michael Oakeshott, politics is a practical activity concerned with the choices made in political situations, a political situation being 'a condition of things recognized to have sprung, not from natural necessity, but from human choices or actions, and to which more than one response is possible' (Oakeshott, 1991, p. 70). On this account, we can see that the international has become part of the political, because it is now recognized that international arrangements have sprung from human choices, but this does not mean that a formula is available to guide action in this sphere. Politics is about practical action in a realm where no answer can be other than provisional, not about the creation of ideal theory – and it ought not to be surprising that when the latter is applied to subjects such as the legitimacy of borders or global social justice the argument quite soon breaks down.

A good part of the argument here concerns the role of power in political/international life. Whereas conventional international relations theory has, if anything, overemphasized the role of power, the tendency on the part of cosmopolitan theory has been in the other direction, towards regarding the exercise of political power as a signal that legitimacy is lacking. Rather, it may be more helpful to recognize that politics is always a contest; Carl Schmitt's conception of the political as essentially defined by the existence of friends and enemies and Chantal Mouffe's espousal of 'agonistic pluralism' in post-Marxist terms point in this direction; the unpleasant nature of Schmitt's politics ought not to distract us from recognizing the precision of his critique of liberalism's apolitical nature (Mouffe, 1993; Schmitt, 1996).

From this perspective there may be a role for ideal theory in the sense that it establishes some kind of goal to aim at, but this needs to be combined with a more overtly political account of how the present system of international economic inequality came into existence, whose interests it serves, and how, politically, it can be adapted or changed to serve the interests of the poor and downtrodden. Still, one should not underestimate the importance of ideal theory. Rawls ends the *Law of Peoples* by making the point that, although there is no guarantee that a just society of peoples *must* come into existence or that it *will*, the very fact that it *could* has, in itself, significance – it affects our attitude towards the world, it makes us appreciate that political action need not simply be about compromise. 'By showing us how the social world may realize the features of a realistic utopia,' says Rawls, 'political philosophy provides a long term goal of political endeavour, and in working towards it gives meaning to what we can do today' (Rawls, 1999b, p. 128). This is the ultimate justification for cosmopolitan political theory.

Conclusion

One feature of liberal political theory – regarded as a virtue by its adherents – is its universalism, its belief that the individual at the heart of liberal political theory is a universal subject, with, ultimately, the same kind of interests wherever he or she is located across time and space. When Rawls refers to 'human nature as it is' as the realistic dimension of his realistic utopia, it is to this anthropology that he is referring. Projects for global social justice characteristically rest upon a similar anthropology – we can know what a globally just world would look like, because we know what human beings in general are like. We have already seen this argument in the context of human rights, and it is now time to investigate more clearly the cultural dimension of contemporary international political theory, if only to see whether this position can be sustained.

Cultural Diversity and International Political Theory

The demands for an effective human rights regime and for global social justice, set out in the last three chapters, jointly and separately constitute a challenge to the norms of the Westphalia System. The latter are based at root on sovereignty and a distinction between the domestic and the international, and cannot be sustained if human rights and global socio-economic arrangements are to be judged in the light of international standards. Westphalian norms have been defended by statist writers and authors who place a great deal of emphasis on a general right of political communities to determine their own fate, but the drive to establish universal standards, represented by notions of human rights and global social justice, has also come under attack from those who argue that the universal standards in question are, in fact, those of the West. The international human rights regime – at least in its current elaborate form – establishes, it is argued, a template for political legitimacy in the modern world that privileges a particular, Western, conception of politics; moreover, while the impulse to redistribute wealth might be welcomed by some critics, theories of justice elaborated by liberal cosmopolitan thinkers are equally open to the charge of being based on specifically Western values.

Before moving to an examination of the substance of this issue, a few preliminary points may be helpful. First, this is one area where conventional political theory and international political theory are covering, if not the same, then very similar ground. The debate over multiculturalism that has been of such great interest to liberals for the past generation is replicated at the international level (Kymlicka, 1995a and 1995b; Parekh, 2000). The international issue of the rights of 'indigenous peoples' cannot be seen in isolation from the rights of the same peoples in the domestic context. Arguments in favour of 'Asian values' are not dissimilar to those in favour of special rights on religious or cultural grounds within established societies (Barry, 2000). Similar issues concerning gender emerge at each level (Cohen, Howard and Nussbaum, 1999; Nussbaum, 2000).

Rather more important is what might be termed the 'Westphalia Paradox', which is that the one part of the normative framework of contemporary international relations that is incontestably Western in origin is also that part which is most enthusiastically adopted by non-Western critics of the Western origins of that framework. As established in chapter 2, the origins of the 'Westphalia System' are clearly to be found in early modern Europe. There have been earlier political formations based on the interactions of independent, territorially based, political actors but such proto-international systems have generally been short-lived, whereas the European states-system has survived and prospered over the last 400 years (Bozeman, 1960). This is partly to be attributed to the system of political economy which it fostered and which produced for the European state productive (and military) capacities no other political formation could equal, but it is also to be attributed to the moderating impact on power politics of the institutions of 'international society'. And, as eighteenth-century writers such as Vattel and Burke noted at the time, international society in turn was based on the common values left behind for the European states by their Roman and medieval predecessors. The sovereign state, diplomacy and international law – the institutions of this society – are incontestably tied to that common past.

As Europe's formal political dominance over the globe receded, colonies achieved their independence and notionally independent states achieved the abolition of regimes of 'capitulation' and other symbols of their second-class status, so this Westphalian order was generalized, and the society of states expanded to its current near-200 members. The model of the sovereign state was adopted generally not because it was particularly appropriate to the social circumstances in which many of the new states found themselves – which was clearly not the case – but because of the 'lock-in' effect identified at the beginning of chapter 3; there was, genuinely, no alternative to this model. What is interesting is that, although the Westphalian model has indeed been inappropriate for many of the new states, they have adopted the norms of sovereignty with great enthusiasm. Whereas within the original home of the system, Western Europe, the notion of sovereignty is challenged by the European Union and, more generally in the Western world, by the impact of globalization, in much of the 'South', especially in Asia, sovereignty is fiercely defended. The People's Republic of China resists what it regards as 'Western' critiques of its human rights position by reference to the notion of sovereignty, even though no precedent for the idea of an international society based on sovereign states can be found in Chinese history. Predominantly Muslim Malaysia and Indonesia defend their sovereignty with equal vigour, yet the notion of the sovereign state is even less compatible with Islam than it was with medieval Christian doctrine. Even India, committed by its constitution to secularism and human rights, has joined the other three named Asian powers in not even signing, let alone ratifying, the Rome Statute for an International Criminal Court, on the grounds that such an institution would undermine its sovereignty – on which basis they join in unlikely alliance with the 'New Sovereigntists' in the United States and Senator Jesse Helms, the indefatigably right-wing former chair of the US Senate's Foreign Relations Committee (Helms, 2000/2001).

The reason for this apparent paradox is, of course, easy to identify – and it is important that it should be identified at the outset because it underlies a great many of the issues to be discussed in this chapter. These states defend the norm of sovereignty because they recognize their political weakness in the current world order, and are concerned in any way they can to buttress their position and resist external inter-ference in their affairs. The incontestably Western norm of sovereignty serves this purpose, as does a critique of human rights norms as based on alien values. In each case, states are attempting to shore up their lack of effective political power by articulating their position in nor-mative terms. This ought not to be seen as surprising, nor ought it to be regarded as particularly shameful. The important issue here con-cerns the nature of the states in question, and, in particular, whether the leaderships of those states which resist external interference in the name of their peoples are, in fact, better seen as defending their own privileges rather than some common good.

In so far as they are preserving their societies' right to be different, as opposed to simply their own right to rule, their position is wholly compatible with the 'pluralist' conception of international society described and largely endorsed by Hedley Bull, and with the notion of international society as a practical association set out by Terry Nardin (Bull, 1997/1995; Nardin, 1983). Their opposition to the new human rights norms can be seen as a principled rejection of the direction that international law has taken since the 1940s. This is not to say that they have chosen the right principles or that their resistance to the new norms is justified, but it does no harm at all to establish early in this discussion that the defenders of cultural diversity have solid argu-ments on their side which are well established in conventional inter-national thought.

The 'rights of peoples'

The issue of human rights has been at the centre of discussions of cul-tural diversity and international political theory, for obvious reasons –

the very notion that there are 'human' rights, that is to say rights that individuals possess simply by virtue of their humanity, constitutes a challenge to the notion of diversity. The Universal Declaration of Human Rights, the two Covenants on Civil and Political Rights and Economic, Social and Cultural Rights, and a raft of other international agreements are all designed precisely to set limits to the extent to which one political system may vary from another. In principle, such documents do not tell states how they ought to arrange their affairs, rather, they simply forbid certain practices – but the level of detail they contain is such that, in practice, states that wish to be compliant have little scope for manoeuvre. It is difficult to see how any state that was not a fully functioning liberal democracy could meet all the requirements of the international human rights regime, and, for that matter, most 'actually existing' liberal democracies would be in difficulty. Taking international legislation in this area at face value, all political systems that are not liberal-democratic are delegitimized by the international human rights regime. In fact, of course, for most of the last fifty years the terms of the regime have not been taken at face value for contingent political reasons mostly connected to the Cold War – it was only with the end of the Cold War that Western, especially US, 'democracy promotion' led to explicit conflicts in this area, of which the Asian values debate is exemplary. The latter is the subject of the next section of this chapter; first, the one part of the international human rights regime that does allow for difference will be examined – the so-called 'third-generation' rights of 'peoples' seen as collectivities, not simply as aggregates of individuals.

The Universal Declaration of 1948 refers to a putative collective right of national self-determination, but the overwhelming thrust of this document is individualist; it is not until the 1980s that collective rights come to be seen as not necessarily composed of the rights of the individuals who make up the collective body. Two factors are important here – regionally specific declarations of human rights, and the global protection of the rights of indigenous peoples. As to the first, the African Charter of Human and Peoples' Rights 1981 (generally known as the Banjul Charter) is instructive. Its very title suggests a shift in emphasis, as does its specific commitment to the values of African civilization; in the Preamble it is stated that 'on the one hand, fundamental rights stem from the attributes of human beings, which justifies their international protection and on the other hand, that the reality and respect of peoples' rights should necessarily guarantee human rights'. What exactly this means is not clear, and as with many such international agreements, the obscurity is no accident; the wording represents an attempt to reconcile universal values with the notion that there are specifically African values which revolve around the family and extended kin-groups. The implication is that universal and African values are wholly compatible, but if that were actually the case there would be no issue here; in practice, there is a potential conflict here between the individualism of the universalist position and the collectivism of an endorsement of family and community life. A similar disjuncture is to be found in the Vienna Declaration of 1993, which combines a restatement of universalism with the recognition of 'the significance of national and regional particularities and various historical, cultural and religious backgrounds'. Once again, a degree of double-think is involved here.

These issues become clearer when the rights of indigenous peoples are under consideration. Such rights were brought into focus in the 1980s, largely by New Zealand Maori, Canadian and US 'First Nations', and Australian Aborigines, although the majority of indigenous peoples actually reside in South American and Asian countries rather less sympathetic to their cause than the aforementioned liberal democracies. The 1984 Declaration of Principles of Indigenous Rights by the World Council of Indigenous Peoples has yet to be adopted as a UN Declaration, largely because of the resistance of countries such as Brazil, Vietnam and Indonesia, which regard the notion of indigenous rights either as likely to interfere with their economic sovereignty, or, indeed, as an actual threat to the unity of the state. Indigenous peoples are peoples with their own customs, practices and institutions who have become outnumbered in their own lands, and obliged to adopt the community standards of the majority; the claim is that this constitutes a form of 'cultural genocide' and that these groups are entitled to resist the majority in the name of preserving their culture. Moreover, because a collective wrong has been perpetrated, a collective remedy is the appropriate answer; indigenous groups are entitled to be different from the majority, even if such difference involves overriding some of the rights of the individuals who make up these groups in the name of collective 'rights' – although whether collective rights are actually rights in any genuine meaning of the term is contestable (P. Jones, 1998).

In practice, the majority of the groups in question do not wish to preserve such common features of indigenous political practice as patriarchy or the anti-democratic rule of the tribal elders, which allows liberal theorists of multiculturalism, such as the Canadian Will Kymlicka, to support their positions while simultaneously arguing that Canadian constitutional protection for the rights of the individual should apply to their members (Kymlicka, 1995a). Still, the possibility of a clash here is evident; the right to be different that is asserted is meaningless unless it involves the potential endorsement of actual meaningful difference and not simply secondary issues such as the right to dispose of tribal lands. In so far as it is the case that the liberal international human rights regime and its domestic equivalents privilege the rights of individuals over communities, and takes to itself the right to determine exceptions to its own rules, then to require indigenous peoples to play by these rules is simply to perpetuate the collective wrong done to them. A kinder, gentler form of imperialism replaces the original physical dispossession of the indigenous by an equally soul-destroying spiritual dispossession if these groups are obliged to play the rights game on the terms laid down by the dispossessors (Tully, 1995).

This is a powerful argument which does accurately identify the roots of the problem and is often articulated by groups who by virtue of the wrong done them are entitled to a respectful hearing; in order to respond effectively it is necessary for the defenders of universalism to address the core issue, which is why the liberal notion of rights should be allowed to dominate the debate. Such a defence can, of course, be mounted, and will be considered below after a consideration of the arguments presented by the defenders of Asian values. The latter use arguments which are structurally quite similar to those used by defenders of collective rights; indeed, there are similarities also to arguments deployed by feminist critics of the current international human rights regime – the various opponents of universalism tend to use similar arguments, albeit to reach radically different conclusions. Before moving on, one further point about discussions of indigenous peoples and their rights needs to be made, because it is apposite to the later discussion. It is often, and rightly, argued that those who speak for indigenous peoples do not always represent all of their constituents, some of whom may hanker to break free from even benign forms of traditional rule. In the same way, many 'Asian' leaders clearly do not speak for all the 'Asians' they represent – but, whether true or not, to regard this as an important point is already to adopt the standard of liberal individualism that is subject to investigation. The views of individuals are only significant if there is some prior reason to regard the views of individuals as significant. There is no natural way of deciding this issue that does not involve providing a reasoned defence of liberal universalism.

The 'Asian values' debate

Indigenous peoples could be regarded as exceptions to a general rule – although to treat their case in this way would, of course, be to accept the terms of reference of liberal universalism – but the proponents of

'Asian values' cannot be treated in this way.* The argument here is that rather than there being a single human rights regime applicable to all, there should be a range of different regimes adapted to particular circumstances, which, needless to say, undermines the very notion of *human* rights, that is, rights applicable to all human beings simply by virtue of their humanity. In fact, the Asian values position conflates a number of arguments, but before unpacking them it may be helpful to provide a certain amount of context.

The end of the Cold War – and, in particular, the terms under which the Cold War ended – provided a context for a new consideration of human rights. During the Cold War, the US and its West European allies had quite frequently found themselves defending regimes that were geo-strategically important, but politically oppressive to their own citizens; in the emerging world order it might still be the case that some such regimes were politically important to the West for one reason or another, but the general exemption provided to reliably anti-Soviet regimes was no longer available. In Latin America and in Africa one-party regimes and military rule became generally discredited and their leaders could no longer rely upon the US to provide either overt or covert support. Bodies such as the IMF and the Commonwealth began to make good government and respect for human rights a condition of aid. As a result, a general trend towards 'democratization' is discernable in this period, especially in Latin America where the number of regimes that were not at least formally democratic dwindled, while in Africa long-standing rulers such as Presidents Mobuto of Zaire and Kaunda of Zambia found themselves isolated and undermined. In East Asia things were rather different; the People's Republic of China had provided a spectacular demonstration of its undemocratic credentials in Tiananmen Square in 1989 and as a major power and permanent member of the UN Security Council had no intention of bowing to external pressure. The mildly authoritarian regimes of Malaysia and Singapore, and the rather less mild rulers of Indonesia, were experiencing a high degree of economic success – the so-called 'Asian Miracle' – which, as far as they were concerned, gave them both the ability and the moral right to resist external pressures to democratize.

* Strictly speaking, the term 'East Asian' is more appropriate than simply 'Asian' in this context, since the most important South Asian country, India, does not officially endorse the positions involved, but Asian values has become the established term and it would be pedantic not to use it here. The debate has been well covered in a number of collections (Tang, 1994; Bauer and D. Bell, 1999; Van Ness, 1999; L. S. Bell et al., 2001) and one outstanding monograph in Daniel Bell's 'signature' form of a set of dialogues (D. Bell, 2000). All of these sources are employed in the following discussion.

This sets the scene for a war of words that broke out in 1993. This year was significant for two reasons. First, a major UN Conference on Human Rights was scheduled for the autumn in Vienna; this was intended to be the most significant event for the human rights regime since the signing of the two Covenants in 1966, perhaps since the Universal Declaration of 1948 – the aim was to restate the fundamentals in the post-Cold War context, and to address issues of compliance in a serious way. Regional conferences were designed to lead up to Vienna, and in the summer of 1993 Asian leaders met in Bangkok to define their position on human rights and put together a coherent response to the pressures for democratization identified above. This all took on greater significance because of the second reason for the significance of 1993, the election of the Democrat Bill Clinton to the US presidency. The Republican Administrations of Ronald Reagan and George Bush (Senior), while convinced of the superiority of Western values, especially after the triumph of the West in the Cold War, had not been particularly enthusiastic supporters of democratization as a general principle. Clinton, on the other hand, was the inheritor of the human rights agenda of his Democrat predecessor, Jimmy Carter, and came into office with a specific programme of 'democracy promotion'; just how serious he would be about this agenda was open to question – in the event, 'not very' was the answer – but, unsurprisingly, in 1993 some Asian leaders thought they could see serious conflict ahead unless they were to establish a defensible position (M. Cox et al., 2000). The result was the Bangkok Declaration of 1993 (excerpted in L. S. Bell et al., 2001) which deplores the politicization of human rights and double standards in this area (Article 7), and, while endorsing universal human rights 'in the context of a dynamic and evolving process of international norm-setting' (Article 8), gives equally strong endorsement to sovereignty and national self-determination, and, further, is clear that 'States have the primary responsibility for the promotion and protection of human rights' (Article 9).

A tense and unsatisfactory conference in Vienna, which was unable to make much progress, finally adopted a Declaration and Programme of Action which contained the following formula:

> Article 5 . . . all human rights are universal, indivisible, and interdependent and interrelated. The international community must treat human rights globally in a fair and equal manner, on the same footing, and with the same emphasis. While *the significance of national and regional particularities and various historical, cultural and religious backgrounds must be borne in mind*, it is the duty of States, regardless of their political, economic and cultural systems, to promote and protect all human rights and fundamental freedoms. (Emphasis added.)

On the face of it, this is an endorsement of universalism, but the emphasized clause – which is lifted from Article 8 of the Bangkok Declaration
– could certainly be interpreted in such a way as to undermine this
endorsement, since many historical, cultural and religious 'backgrounds' do not endorse the notion of equal human rights, and some
regions have a different take on the subject than others. The intention
of some East Asian leaders was that the clause should be read in this
way.

What are the arguments that these leaders have deployed? The first,
and probably the most important, argument from a political angle has
little to do with either values or, specifically, Asia; it is the general point
that the West's record in the world over the last four centuries undermines the legitimacy of its present backing for human rights. For the
last half millennium, Europe has imposed its will on the world by brute
force, abusing the rights of 'natives' the world over; now, barely a few
years after the end of formal colonialism, Europe is once again telling
people what to do, this time in the name of universal rights. Common
politeness ought to have led to a period of silence! Of course, it will be
argued, perfectly correctly, that promoting human rights is not the
same as imposing alien control, but it is not too difficult to see how
those on the receiving end of democracy promotion might see things
differently. It is interesting to see the same issue arising in the context
of recent British criticism of President Robert Mugabe of Zimbabwe;
the then British Foreign Office Minister responsible, Peter Hain, had a
cast-iron record as an opponent of Apartheid and racism in southern
Africa and clearly believed that this gave him the right to speak frankly
when faced with evidence of racism by African leaders. Equally clearly,
Mugabe was not the only African who found the spectacle of a white
leader from Britain laying down the law in this way somewhat
offensive.

The argument from anti-imperialism has been an important element
of the East Asian critique of the international human rights regime; less
important but also heard, albeit *sotto voce*, has been the proposition that
the full human rights package is only deliverable once a certain level
of socio-economic development has been reached. At the earlier stages
of development, the rights of, for example, trade unionists may need
to be restricted; likewise, it is argued, an official 'loyal' opposition is a
luxury only the rich can afford. This is actually, of course, a universalist argument; the case is not that there is anything un-Asian about the
international human rights regime, rather that less-developed Asian
countries are not yet ready to comply with it – this is clearly not an
argument that would be likely to appeal to anti-imperialists and
defenders of the view that there are genuinely Asian values. It is also
clearly the case that a rich country such as Singapore could hardly

claim that these kinds of restrictions are still necessary, even were it to be conceded that they once were. As to the merits of the argument, taken to extremes it is clearly false. As Armartya Sen has argued convincingly, political freedom and development are not antithetical one to another (Sen, 2000a). On the other hand, high growth rates require higher rates of saving than may sometimes be easy to achieve in a fully democratic regime, and it is not wholly implausible to argue that the Singapore, South Korean and Taiwanese success stories owe at least something to the mildly authoritarian nature of rule in those countries – although the latter two have democratized without apparent ill effects.

Politically important though these arguments have been, they do not address the core of the Asian values debate, which is the proposition that the contemporary human rights regime privileges the Western conception of the individual as a 'rights-bearer' as opposed to alternative conceptions of human dignity which are less individualist, less inclined to set the individual against the community. Western values, so it is argued, stress the rights of the individual against the community; Asian values, on the other hand, stress the duties of the individual to community and family. It should be noted that this position does *not* deny that individuals ought to be seen to have rights, rather that these rights need to be understood as existing within a complex of social relations; the Western emphasis on the individual asserting himself against society is not an appropriate way of understanding this latter complexity. My use of gendered terminology here is not accidental; this critique of the heroic individualist rights-bearer is structurally very similar to that produced by some feminist writers. In each case, it is the assumption that social life is divided into public and private spheres and that rights are particularly relevant to action in the public sphere that is contested – although to very different effect.

Quite frequently, the difference between Asian and Western values are seen to rest on different attitudes to religion. Hindu and Buddhist thought rests on the idea of 'life' as ultimately one, and rejects the notion, common to the religions of the Book (Christianity, Islam, Judaism) and to Western secularism, that individual human lives can be seen as projects, with beginnings, middles and endings (and, perhaps, judgement after death). Such differences could quite plausible be seen as feeding into different conceptions of human dignity – but the force of this point is certainly lessened by the fact that, for the time being at least, India, the largest home to Hindus and Buddhists, remains officially strongly committed to the international human rights regime. How far Indian popular culture has internalized the vales of that regime is, however, open to question, and the rise of Hindu nationalism at the expense of secularist political parties is perhaps significant. Indian feminists are certainly aware of the tensions here (Coomaraswamy, 1994).

Islam, on the other hand, is a religion whose notion of the individual soul is similar to that of the other religions of the Book, and notions of reincarnation and karma do not apply here. However, as Malaysian critics of the international human rights regime have stressed, the Islamic emphasis on submission to the will of God – and the belief that God's will has been definitively revealed – provides the basis for a critique of contemporary Western society as over-concerned for the rights of the individual. Malaysia's leader Mahathir Bin Mohamed has consistently described contemporary Western society as degenerate, citing the toleration of homosexuality, concern for the rights of women and an unwillingness to be sufficiently rigorous in combating crime (Mohammed and Ishihara, 1996). Such critiques are also to be heard in the Arab world and from the Islamic Republic of Iran. Certainly, it is the case that the way in which Islamic religious law is interpreted in, for example, Saudi Arabia, Iran or the Sudan is incompatible with the current international human rights regime; whether such interpretations are actually mandated by Islam is a matter for dispute, although even the most 'liberal' interpretation of the requirements of Islamic law cannot acknowledge full sexual equality or fully equal rights for believers and non-believers in a society where the former are in the majority.

Whether 'Confucianism' should be seen as a religion or not is debatable, but it is certainly a system of ethics whose adherents, in China proper and the Chinese Diaspora, frequently argue that it imposes obligations on the individual which are incompatible with the international human rights regime. The respect mandated under almost all circumstances to parents and to age has anti-individualist implications, and, it is argued, is accompanied by an approach to the authority of political leaders which makes the latter, in effect, *in loco parentis*. To set oneself against the authority of the state, far from being a potentially heroic act, shows lack of respect and is to be condemned. Certainly, the powers that be ought to rule with justice and moderation, but they ought not to be held to account too readily by the ruled – it is easy to see the attraction of such a position to authoritarian rulers. To what extent this position is authentically Confucian is a matter for debate, but Confucian ideas have been cited by Singapore's Lee Kuan Yew (Zakaria, 1994).

Rather more convincing than Neo-Confucianism, as such, is the position of the Singapore diplomat Kishore Mahbubani, who argues that Singapore's policies on such matters as the rights of the accused in criminal cases are simply a matter of defensible social choices which ought not to be subjected to external critiques. His most famous intervention has been an essay in *The National Interest*, 'The West and the

Rest' (1992), but a conference presentation on press freedom in 1993 conveys his point very precisely and energetically: pointing out that while you would be placing your life in jeopardy by strolling a few hundred yards off course from the offices of the major US newspapers, for their editors and writers

> danger from habitual crime is considered an acceptable price to pay for no reduction in liberty. This is one social choice. In Singapore you can wander out in any direction from the *Straits Times* and not put your life in jeopardy. One reason for this is that habitual criminals and drug addicts are locked up, often for long spells, until they are clearly reformed. The interests of the majority in having safe city streets are put ahead of considerations of rigorous due process, although safeguards are put in place to ensure innocent individuals are not locked up. This is another kind of social choice. (Van Ness, 1999, p. 93)

Two points are noteworthy here; first, Mahbubani endorses the notion that there are basic universal rights. It is the scope of these rights that is in question – not entirely flippantly, one might say that 'due process' is mandatory, but not 'rigorous' due process. Second, it should be said that the attitude he describes is by no means confined to citizens of Singapore or indeed Asia. Policies of 'zero tolerance' and large-scale incarceration have been employed in the US and the UK in recent years, although whether such policies have produced reformed criminals is open to doubt. Fareed Zakaria has written helpfully of the rise of 'illiberal democracy' in East Asia and elsewhere, but there are clearly illiberal democrats closer to home in Europe and the US (Zakaria, 1997).

There is a wider point here about 'essentialist' definitions of Asia and the West (Sen, 2000b). Clearly these broad categories conceal more than they reveal, and the same is also true of religious catch-all terms such as Islam and Christianity. The notion that something called 'Christianity' is necessarily supportive of human rights such as freedom of speech and freedom of conscience would have surprised the majority of Christians over the last two millennia, and many Christian leaders today; the West may provide support for the international human rights regime today, but it is also true that the regime owes its very existence to the atrocities committed by Westerners in the 1940s. In any event, Christianity and Islam, Buddhism and Confucianism are not closed systems of thought; they are now, and probably always have been, influenced by one another, as, for that matter, are the 'civilizations' that Samuel Huntington has observed clashing. Huntington's article 'The Clash of Civilizations' fed into the Asian values debate by criticizing the West's emphasis on human rights as productive of inter-civilizational conflict, but the spatial definition of civilization employed, with its accompanying notion of border zones and 'fault lines', is deeply suspect, even in the rather less tendentious form advocated by Eisuke Sakakiba (Huntington, 1993a, 1993b, and 1996; Sakakiba, 1995; C. Brown, 1999a).

What all this suggests is that the notion of 'Asian' or 'East Asian' values makes little sense; most of the time it makes more sense to think of certain values as being held by (some) Asians – along with other non-Asians – rather than of the values themselves as being in some sense Asian. However, it must be noted that this does not do away with the problem; the essential question posed by the East Asian critics is why one particular conception of what it is to be human – the rights-bearing individual – should be privileged over others, and the fact that there are Western critics of this account of the individual, and, for that matter, Asian supporters, does not undermine the relevance of this question. Supporters of the current human rights regime are still being challenged to defend its universalism.

The undoubted existence of Asian supporters of the current regime does, on the other hand, raise one obvious question, which is whether the Asian opponents of universalism are actually speaking for anyone other than themselves, a point raised above in connection with indigenous peoples. The charge here is clear; governing elites in East Asia are simply defending their own positions by claiming that the undemocratic nature of their rule is validated by their 'culture' and that their critics, domestic as well as foreign, are attempting to impose alien values on their peoples (Lawson, 1998). Democratization is resisted in the name of cultural difference, but the real motive of rulers is the less noble desire to preserve their own privileges, and, in many cases, perhaps particularly in the Middle East, lifestyles which owe more to the values of the international jet-set than to the traditions they allegedly defend. As noted above, it is difficult to find a neutral way of assessing this argument; to use opinion polls or referenda to find out what the people really want is to adopt methods which are tied to Western conceptions of politics – perhaps there may be some mileage in more informal ways of getting at local attitudes by, for example, as Daniel Bell suggests, the analysis of the kind of people local cultures adopt as heroes (Buruma, 1984; D. Bell, 2000, p. 179). In fact, the most telling point in this debate can be made by assuming that the rulers are, indeed, in bad faith, but then asking why they employ the particular rhetoric they do to defend their positions – presumably this can only be because they assume that this rhetoric will be effective in mobilizing their supporters, or, to put the matter differently, they can only be cynical about the values they supposedly promote if they have reason to think that their peoples are *not* cynical. For this reason, it would be unwise to reject criticisms of universalism simply on the grounds that they are self-serving – especially because much the same might be said of campaigns to promote democracy by rich and powerful Western countries (C. Brown, 2000a).

In defence of universalism

One of the more positive effects of the Asian values debate has been to oblige the defenders of universalism to marshal their arguments, and decide exactly what it is that they want to defend; the result has been the emergence of several different kinds of universalist argument. At one extreme these arguments make no concession to their opponents; writers such as Brian Barry or, from a different tradition, Jürgen Habermas are happy to assert the general superiority of the values incorporated in the international human rights regime and to meet head-on those who challenge them. At the other end of the spectrum are those who defend the notion of a minimum set of universal rights; writers such as Bikhu Parekh and, in his later work, John Rawls fit into this category, in both cases with arguments that might be acceptable to at least some of those who argue anti-universalist positions. Set somewhat to one side are those who defend universalism with arguments that are not canonically liberal; Richard Rorty's post-modernist defence of the 'human rights culture' comes into this category, as does Martha Nussbaum's 'human capabilities' approach.

Brian Barry's approach to 'justice as impartiality' was briefly described in the previous chapter; his cosmopolitanism is based on a strong account of the implications of equal treatment for all, and he argues, persuasively, that the existing global order cannot be seen as just from an impartialist perspective. Anyone committed to reaching agreement on the terms of a just world order would not consider it reasonable that there should be the dramatic inequalities that actually exist in the world today, and the appropriate response to these inequalities is large-scale transfers from rich to poor; in so far as the sovereign state constitutes an obstacle to this process it should be, as far as possible, undermined by the development of more effective global institutions (Barry, 1998). The same commitment to radical egalitarianism makes Barry a strong supporter of the notion of universal human rights, although the consequentialist, quasi-utilitarian nature of his approach makes him a little suspicious of the notion of 'rights' as such. He is not a rights 'fundamentalist' but he is committed at a deep level to universalism. His recent *Culture and Equality* is explicitly a defence of universalist egalitarianism against the charge that such a universalist perspective is insensitive to the need to respect culture and difference; although this extended, entertaining and scholarly polemic is designed specifically to respond to domestic 'multiculturalism' the arguments he deploys are clearly relevant to the international debate (Barry, 2000).

These arguments are, in essence, very simple and would have been regarded as uncontroversial by most liberals until comparatively recently; they rely on one basic assumption – of human equality – and the central proposition that reason, properly applied, can tell us what the implications of human equality are. The main thing that reason tells us is that equality requires that whatever rules are necessary to regulate human conduct should, as a matter of principle, be applied across the board, and that only in very exceptional circumstances is it right that different rules should be applied to different people because of some secondary fact about them such as their culture or religion. Thus, if, say, equal rights for women is a reasonable implication of the basic assumption of human equality – as it surely is – then the fact that certain religions and/or cultures hold a contrary view is neither here nor there. If particular religions wish to preserve an all-male priesthood, or even preach that women are inferior to men, then liberal principles hold that there is nothing to stop them from so doing – always assuming that no one is required to join the denomination in question or prevented from leaving and that no one is forced to listen – but such discriminatory behaviour ought not to be backed by the force of law even if it is, allegedly, supported by the majority of the people of a particular society. The whole point of rights is that they ought *not* to be subject to the will of the majority.

This argument is presented by Barry in the context of the domestic politics of liberal societies, and in response to those theorists who argue that liberal principles should be adapted to take into account the multicultural nature of most contemporary polities. However, Barry's position clearly has international implications; if, to continue the above discussion, polygamy or female genital mutilation ought not to be tolerated in present-day America or Britain because they are practices that oppress women and thereby are anti-egalitarian, then exactly the same argument applies elsewhere in the world. To accept the pluralist position that different cultures are entitled to pursue different conceptions of the good would be, for Barry, to deny the reasonableness of his core position on human equality, and, although his argument in *Culture and Equality* is largely directed against fellow liberals who are presumed to share this position but who, unaccountably, do not seem to realize its implications, and not towards the opponents of liberalism, he clearly holds that the latter are wrong.

Critics of universalism would argue that Barry's position rests on a suspect anthropology. Barry regards human equality as the appropriate starting point and religion and culture as distinctly secondary characteristics of the human animal; they are, more or less, analogous to what

liberal political theorists call 'expensive tastes'. Thus, I might decide to
dedicate my life to dining every night in the best restaurants in London,
drinking the finest wines, but it would not be reasonable for me to
expect the public to provide me with a special supplement to my income
to allow me to pursue this very expensive taste simply because I have
chosen it as my goal in life. Analogously, the adherents of Islam, Sikhism
or Christianity are entitled to hold to their faith and to bear whatever
costs that faith might require of them, but they are not entitled to impose
it on others, or call on the public authories to assist them to meet its
burdens. The problem with this analogy is that people do not generally
regard their religion or their culture in these terms – rather than thinking of the latter as life-style choices, they see these features of their lives
as defining who they actually are. On this account, we are not individuals who have chosen to be Christians, or Maori or whatever; we are
simply 'Christian' or 'Maori' – these are defining identities, even if they
are identities we have chosen through conversion.

It is interesting, as noted above, that Barry does not spend much time
in *Culture and Equality* defending his individualism or his assumption
of human equality. He has little to say to those who would, in principle, reject at least a secular notion of human equality. Reason tells us
that they are wrong, in so far as there is no reasonable argument against
political equality, but is there actually a single 'reason' that is self-
authorizing in this way? Such is the Enlightenment faith – and Barry
has been described in the *Oxford Companion to Philosophy* as an intellectual descendant of the Scottish Enlightenment project – but it is precisely this faith that is at issue. Those who reject the authority of reason
in the first place are unimpressed by this line of reasoning, and, in
effect, Barry talks past the actual adherents of, for example, Asian
values. Perhaps this is unavoidable and there is no way to get beyond
some bedrock set of beliefs, but some writers whose allegiances are
similar to Barry's have attempted to make the effort, most noticeably
the Frankfurt School critical theorist, Jürgen Habermas.

Habermas shares with Barry a commitment to the values of the
European Enlightenment and a willingness to defend these values as
genuinely universal; whereas Barry has taken on back-sliding liberals,
Habermas has engaged in polemics with post-modernists and post-
structuralists of one kind or another, the 'young conservatives' whose
alleged relativism in his view undermines their ability to be critical of
existing practices, and, of course, makes cross-cultural criticism impossible (Habermas, 1987). Along with Barry, Habermas wishes to defend
a cross-cultural notion of 'reasonableness' but, unlike Barry, he has provided himself with what he takes to be a foundation for his position
with his theory of communicative action, and the notion of an 'ideal-
speech situation' (Habermas, 1984). Again, like Barry, Rawls, and

modern liberal theory in general, Habermas subscribes to an account of truth as the product of consensus under ideal conditions. There is no notion of truth or justice 'out there'; what is true is what we consensually believe to be true, but not any consensus will do; there has to be some way of excluding from our thought processes the biases that stem from the existing order. For Rawls, this is the role of the original position and the veil of ignorance; for Barry Scanlonian contractualism is the right approach; but Habermas's ideal speech situation works in a slightly different way from that envisaged by his Anglo-American colleagues.

Ideal speech refers to discourse that is free from the distortions of power and privilege, in which all points of view can be entertained and the force of the better argument alone will win through. Habermas argues that the possibility of ideal speech is underwritten by the very nature of language; the act of speech implies an underlying commitment to truth – even the intent to lie makes no sense unless truth is the normal basis for language. The argument here is complicated, and cannot be replicated within the scope of this chapter, but it allows Habermas to claim that the ideal speech situation has an ontological grounding denied to thought-experiments such as the Rawlsian original position. Further, the ideal speech situation provides a kind of model of the requirements of an ideal society, in so far as ideal speech could only exist in a particular kind of egalitarian society dedicated to social justice. In effect, Habermas is arguing that the (radical) liberal conception of society is underwritten by the nature of language, and therefore, by the nature of human beings as such. There is, thus, no necessity to apologize for the Western origins of liberal individualism and human rights; it may be that the West has come closer to achieving the conditions for ideal speech than other societies, but this claim to higher cognitive adequacy is not based on criteria established by the West to validate its own way of life. The emancipation promised by human rights and a scientific culture is grounded in the very nature of human speech not in the customs of the West – in any event, the contribution of all different cultures and religions can be heard within the ideal speech situation, each contributing to the search for intersubjective truth, a point particularly stressed by one of Habermas's leading followers in International Relations (Linklater, 1998).

These are, of course, very strong claims, and, predictably, they are not widely accepted even by some other adherents of discourse ethics, much less by those who are critical of his initial starting point. The foundationalism of Habermas's position jars; the idea that scientific knowledge about the nature of language, or of developmental psychology, another of Habermas's recent interests, could underpin political values rouses suspicion. Those who already hold the values in question may regard his argument as supportive, but those who are not liberals are rarely convinced by arguments that assert the underlying truth of liberalism. The central point here is clear – what seems from a liberal universalist perspective to be obvious and reasonable is by no means so from the perspective of, say, a Muslim or a Christian fundamentalist, and to require of the latter that they adopt a liberal perspective is to invite them to abandon their firmly held beliefs for reasons which will only become valid once those beliefs are abandoned. Bikhu Parekh describes this demand as the product of 'moral monism', a solipsistic view of the world which cannot be defended (Parekh, 1999). Parekh himself, however, wishes to resist what he calls 'moral relativism' as much as do the liberals he criticizes, and his own approach involves attempting to establish cross-cultural principles which can underlie a minimum set of human rights (Parekh, 2000).

Minimum standards?

The idea that a minimum set of general principles might be discovered that can serve as the basis for cross-cultural dialogue has already come up in a number of different contexts. For example, Michael Walzer, it will be recalled from chapter 5, identified some minimum sense of what could be described as a habitable human environment, while John Rawls made respect for a minimum set of rights a defining characteristic of well-ordered hierarchies, the 'decent' peoples that are full members of his confederation of peoples along with liberal peoples. The proponents of Asian values have, in the Bangkok Declaration and elsewhere, stressed their commitment to at least a minimum set of human rights. And, further, there is some evidence that cross-cultural similarities exist at a level sufficient to form the basis for a kind of minimum moral code, if not the 'common morality' advocated by Alan Donagan (Donagan, 1977; Renteln, 1990; D. E. Brown, 1991). The underlying thinking here is that the 'hard-line' liberal position that all societies that are not liberal are, in some sense, defective – albeit to different degrees – is insufficiently discriminatory. The key task is to establish which kinds of 'difference' are deserving of respect and which are not, and to lump all non-liberal codes into the same category does not contribute to this task – rather the need is to distinguish between those societies where human dignity is generally respected and those societies which are based on such obviously inhumane principles that this cannot be held to be the case. The existence or not of some kind of minimum set of rights would seem to make this distinction, and to form the basis for an ongoing cross-cultural dialogue.

On the surface, this is an attractive position. Unfortunately, when investigated a little more closely it becomes less so, largely because it is clear that the notion of what constitutes a minimalist set of principles varies dramatically depending on who one is talking to. Walzer's minimum rules out slavery and genocide, which is comforting but not very discriminatory. The minimalist principles advocated by Parekh, and Rawls' basic human rights support freedom of religion and regard discrimination on the basis of gender as unacceptable, but those societies that are potential candidates for 'decent' status mostly do not. It is interesting that when Rawls wishes to illustrate what a decent society would look like he invents a Muslim society, 'Kazanistan', where gender equality and religious freedom is guaranteed, and non-Muslims have access to all the rights and positions of Muslims except the right to hold the highest political and judicial offices (Rawls, 1999b, p. 75). Needless to say, this is an exercise in ideal theory, but even so the gap between Kazanistan and 'really existing' Islamic republics is far greater than the gap between actual liberal democracies and Rawls's liberal peoples.

Parekh places a great deal of emphasis on dialogue, the importance of arguing through issues such as polygamy, but, attractive though the idea of resolving differences in this way may be, there is no guarantee that it will work, and, more to the point, dialogue itself is not culture-neutral. Fundamentalists of all ilks reject the idea that moral progress comes from talking things through. Part of the problem here is that the most compelling objections to the full-blown liberal notion of universal human rights are also objections to minimal codes, and so it is not clear what is gained by liberals when they move to the latter position. The kind of anti-foundationalist objections to human rights in general apply just as firmly to minimalist notions of rights – and if rights are fictions, why write a short story rather than a novel?

Relativism and universalism

Retracing some steps in the argument, it is clear that the universalists examined above all appear (a) to rest their account of human rights on some conventional construction – a contract, the ideal speech situation – defensible by reason and (b) to assume that unless this can be done moral relativism follows, with allegedly disastrous consequences. Both positions can, in fact, be challenged, as can the connection between them. Taking this connection first, it does not follow that those who deny the possibility of firmly establishing the meaning of terms such as human rights are necessarily 'relativists'; one might take the view that a 'right' is an essentially contested concept which means that no definition could be final but does not mean that any definition of a right is as good as any other (Connolly, 1983). Moral relativism is a tricky position and it is by no means clear that most of those accused of holding it are actually guilty (Herskovits, 1973; Matilal, 1989). It is certainly not the case that the majority of participants in the Asian debate are relativists; Muslims, for example, believe that the way of life they espouse is valid for all, which is a different kind of universalism rather than any kind of relativist position. There are, however, a few genuine relativists around, and one such, Richard Rorty, has actually defended the notion of human rights quite effectively.

Rorty uses the language of rights, but with a particular spin (C. Brown, 2000f). Rights act to 'summarise our culturally influenced intuitions about the right thing to do in various situations'; such summarizing generalizations increase 'the predictability, and thus the power and efficiency, of our institutions, thereby heightening the sense of shared moral identity which brings us together in a moral community' (Rorty, 1993; p. 117). Since the Enlightenment, Americans and Europeans have created a 'human rights culture' in opposition to prejudices of one kind or another – racial, religious, most recently, misogynist and homophobic – and thereby extended the scope of this shared moral identity. This is an achievement which is both based on and reinforced by 'security' – 'conditions of life sufficiently risk-free as to make one's difference from others inessential to one's self-respect, one's sense of worth' (ibid., p. 128) – and 'sympathy', the ability to put one's self in another's shoes, to perceive the Other as a fellow human being. It is also an achievement which is continually open to question; our sense about 'the right thing to do in various situations' is always corrigible – prejudice is never conquered once and for all, and what counts as prejudice is never a closed issue.

Overall, Rorty's suggestion that in the West the scope of shared moral identity has expanded in this way seems broadly accurate, if a little self-satisfied, but what does this tell us about societies where these extensions of shared moral identity have not taken place, or where a shared moral or religious identity does not lead to the elimination of prejudice? Rorty's explicit relativism means that he cannot argue that those who think this way are wrong or irrational, because there is no human nature that could ground rights. UN Declarations, Covenants and the like cut no ice, because human beings create themselves and if they have not created themselves in ways that are amenable to a human rights perspective, nothing can get through to them. Rorty suggests that the best way to see such people is not as 'wrong' or 'irrational' but as 'deprived', deprived of the security and sympathy that has allowed us to create a culture in which rights make sense. They are in need of an environment in which they can reflect on these matters in relative safety; they are in need of a sentimental education. In any event, he suggests, the only way to argue for and promote the extension of the human rights culture is explicitly as a *culture*, and not as a movement that could be grounded by some form of knock-down moral reasoning.

Rorty's, occasionally rather smug, endorsement of Western values may grate, but this should not be allowed to undermine the strengths of his position. He endorses a dialogic approach to cross-cultural criticism, but his explicit relativism means that he is genuinely able to claim not to be privileging any particular voice in the dialogue. Still, for the liberal cosmopolitan notion of 'reasonableness' he substitutes his own reference point, 'suffering' – and it is by no means clear that it is possible to establish what it is to suffer in a culturally neutral way with any more ease than it is possible to establish what it is to be reasonable. All people of good will think that unnecessary suffering is wrong, but they do not agree as to what constitutes unnecessary suffering, which is why there is a problem with universal values in the first place.

If he has not solved the problem, Rorty has at least redescribed it; specifically he has highlighted the way in which the international human rights regime promotes a particular account of what it is to be human, but is unable to show why this account should be accepted by those who do not share it. The reason for this is that while most liberal universalists deplore moral relativism, their own account of human rights as the product of conventional constructions such as the social contract, or the ideal speech situation, leaves them open to the charge that they too are, at root, relativist. Relativism is, for Rorty, simply a defining feature of liberal thought; he regards the term as empty because he does not recognize any non-relativist way of approaching moral issues.

One liberal who has focused explicitly on the issue of relativism is the classicist Martha Nussbaum, who found herself obliged to confront this issue during work with the UN University, and in response developed with Armatya Sen the 'human capabilities' approach discussed in chapter 7 (Nussbaum and Sen, 1993; Nussbaum and Glover, 1995). Nussbaum was horrified by the prevalence in development studies circles of what she took to be a crude form of moral relativism that disabled the possibility of cross-cultural criticism. The human capabilities approach is designed to provide the basis for such criticism. It rests on the proposition that, in order to combat relativism, it is necessary to be able to describe, at least in outline, the shape of a flourishing human life; this description cannot simply be based on the preferences or customs of a particular society. Sen had come to similar conclusions from a different direction in his critique of rational choice reasoning in economics; if rationality is simply connected to instrumental reason-ing, and revealed preferences are the only basis for judgement, then no criteria exist whereby 'rational fools' who devote their lives to harmful activities can be distinguished from those not so inclined (Sen, 1977).

Even a consensus arrived at under ideal conditions cannot tell us what human being are really like – for this the anti-essentialism of moral theory in the twentieth century must be rejected, and Nussbaum and Sen explicitly hark back to earlier moral theorists, the young Marx in the case of Sen, thinkers of the ancient world in the case of Nuss-baum. In her writings of the early 1990s, Nussbaum presents a neo-Aristotelian account of 'non-relative' virtues. The 'virtues' are frames of mind which orient one towards characteristic human experiences, and, as Nussbaum puts it (paraphrasing Aristotle):

> Everyone has some attitude, and corresponding behaviour, towards her own death; her bodily appetites and their management; her property and its use; the distribution of social goods; telling the truth; being kind to others; cultivating a sense of play and delight, and so on. No matter where one lives one cannot escape these questions, so long as one is living a human life. (Nussbaum, 1993, p. 245).

On the basis of these characteristic human experiences it is possible to give at least an attenuated account of the circumstances under which the virtues can be practised and human flourishing can occur. There will be many different ways in which human beings can live a human life, but there are limits to the acceptable range of differences. There are some kinds of lives that preclude human flourishing and which ought not to be tolerated, but the claim is that this position relies on an account of what human beings are that is not simply the self-descriptions of one culture writ large. There is, of necessity and delib-erately, a great deal of vagueness here, and, unlike human rights documents which attempt to fix meanings, what is on offer is a lan-guage which can usefully be employed to set the parameters of debate in contexts where a particular cultural practice is being questioned, rather that the basis upon which definitive quasi-legal judgements can be made about such practices. It establishes clearly that to say 'we do things that way here' is not good enough; the defenders of such prac-tices as female genital mutilation in East Africa, or capital punishment in the US, are required to show how, contrary to what appears to be the case, such practices are actually consistent with human flourishing – but the possibility that they can do this, unlikely though it may be in both cases, is not excluded in advance or by definition.

It is, however, striking that the way in which Nussbaum has devel-oped her thought in the last decade has not been in this direction, but towards an increasingly explicit liberal agenda. In works culminating in *Women and Human Development* the virtues are replaced by a far more detailed list of 'Central Human Functional Capabilities', which are said to be established as a cross-cultural, Rawlsian 'overlapping consensus' (*Ethics*, 2000; Nussbaum, 2000). The list remains vague; the very first and most basic functional capability 'being able to live to the end of a human life of normal length' remains what it only can be, the basis for an argument and not a definitive statement – is this capability denied by the practices of capital punishment, or abortion? But, without removing the contestable nature of the position, the additional detail takes us away from the notion that what we have here is an anthropology that does not privilege any particular way of life. Moreover, the way in which the additional detail is arrived at is problematic. Consider, for example, the proposition that the human capability for affiliation involves the 'social bases of self-respect and non-humiliation'; this seems reasonable and the basis for the kind of criticism of particular cultural practices outlined above – but this is then fleshed out by the more question-begging proposition that this requires 'protection against discrimination on the basis of race, sex, sexual orientation, religion, caste, ethnicity, or national origin' (Nussbaum, 2000, p. 79). What begins as a general proposition which sets out quite plausibly the basis for a discussion becomes a specific set of propositions that closes down certain kinds of argument by ruling them out in advance. What begins as something that *everyone* can be invited to give assent to as a preliminary to a discussion, is turned into the expression of a particular view of the world: many potential partners in a dialogue will feel they are being invited to play on someone else's ground – and so are unlikely to take part.

Revealingly, Nussbaum remarks that 'sexual orientation' was not on earlier versions of the list because she believed that there was too little consensus on the item, but has now been added because recent developments in India suggest that this is no longer premature (ibid., footnote, pp. 79–80). One immediate response to this might be that on this basis recent developments in *Africa* suggest it is indeed premature, and Indian thinking alone cannot be the basis for a truly universal list of capabilities – but rather than argue that particular case, it is the wider issue of how the terms of this overlapping consensus are to be determined that is important. This seems to be an empirical issue, but if, for example, gay rights are 'in' because (now) most cultures accept that they should be, we might ask if this is actually the case, and how would we know. Most important, where is the critical edge if the list of capabilities simply follows what is already defined by a consensus? The Rawlsian notion of an 'overlapping consensus' relies on the prior commitment of parties to a notion of 'public reason' and this is what enables the notion to do its work; it is not intended to represent some kind of actual 'real-world' consensus, for the obvious reason that no such consensus exists. But if the existence of a consensus is not determined empirically, what is the equivalent of 'public reason' for Nussbaum? Aristotle relied upon biology to tell him what human flourishing entailed; this is not a move available to Nussbaum, but it is not clear what its contemporary equivalent might be.

This is not intended to undermine the overall importance of *Women and Human Development*. The specific focus on the experiences of women, and, in particular, Nussbaum's very personal and detailed account of the experiences of particular women in India, are very valuable. Nonetheless, even here, there are problems. The focus on India allows Nussbaum to avoid some problems that occur in other societies; the official commitment enshrined in India's Constitution to human rights and non-discrimination, and the existence of the rule of law in that country provides a framework for women's rights in India that simply does not exist in many other parts of Asia – even though these features of Indian life may be at odds sometimes with tendencies existing in Indian civil society (Coomaraswamy, 1994).

In summary, whereas a decade ago it seemed that Nussbaum might be providing a way of breaking open, transcending even, what was becoming an increasingly sterile and repetitive debate between liberal cosmopolitanism and its critics, it is now clear that her work is unconditionally based in the first camp (Connolly, 2000). This is confirmed by the *Boston Review* debate on cosmopolitanism, initiated by her dismissal of Rorty's attempt to show that, properly understood, an education in being an American entails a cosmopolitan education (J. Cohen, 1996). Other polemics, for example against the feminist writer Judith Butler, make it clear that the 'relativists' she opposes are a very broad church indeed, pretty much identical to the liberal multiculturalists attacked by Barry in *Culture and Equality* (Nussbaum, 1999).

In this chapter, cultural diversity has been approached as an issue in international political theory, but this may be somewhat missing the point, avoiding the real agenda. An alternative account might say that universalism is a by-product of globalization, and that anti-universalist positions are a reaction to the latter (Barber, 1996). On this account, the human rights culture is being carried through the world by the same process that has seen the emergence in recent years of a global economy with global corporations and global brands. Putting the matter differently, human rights developed in the West in order to provide ordinary folk with some kind of protection from the power of the over-mighty states that the combination of the Westphalia System and industrial capitalism has created. Now that such states have been exported throughout the world, such protection is required by everyone, everywhere.

There are wider issues involved here. While it would be a mistake to think that globalization has wholly displaced the concerns examined in this and earlier chapters, it would be difficult to deny that the recent changes in global society have changed quite radically the context of international political theory. This is the subject of the next chapter.

11

Post-Westphalian International Political Theory

While early chapters of this book described the evolution of Westphalian international political theory from the early modern origins of the system to the characteristic conceptual formulations of the twentieth-century discipline of International Relations, much of the rest has demonstrated the problems Westphalian theory has increasingly encountered in trying to make sense of contemporary conditions. The notion that individuals as well as states have rights is problematic from a Westphalian perspective, as is the idea that social as well as procedural notions of justice might be appropriate in international relations. Over the last half century, the meaning of sovereignty itself, the core Westphalian concept, has been a subject for contestation. The Westphalian order has not lacked defenders, but, overall, it is difficult to ignore the sense that there is increasingly perceived to be a lack of fit between the 'sovereignty system' and the modern world. Part of the purpose of this book has been to challenge the idea that a clear-cut divide between domestic politics and international relations is possible, but whereas once such a challenge looked like a radical step, it is now becoming a commonplace; only the most crusty of IR theorists now believe in the existence of such a divide. To put these points differently, most of this book has been devoted to examining international political theory in a *partially* Westphalian world. But, while the world of 'nation-states' still conditions a great deal of modern thought, it is increasingly the case that this world does not offer even a partially adequate account of contemporary reality. The pace of change over the last two decades has accelerated to a such a degree that the lack of fit is now such that we are moving into a post-Westphalian world – such, at least, is the claim of theorists of globalization.

The story of globalization has been told by a great number of writers – most recently by David Held and his colleagues (1999 and 2000) and

Jan Aart Scholte (2000), but earlier by *inter alia* Kenichi Ohmae (1990), Peter Dicken (1992), Manuel Castells (1996/7) and Anthony Giddens (1999). Although globalization involves political, social and military changes, the basic argument concerns the global economy, and takes the following form. The Westphalian political order used to make sense because it corresponded to economic realities; the Westphalian state was an economic as well as a political unit. In the nineteenth and early twentieth centuries most economic activity was based within a national context; trade occurred but was conducted by nationally based firms; capital movements took place but largely in the form of portfolio investment; stock exchanges were sensitive to each others' movements but still operated as separate entities – thus it made sense to think of the national economy as the prime global economic actor, and for individuals to look to the nation-state as the provider of economic and military security, or, another, socialist, variant, for the capitalist class to be organized on national lines. Politics within nations was, therefore, different from politics among nations, and Westphalian (international) political theory reflected this difference. Now, however, things are very different. Economies are closely intertwined; multinational corporations (MNCs) control a great deal of trade which is now substantially based on transfers between branches of the same firm; global capital markets have replaced local markets and the capacity of the state to control national economic activity is severely weakened (Strange, 1996).

These economic changes are at the root of the process but, as the literature cited above amply illustrates, a much wider account of the transformation of contemporary society is entailed by the globalization thesis. To a great extent, this transformation takes the form of a process of homogenization. Global firms and global markets are increasingly producing the dominance of global brands and the emergence of global consumption patterns; this process is both productive of and driven by the technological revolution associated with the microchip and the emergence of global media, especially the worldwide dominance of entertainment and infotainment TV channels symbolized by MTV and CNN. Gradually, so it is argued, the distinctive character of particular societies becomes lost as consumers everywhere eat their burgers under the giant M of the McDonalds' arch, and watch MTV or surf the Internet while wearing their Nike trainers. Sociologists of the 'Stanford School' have generalized the argument here, seeing nation-state identities, structures and behaviours as increasingly shaped by a world society, that is, by worldwide cultural and associational processes (Mayer et al., 1997). Manuel Castells, Anthony Giddens and Ulrich Beck, amongst others, have given content to this argument with notions such as the 'information society', the 'third way' and 'risk society' (Castells, 1996/7; Beck, 1999; Giddens, 2000). The possibility that a global civil society might be emerging is widely entertained (Walzer, 1995; Lipschutz, 1996).

This brief summary might give the impression that the globalization thesis is simply about homogenization, which, of course, is not the case. The drive towards homogenization has created its own antibodies – the anti-globalization coalition that has made its presence felt so forcibly at recent meetings of the World Trade Organization and the G7/8 is itself quite obviously the product of globalization, relying as it does on the new technologies – the Internet, mobile and satellite phones and so on – for its organization and creating global slogans and heroes such as the Chiapas leader 'Subcomandante Insurgente Marcos' and the French farmer turned activist José Bové. Benjamin Barber has hypo- thesized that 'McWorld' and 'Jihad' – his, rather inappropriate, term for the traditionalist forces mobilized against globalization, most of which, of course, have nothing to do with Islam – exist in a symbiotic relationship (Barber, 1996). The very technologies that create a world society may also help individuals to preserve their local affiliations. Arjun Appadurai has traced the way in which the meaning of migra- tion has changed in the modern world; cheap air-fares, fax, telex, satel- lite TV and the Internet mean that populations can relocate around the world without losing touch with their home base – Kurds in Germany and Sikhs in Canada and Britain are no longer necessarily cut off from the politics of Kurdistan or 'Khalistan'; indeed, their contribution to this politics may be more intense than that of many who have stayed at home (Appadurai, 1996). In addition to these forces of homogeniza- tion and counter-homogenization, it should also be acknowledged that the global social and economic forces that lie behind globalization create new kinds of global stratification. Nike sweatshirts and trainers may be worn more or less everywhere, but they are mostly manufac- tured in the newly industrializing countries and often in deplorable working conditions. Access to the new technologies is very unevenly distributed in the world – witness the low number of Internet sites in sub-Saharan Africa, where the general unreliability of telephone ser- vices outside of a few major cities makes it difficult for even local elites to go on-line.

As will be apparent, the exact meaning of globalization is con- testable, but it is difficult to contest the idea that something fairly fun- damental has changed in recent years, however difficult it is to give precise content to that 'something'. This and the next, and final, chapter will try to offer, if not precision, then at least some thoughts on what that something might be. In this chapter the focus will be on the puta- tively changing nature of the international, or global, community; as a way into this subject recent changes in international law, and in par- ticular the emergence of the individual as the subject of international criminal law, will be examined. It will be suggested that these changes implicitly rely on the notion that a deeper sense of community is immanent in the changes brought about by globalization, which notion will then be investigated. In chapter 12, more speculatively, the future of the global order will be discussed in the light of the challenge from anti-globalization protesters – is Westphalia now 'Westfailure'? Do we live in a world gone wrong?

Before embarking on this agenda, however, two quite important caveats must be entered. First, the economic dimension of the globalization thesis can be challenged in its own terms. Paul Hirst and Graham Thompson have argued quite convincingly that many of the changes referred to above took place in the nineteenth century rather than the twentieth, and that the statistical evidence on investment and capital-creation suggests that the national economy remains far more central than globalist rhetoric would have it, 'internationalization' rather than 'globalization' being their preferred term for recent shifts, while the thesis that national political action will always be ineffective can be criticized as defeatist and serving the ends of the rich and powerful (Hirst and Thompson, 1999). Of course, substituting 'internationalization' for 'globalization' does nothing to undermine the proposition that the social changes identified above are important, but it is salutary nonetheless to be reminded that sometimes the rhetoric here does get out of hand.

Second, and rather more important, it should be noted that even if the economic side of the globalization thesis is accepted it does not *necessarily* follow that Westphalian political theory is outmoded. It is clear that the latter did not come about because of the conjunction of the nation-state and the national economy; the Westphalian order existed before either national states or national economies existed. The capitalist nation-states that came to dominate world politics in the nineteenth and twentieth centuries operated within the only structures they had available, which were those which had been established two centuries earlier by dynastic states whose economies were neither industrial nor national, and perhaps not capitalist. The Westphalian political structure and Westphalian international political theory pre-dated the capitalist nation-state, and there is no reason in principle why they should not post-date them as well.

A further reason for a degree of scepticism about the more extreme claims on behalf of globalization raises the wider issue of the relationship between changes in the world of 'brute facts' and changes in the normative categories employed by theorists and practitioners to create the moral universe. One version of this relationship has already been encountered in chapter 9 in the form of the argument by critics of John Rawls such as Charles Beitz and Thomas Pogge to the effect that

Rawls's assumption that societies can be treated as bounded and self-contained can be undermined by pointing to the undoubted existence of international interdependence; indeed, a recent critic of *The Law of Peoples*, Allen Buchanan, explicitly accuses Rawls of providing theory for a 'vanishing Westphalian world', thereby linking this interdependence to the globalization argument (Buchanan, 2000). The problem is that there are arguments being made at two levels here which cannot easily be forced on to the same plane, even though they address points which are clearly related. Rawls is concerned with who *ought* to be considered members of a co-operative scheme for purposes of deciding upon the distribution of the proceeds of co-operation. This is not something that can be decided upon on the basis of an appeal to the facts of economic interdependence/globalization, because these facts do not speak for themselves; their normative implications have to be drawn out on the basis of criteria supplied by the theorist. Whether or not a group of individuals constitute a society is not something that can be determined a-theoretically. Certainly some brute facts are unavoidable – a random collection of individuals could not constitute a society – but what kind of relationship between individuals is required and at what level of contact, is not something that can be decided on empirical grounds by some kind of frequency count.

In short, taking these two caveats together, the notion that globalization necessarily changes everything and forces a complete rethink of international political theory – indeed, perhaps its abolition – is taking the argument a step or two beyond what can be justified by an appeal to the facts. The key task, rather, is to produce a more nuanced account of the impact of the changes that have taken place in recent years. The categories of Westphalian political theory most likely will require quite considerable amendment as time goes by, but they are unlikely to be found completely irrelevant.

The individual and international political theory in the twenty-first century

One area where change of a quite dramatic nature has taken place in recent years concerns the status of the individual in international political theory. In principle, of course, the fifty-year-old international human rights regime is itself profoundly anti-Westphalian in so far as it purports to regulate the ways in which states are entitled to treat their own nationals; such regulation is consistent with some pre-Westphalian ideas about natural law and the limits on sovereign power, but, on the face of it, goes against the norms that were allegedly established in the mid-seventeenth century (although, as we have seen, what exactly those norms were is still a matter for debate). In practice, however, the human rights regime has been, until very recently, statist in its origin and modes of operation. It comprises Declarations made by states, Covenants signed and ratified by them and institutions subordinated to them. Only in one case, that of the European Convention on Human Rights, can it be said that effective mechanisms exist for ensuring that states live up to their treaty obligations. Even the limited system of oversight that exists at the global level, in particular the office of the UN Commissioner for Human Rights, was only established with great difficulty, and the current occupant of the post, Mrs Mary Robinson, has been in two minds as to whether or not she could be a more effective campaigner without the notional support provided by the office. In effect, states have, somewhat grudgingly, acknowledged that their citizens have some claim on them to be treated in accordance with universal standards, but then, everywhere except in Europe, they have preserved the right to police themselves in this matter, and to interpret the implications of the documents they have signed.

There are signs that this situation is changing. The Pinochet case in Britain in 1998–2000 is one straw in the wind. Senator, formerly General and then President, Pinochet had become head of state in Chile as a result of a military coup and had, undoubtedly, presided over violations of human rights. He left office in 1990, allowing a civilian government to be elected after coming to an understanding that he would have immunity in Chile for past acts – his appointment as a Chilean senator (for life) conveyed this immunity. In October 1998, while in London for medical treatment, he was arrested and subjected to extradition proceedings; a Spanish magistrate had issued a warrant for his arrest on charges relating to the torturing of Spanish citizens in Chile while Pinochet was head of state. The legal issues surrounding this case were very complex and the detail is not of great interest for this study, but the final outcome is that in early 2000 the Law Lords (Britain's highest court) declared that Pinochet could be extradited. Their reasoning was that, after the adoption of the International Convention against Torture of 1984 by the Criminal Justice Act of 1988, torture became a crime under English law even when committed in another jurisdiction, and, crucially, that the immunity that normally attaches to the head of a state cannot be extended to cover crimes of this nature. Pinochet could be extradited to Spain on the basis of crimes allegedly committed between 1988 and his leaving office in 1990.

In fact, Pinochet was not extradited but deported to Chile on health grounds, to the relief of all three governments involved, in Britain, Chile and, indeed, Spain, where the arrest warrant had been issued without the support of the Spanish government. Nonetheless, and in spite of the restrictive nature of the ruling, the decision of the Law Lords constitutes a quite remarkable challenge to the norms of the Westphalia System. One of the first principles of the latter is the notion of 'sovereign immunity', the principle that individuals who happen to be the head of a particular state, or members of its government, cannot be held personally responsible for the conduct of their office by anyone other than the nationals of the state in question; this is, of course, related to the similar, and even more firmly established, principle of 'diplomatic immunity', which provides diplomats with absolute protection from prosecution for offences allegedly committed in the country to which they are accredited (unless, of course, their immunity is waived by their government). These immunities follow naturally from the assumption that it is *states* themselves who are the subjects and objects of international law, and not those individuals who hold particular offices within the state – on the same basis, international treaties bind states, and not simply the particular governments that have signed and ratified them. States possess legal personality in international law, while, conventionally, individuals do not.

The decision of the Law Lords consciously undermines this principle, arguing that individuals can be held to account for their actions in accordance with international standards, even if these actions were perceived by them to be necessary for the exercise of their official function. No one has suggested that Pinochet presided over torture for reasons of personal animosity; bizarre and unpleasant as it may seem, he and his supporters clearly believed that he was doing the right thing for his country by acting as he did, and the traditional doctrine of sovereign immunity supports his right to make this choice. The Law Lords did not; on their account a head of state has the right to exercise authority but only in accordance with international law, which now forbids torture. On the face of it, this is a real step forward in international human rights law, and it ties in with another recent international legal development, the Rome Statute to create an International Criminal Court (ICC), which was signed in 1998, and will come into force if and when it receives the necessary sixty ratifications, probably sometime in late 2001 or 2002.

Pace the principle of sovereign immunity, there have been in the past ad hoc tribunals at which particular individuals have been required to answer for acts carried out while they have been in government – most notably the post-Second World War tribunals at Nuremberg and Tokyo, where particular office-holders of the defeated Axis powers were tried for crimes against humanity, planning aggressive war and crimes against the laws of war. Valuable though Nuremberg may have been in collecting evidence of Nazi atrocities, it was in no way an impartial tribunal; possible Allied war crimes (such as the saturation bombing of cities) were not investigated, and, given Soviet aggression in conjunction with the Nazis over the Baltic republics and Finland – not to mention the USSR's treatment of its own citizens under Stalinism – the Russian presence amongst the judges inevitably undermined the legitimacy of the exercise. In the 1990s the reaction to the genocide in Rwanda and crimes against humanity in former Yugoslavia was more measured; the Security Council established separate independent tribunals, in Arusha and The Hague respectively, and appointed prosecutors to bring to justice the miscreants. In neither case has a great deal of progress been made, but some, largely symbolic, trials have taken place; most important, Yugoslavia's former President Milosevic is currently (summer 2001) held in The Hague under indictment for offences allegedly committed in Kosovo, and may yet face charges connected with his alleged involvement in war crimes in Bosnia and Croatia earlier in the 1990s. Milosevic was extradited to The Hague following his defeat in elections in Serbia in 2000, and after the exertion of Western financial pressure; his eventual trial will constitute even more of a break with the past than did the Pinochet case.

These ad hoc tribunals set a kind of precedent, and, faced with the possibility of establishing further ad hoc bodies to deal with future conflicts, a number of countries, including, ironically as it turns out, the US, pressed for the alternative strategy of establishing a permanent International Criminal Court (ICC) – hence the conference in Rome in 1998 which produced the Rome Statute. Under the Statute, the ICC will have complementary jurisdiction with national courts, taking up cases only if the latter are unable or unwilling to do so; its remit covers crimes against humanity, genocide and war crimes – the crime of aggression is currently on hold because of the inability of drafters to come up with an acceptable definition, and 'terrorism' is off the agenda for much the same reason. War crimes and crimes against humanity are defined quite widely and, for the first time in such a document, rape in wartime and other gender-based offences are specifically recognized as war crimes. Prosecutions may be initiated by the Prosecutor, or at the initiative of states that have ratified the Statute, or by the Security Council. The Court will have jurisdiction over offences committed by nationals of member states, or where offences by non-nationals are committed on the territory of member states; in the absence of such a 'territorial hook', the Security Council can still refer specific cases to the Court even if non-member states are involved. The permission of the Security Council is *not* needed for a prosecution to take place, but the Council may *suspend* a prosecution by a positive vote – which means that the five permanent members of the SC would have to agree amongst themselves not to proceed; the P5 themselves wished for things to be handled the other way round, with any permanent member being able to prevent a prosecution.

How all this will work out in practice remains to be seen (*American Journal of International Law*, 1999a). The relationship between national jurisdictions and the ICC will only become clear once some precedents have been established as to, for example, what constitutes an unwillingness to prosecute effectively offences allegedly committed by a member-state's own nationals – would, for example, the rather token punishment handed out to Lieutenant Calley by a US court-martial for his role in war crimes committed in Vietnam have been considered evidence of effective procedures were the Court to have retrospective jurisdiction (which it does not)? It is only after Prosecutors have tested similar current cases before the Court that this kind of question will be answerable. Human rights activists have been generally critical of the limits set on the authority of the Court, but from the perspective of Westphalia, the ICC represents a genuine revolution. For some, it constitutes a step too far; at the Rome Conference in 1998, the US was one of half a dozen states that apparently opposed the Statute in an unrecorded vote – others including such unusual American bedfellows as China, Iraq and Libya. Although President Clinton eventually signed the treaty, at the last moment for signatures on 31 December 2000 and as one of the last acts of his presidency, it is highly unlikely that the Bush Administration will present the treaty to the Senate for ratification, or that it would pass if it were to be presented. Clinton's decision to sign was partly designed to embarrass the incoming administration, but mainly to ensure that US State Department lawyers would still be able to be involved in the work of arranging the detailed procedures of the Court. US opposition to the Rome Statute is particularly disturbing because the Clinton Administration had been one of the originators of the idea of a permanent tribunal. It seems that the decision at Rome not to allow the permanent members of the Security Council the right to block the initiation of prosecutions was the deciding factor in changing their mind.

US opposition to the Court is over two issues, one of limited general significance, the other of much greater import. US forces are widely engaged across the world in response to obligations to NATO, other alliances and sometimes even the UN, and there is a genuine and not wholly unrealistic fear of US servicemen being at risk of being brought before an international tribunal as a result of malicious or vexatious prosecutions – it should be said that France has similar reservations and in ratifying the Rome Statute has taken the opportunity the latter offers for a seven-year gap before its terms apply to servicemen stationed abroad; Britain may well take the same step. The Statute actually creates no new crimes, and so US or other service personnel would be liable to prosecution in their national courts for any offence that would attract the attention of the ICC, but in spite of this – and although the idea of, for example, Bill Clinton being hauled up before the ICC to account for his conduct of the Kosovo Campaign is somewhat fanciful – the possibility of perverse prosecutions cannot be ruled out altogether. Opposition to the Statute on these grounds is not wholly silly – although the draft Senate resolution that would end all US military contact with any state that ratifies the Statute is patently absurd and unlikely ever to come to a vote.

The more interesting opposition to the ICC in the US comes from the so-called 'new sovereigntists' – a group of international lawyers who reject the whole trend of post-1945 legal developments (Rivkin and Casey, 2000/2001; Spiro, 2000). Their, very traditional, argument is that the role of international law is to regulate relations between sovereign states, thereby promoting co-existence. The rights and duties of US citizens are set out in the US Constitution and Bill of Rights, and cannot and should not be tampered with by outsiders; these writers recognize that a state's obligations under international law take precedence over domestic legislation, but hold that this general position applies only to those aspects of international law that regulate relations between sovereigns. When international law purports to deal with matters that are, in fact, none of its business, such as, it is said, the rights of individuals, this position does not apply and local jurisdictions are entitled to ignore the obligations such pseudo-law attempts to create. The new sovereigntists are, it should be said, consistent in their arguments, holding that just as it would be wrong for Clinton to face a tribunal over Kosovo, so it was wrong for the US to push for the extradition of Milosevic to face the Yugoslavia Tribunal in The Hague.

It would be easy to dismiss the new sovereigntists as simply providing an ideological justification for superpower irresponsibility, and certainly the US approach to its international legal obligations has often been deplorable in recent years – witness, for example, the failure to ensure consular access to foreign nationals accused of capital crimes. However, it is worth noting that many of the positions advocated by these lawyers and given political force by right-wing senators such as Jesse Helms are very similar to those held by a number of Asian countries which have also refused to sign, much less ratify, the Rome Statute – these countries include authoritarian and quasi-authoritarian regimes such as China, Indonesia and Malaysia, who might be thought of as having their own reasons not to see the spread of the rule of law internationally, but also democratic India. Far from seeing the ICC as an institution that could be used against the US, these countries – rather more plausibly, it has to be said – see it as far more likely to be used against those the West or the US decides are wrongdoers. In other words, this is seen as yet one more example of the West imposing its values on the rest of the world.

The key issue here is whether there exists a sufficient global consensus on basic values to support the extension to the international human rights regime that an ICC would entail. It will be recalled that at the outset of this section it was noted that only in Europe was there an effective enforcement mechanism for human rights; the European Convention on Human Rights is accompanied by a court which has jurisdiction over member states, most of whom have, in any event, enacted the European Convention as domestic legislation. This clearly represents a step away from traditional notions of sovereignty; it was and is possible because the countries are able to draw upon shared commitments. All of the states concerned are modern liberal democracies, at broadly similar levels of socio-economic development with broadly similar procedures for protecting the rights of their citizens; the European Convention acts as a kind of pooling of good practice in this area, and although the decisions of the European Court sometimes irritate particular members, they seldom if ever challenge them on the basics. It must be doubted whether this degree of consensus exists at a global level. Most likely the Rome Statute will reach the sixty ratifications it needs in order to come into force, but on current form they are likely to be drawn overwhelmingly from Europe and Latin America, with very few Asian or African members; whether such a body will have the necessary legitimacy to act as a *global* institution might be doubted, and not simply because of the absence of the only superpower.

Such legitimacy could only come from a wider sense of community than exists at the moment, and the next section will examine the prospects for a transformation of the nature of political community, but before moving on, one final point about recent changes in international law needs to be addressed, namely the relationship between law and the processes of conflict-resolution, or, more generally, between law and international politics. It is often said that after the Pinochet decision the travel plans of former dictators will be much amended; they will be obliged in future to forgo the delights of most European capitals and watering-places (Weller, 1999b). This may be so, but it is also the case that dictators contemplating giving up power on the basis of a negotiated amnesty for past misdeeds may be disinclined to do so. Consider, for example, the transition to majority rule in South Africa; it is clear that, in the end, this took place relatively peacefully because it was understood that there would be no legal sanctions directed against the old regime – the latter would be required to confess past misdeeds to a Truth and Reconciliation Commission but would then receive amnesty. Many people felt that this did not serve the ends of justice, but it is difficult to argue with the political decision taken by the new rulers that the price paid for retribution, however justified, would be too high; the latter would not have been best pleased if this political judgement had been challenged in a British court by, for example, the arrest of former President De Klerk on a visit to London.

In retrospect, so far at least, it can be argued that the Pinochet case has proved to be a positive experience for Chilean democracy, forcing the country to come to terms with its recent past, even though the attempt to put Pinochet on trial there has been abandoned on the grounds of his senility. Still, there is no doubt that the civilian rulers of Chile were genuinely and reasonably concerned that Pinochet's supporters in the army would act unconstitutionally had he been sent for trial in Spain. Moreover, the irony of a Spanish prosecution would have been clear, because Spain is also a liberal democracy with an authoritarian past, and part of the process of successful democratization post-Franco in that country was a tacit agreement that no Franco-era officials should be put on trial for past misdeeds, misdeeds it should be said that, quantitatively and qualitatively, far exceeded those of the Pinochet regime in Chile.

The politics of the Milosevic case are also open to interpretation in a number of ways. As noted above, the Serbian authorities extradited Milosevic to The Hague under considerable Western pressure, political as well as financial, and the medium- to long-run effect of this decision on Serbian politics is uncertain. Two undesirable effects seem possible; on the one hand, Milosevic may come to be seen as a martyr tried and convicted in a Western kangaroo court, or, on the other, the crimes of Serbian nationalists over the last decade may all be attributed to him and a few other scapegoats, allowing ordinary Serbs to forget their own complicity in murder and ethnic cleansing. Had Milosevic been tried by a national court in Belgrade for the same offences, the Serbs might well have found it more difficult to ignore what had been done in their name, and often with their tacit approval. Still, such a local solution would also involve passing up the opportunity to assert the legitimacy of the new international criminal law, and supporters of the decision to try Milosevic in The Hague will argue that the general precedent set thereby is more important than whatever political price is paid in Serbia. As the saying goes, the jury is out on this – the key issue here relates to the degree to which there exists a worldwide consensus on values; the most telling critique of the Pinochet decision, the establishment of the ICC, the trial of Milosevic and the general trend they represent, is that to regard the issues these moves are designed to address as legal, as opposed to political, problems is to presume the existence of a global base for the rule of law which simply does not exist. But perhaps such a base is coming into existence?

Political community transformed?

Community is a word with generally positive connotations, and the 'international community' is a term sometimes employed by publicists, diplomats and careless academics (including, sadly, the present writer on occasion) when they wish to express approval of some collective international action, or, perhaps, to criticize the failure to act. In fact, the term is pretty much meaningless or even misleading – in so far as it translates into anything nowadays it generally stands for something like 'the US and its allies'. It is meaningless or misleading because the positive connotations of the term community are almost entirely associated with particularism – a community is generally thought of as bounded, tied to a particular place and a particular group of people who in some sense form a whole. The idea of an international community implies that the kind of positive qualities associated with such a bounded group could exist as between states, or, even more ambitiously, on a global scale encompassing all people (C. Brown, 1994d). We are used to the idea that nowadays 'imagined communities' have replaced the older face-to-face variety, but most people do not have the imagination to see themselves in communion with the rest of humanity (Anderson, 1983). As noted in earlier chapters, communitarian thinkers from Hegel and Mill to Michael Walzer have set themselves against such a cosmopolitan outlook, arguing that the virtues associated with community – fellow-feeling for one's co-nationals, a willingness to make sacrifices on behalf of the less advantaged – can only be developed in a context where membership is controlled and a system of inclusion and exclusion is in place.

Communitarian thinkers have never denied the existence of ties that cross national boundaries; Walzer, for example, envisages himself as a member of more than one 'tribe' – an American, a Jew, and easterner, an intellectual, a professor – but he also makes the point that such a complex identity is the product of security; when identities are threatened the tendency is to become radically parochial (Walzer, 1994, p. 200). To put the matter differently, from his perspective the key identity we all possess, the basis for community in the full sense of the term, is political and bounded, something that distinguishes 'us' from 'them', even though, in quiet times, we may share much with some of them that we do not with some of us. But what is it about 'us' that is really distinctive and brings about this effect? Two related answers to this question come to mind. First, 'we' in the bounded community are joined together in so many different ways and at so many different levels. I may have a great deal in common with a fellow political scientist in New Delhi or Berlin or wherever, but with my fellow academics in Britain, political scientists or otherwise, I have additionally in common our shared handicap of one of the most oppressive state educational bureaucracies in the world; with all my fellow-citizens I share the frustrating experience of coping with the worst transport system and health service in Europe, we watch at least some of the same TV programmes, read some of the same newspapers and so on – most of all we share the same familiarities with the unwritten rules of everyday life, the ways of going on that make up so much of what we are and do. Occasionally, particular individuals may feel more or less at home in more than one place, but this has not been the common experience over the last few centuries.

Perhaps more important, and developing from this high level of interconnectedness, one of the things that has been distinctive about 'us' in the past has been at least the possibility that we might share a political project. We may live in 'communities of fate' thrown together by accident – and given the arbitrariness of borders all communities were once accidents in this sense, however long established they may be – but we have had the possibility of becoming a 'people', of forming ourselves in some distinctive way in response to values we believe ourselves to share. No modern political communities have been democratic in *origin*, but it is only within bounded political communities that democracy has been possible, at least partly because democratic forms of rule require of individuals that they have a degree of trust in one anothers' basic willingness to abide by convention, and this level of trust seems to be associated with the kind of familiarity with the unwritten rules of everyday life referred to above. In short, it is no accident that both in its origins in the early nineteenth century, and via contemporary writers such as David Miller, nationalism is associated with democratic self-rule (Miller, 1995), although it is also no accident that this association can easily turn sour, and democratic mobilization on national lines can create a movement such as the Nazis.

This last point emphasizes that the account of the value of community given above is by no means unchallenged in the literature, but, setting this aside, the issue under discussion here is whether, under contemporary conditions and given all the factors summarized by the term globalization, the conventional case for bounded communities still stands, even in its own terms. In the first place, although it is certainly still the case that in most parts of the world, for most people, parochial ties are closer than those to the wider world, this is no longer quite the obvious proposition it once was. Only a relatively small number of international businessmen, bureaucrats and media personalities of one kind or another can genuinely be described as part of a global cosmopolitan elite, but most of the citizens of the advanced industrial world, in one way or another, have connections across borders that exceed in number and complexity anything to be found amongst ordinary people in the past. The existence of virtual communities created by high-speed transportation links and the Internet is genuinely unprecedented. Transnational pressure groups have proliferated in recent years, and although a 'global civil society' is still in embryo, the level of transactions that cross national borders makes a purely parochial account of community less than persuasive (Hall, 1995; Lipschutz, 1996; C. Brown, 2000c).

More important, the intensity of these links, and, more generally, the growth of the global economy, has made it more difficult to imagine that the bounded community of fate can still develop a distinctive democratic political project. Democracy is about a community ruling itself, determining its common arrangements, setting itself goals, and these are only meaningful activities if it can be assumed that communities actually have the capacity to make decisions on the key issues that affect them. Such an assumption has always been a little optimistic, but under current circumstances it has to be seen as highly implausible. Contrary to the position of hyper-globalists like Kenichi Ohmae, communities certainly retain some capacity for self-determination, but how much is debatable (Ohmae, 1990). It could well be argued that while many countries do possess the ability to manage the impact of globalization, even the largest and most powerful among them no longer have the quite the kind of capacity for self-government that was routinely available to small communities even a half-century ago.

If this account of the impact of recent changes is accepted, then the argument can be taken in a number of different directions. David Held and his colleagues have argued for the democratization of international relations (Held, 1995; Archibugi and Held, 1995; Archibugi, Held and Köhler, 1998). Their position is that the automatic association that links the nation-state and democracy must be broken. Since the power to change things no longer exists at the national level, the impulse to self-rule must be redirected towards global institutions. The UN and other inter-state bodies are, at the moment, in no sense democratic. Some incorporate a 'one state one vote' rule, which, given inequalities of population, can only be justified in terms of an account of international society in which, to quote again Vattel, a dwarf is as much a man as a giant. In others, such as the UN Security Council and key economic agencies such as the IMF and the World Bank, the most powerful states have their power actually amplified by institutional measures such as weighted voting or the granting of 'veto' power. On Held's account, the need is for a long-term programme of political reform in which these institutions are gradually democratized, perhaps initially by accompanying statist organization with directly elected people's assemblies. And the developments in international law towards recognizing the responsibilities of individuals, noted in the previous section, are part of this programme of reform.

Held and his colleagues represent an old, well-established line of utopian international thought – and that judgement is not intended to be dismissive. One of the features of the dominance of realism in the decades after 1945 was to delegitimize attempts to think about international institutional reform; ventures such as Clark and Sohn's proposed redrawing of the UN Charter were dismissed as hopelessly unrealistic (Clark and Sohn, 1966). What this dismissal ignores is the extent to which what is implausible in one period can become obvious common sense in another. To take an example from a cognate discussion, those who argue that it is inconceivable that the world will ever agree to transfer serious amounts of wealth from the rich to the poor globally should ask themselves whether a century ago it would have been seen as remotely plausible that all of the advanced industrial societies in the world would redistribute *internally* between 35 and 55 per cent of their national product. On the other hand, it does seem that at the moment the conditions for global democracy simply are not present. There is no global *demos* in so far as it hardly seems conceivable that the 300 million North Americans and 400 million Europeans would consent to be governed by a rule under which they could be outvoted by either the 1,200 million Chinese, or the 1,000 million Indians – and the same is equally true for either of the latter groups.

Such consent will only be given, if at all, if individuals are confident that national groupings will *not* vote as blocs, and this stage clearly has not yet been reached. After all, the peoples of the European Union, who share a similar cultural heritage and roughly comparable standards of living, are not yet prepared to elect directly a European executive – and the direct elections for the European Parliament that do take place are almost always dominated by national concerns, turning into a referendum on the national governments of each member-state. This suggests that any movement towards global democracy is likely to be painfully slow – but this is not a reason for not taking the first steps, and in response to the above argument, David Held and his colleagues will quite reasonably point out that to wait for the conditions for global democracy to be established before attempting to democratize the global order is to adopt a policy of indefinite deferral. The more quasi-democratic institutions that can be brought into existence at the global level the more likely it is that the context for a functioning global democracy will emerge, although most probably at a glacially slow pace.

In any event, this does not exhaust the possibilities for the transformation of political community. Andrew Linklater's recent work suggests that it may be possible to think about the notion of political community in new ways, appropriate to an age of globalization. Linklater's project is ambitious, and follows through on themes identified in earlier works. *Men and Citizens in the Theory of International Relations* (1981/1990) is a perceptive historical account of the conflict in international thought between the obligations we owe to each other as fellow citizens, and the obligations we owe as members of humanity as a whole. The final sections of the book present a conflict between the statism and stress on community of Hegel and the moral universalism of both Kant and Marx; the latter two are given the best of the argument, but the merits of the former are not wholly discounted – Linklater's adherence to a form of Frankfurt School critical theory ensures that all three masters of thought are given some weight, but also that a Kantian reading of Marx (or perhaps a Marxian reading of Kant) is privileged. His second book, *Beyond Realism and Marxism: Critical Theory and International Relations* (1990), extends the conclusion of *Men and Citizens* into a consideration of global class relations seen from a 'dependency' viewpoint; the stance adopted is rather further 'beyond' realism than it is beyond Marxism, but, as with the earlier volume, there is no sense in which a wholehearted Marxian universalism is allowed to take over. The tension between the legacies of Hegel, Kant and Marx remains.

In *The Transformation of Political Community* (1998) these tensions are at least partially resolved. The universalism of Kant remains dominant, now explicitly funnelled via the discourse ethics and developmental moral psychology of Jürgen Habermas. Political community is seen as resting upon a system of inclusion and exclusion, because without some such system political life is impossible – Linklater is sensitive here to the case presented above to the effect that democratic self-rule is only possible within communities that are, in some sense, bounded – but a moral obligation to make the community as inclusive as possible is posited, and, to similar effect, it is argued that the distinction between the obligations owed to insiders and those owed to outsiders should be as limited as possible. Rather than political community being seen as synonymous with restrictive, enclosed, morally self-sufficient and self-satisfied bounded groups, the notion needs to be transformed into an outward-looking, generous conception of political life, no longer seen as incompatible with a wider cosmopolitan universal morality.

Realist writers will naturally regard this as 'fantasy' politics, in the words of one dyspeptic commentator, but Linklater would reject the charge of utopianism (Schweller, 1999). He believes the transformation of political community to be immanent in current trends; globalization is not leaving things as they were – whether they will move in the direction he wishes is, presumably, going to be partly a function of political action, but the notion of moral development he adheres to gives him some reason to be optimistic that globalization will not lead to reactionary outcomes. More generally, discourse ethics plays an important role in Linklater's account of the transformation – it is the basis for his answer to the kind of points about cultural diversity and global governance made above and in the previous chapter. On his account, the terms of inclusion and exclusion upon which political communities ought to be based, and which determine their relations one with another, are to be set by open, uncontrolled, discourse in which all voices can be heard and none will be privileged – critics who argue that universal values of the kind Linklater espouses incorporate privileges for an essentially Western (and masculine) perspective are reassured than no such privilege exists in this ethical framework.

It is fair to say that such critics are unlikely to be satisfied by this answer. Although the discourse itself may not privilege a particular ethical point of view, the idea that ethical principles are to be determined by dialogue and unforced consensus cannot be divorced from its origins in a specifically Western rejection of naturalistic accounts of moral obligation. Those who believe, for example, that appropriate ethical principles can be determined by reference to the will of God are unlikely to appreciate being told that these principles need to be validated by discourse – on the other hand, Linklater might reply, in so far as the principles God allegedly sets down involve harm being visited upon non-believers, the latter are entitled to expect them to be validated by some non-circular argument. Equally unsatisfied will be those who do not see the role of ethics as determining general principles, whether or not those principles are validated in discourse. Adherents to a Levinasian ethics of encounter – in international political theory David Campbell is, perhaps, the most notable example – will be suspicious of the Kantian insistence that ethical reasoning implies the creation of moral rules (Campbell, 1993 and 1998).

The projects of global democracy and political transformation promoted by Held and Linklater have certain similarities; each presents compelling arguments why the older political and moral justifications for the state are no longer valid, and each identifies globalization as both at the root of the changes that are made necessary and as pushing those changes in a particular direction. Neither, however, provides entirely compelling reasons to believe that a sufficient global consensus on the nature of political transformation either exists now, or is likely to emerge in the near future. More to the point, it could well be argued that in each case energies are being directed towards long-term solutions to problems that will only continue to exist if short-term problems are successfully addressed. Thus, for example, it is certainly the case that the peoples of sub-Saharan Africa would benefit from a democratic global order – but unless the immediate problems of civil war in

Central Africa are successfully addressed the possibility that a great many of them will live to collect this benefit is remote. Of course, both objectives – just global institutions and effective local governments – should be pursued and there is no reason in principle to think that they are in any way incompatible, but at the moment rather more effort seems to be going into the former than the latter.

There is a wider problem here. It is easy enough to see that the existing international order is, in many important respects, unsatisfactory, than it is to see how it might actually change – and, for this reason, it is, *a fortiori*, much easier to show that the present international order is lacking in legitimacy than it is to get a handle on how actually to create the kind of world order that would be legitimate. It is a commonplace that most of the critics of globalization are better at demonstrating its evils than they are at showing how the good things associated with global change – and there are such good things – could be preserved without these evils. The next, and final, chapter examines this dilemma.

12

A World Gone Wrong?

'Strange things are happening like never before,' sang Bob Dylan, quoting the Mississippi Sheiks, in the title track of his 1993 album *World Gone Wrong*. The leaders of the world's most powerful countries who gathered at the G8 Summit in Genoa in July 2001 could only agree as they met behind a steel security wall, and retired at nights to the secure base of an ocean liner moored in the harbour, while a hard core of anarchists battled the Italian police in the streets, and some tens of thousands of peaceful demonstrators tried to make themselves heard over the din. The disturbances at Genoa followed those in Gothenburg at the US-EU Summit in May 2001; both reflected a pattern set by the Battle for Seattle at the WTO's meeting in November 1999, and what have become a series of annual events at the Davos economic summits, IMF and World Bank AGMs and on May Day. Whenever the symbolic representatives of the current world order meet nowadays they can expect to be greeted by large-scale demonstrations and street violence. In the past, hosting the annual G8 Summit was regarded by the city concerned as an opportunity for positive coverage by the world's media – now things have changed to the point where the Canadian government intends to hold the 2002 Summit in an inaccessible ski-resort in the Canadian Rockies, to the predictable chagrin of the local inhabitants. The next WTO ministerial meeting will be held in Qatar in November 2001, which should cramp the style of demonstrators somewhat.

There is, of course, nothing particularly strange about the idea of demonstrations at international get-togethers, but there are several features of the current crop that are unusual. The sheer scale of the protests is pretty much unprecedented; leaving aside the street-fighting element, the number of organizations that are involved in the protests, one way or another, is large enough, but what is equally striking is the range of interests and positions represented – environmental groups, trade unions, international aid agencies, nationalist French farmers, social democrats, socialists and neo-communists. Moreover, the level of tacit popular support for the aims of the demonstrators seems quite high; although, in the aftermath of the Genoa Summit, world leaders – Britain's Tony Blair to the fore – attempted to focus outrage on the violent demonstrators, most media coverage, even from normally right-of-centre newspapers, actually concentrated on the violence of the *Carabinieri*. Equally unprecedented is the fact that the demonstrators are rejecting the current world order as a totality. Clearly there are specific policies to which the demonstrators take particular exception – most obviously, the US Administration's commitment to strategic missile defence and its rejection of the Kyoto Accords on global warming – and, in this respect, there are points of contact with past examples of mass mobilization, such as the campaigns for nuclear disarmament in the 1950s and 1980s, but the general level of disaffection seems to go far beyond such specifics.

In short, there is today a widespread sense that we live in a world gone wrong, and the aim in this final chapter is to investigate this mood, to ask why so many people appear to have come to this conclusion and explore some of the ways in which the world might change. There is, as yet, very little in the way of academic literature on this subject; the field is dominated by the very popular genre of anti-globalization jeremiads of which even the best, such as George Monbiot's *Captive State*, Thomas Frank's *One Market Under God*, Noreena Hertz's *The Silent Takeover*, Naomi Klein's *No Logo*, make no pretence of objectivity, no attempt to see another point of view (Monbiot, 2000; Frank, 2001; Hertz, 2001; Klein, 2001). Because of the paucity of scholarly comment, this chapter will be rather less literature-based, rather more personal, polemical even, than its predecessors; the reader can take some comfort from the fact that it is one of the shortest chapters in the book. Still – old habits die hard – to start this discussion it may be helpful to examine one piece of academic writing that does do justice to the scale of the crisis faced by the current order.

Westfailure?

Can the existing international order cope with the stresses and strains induced by globalization without some kind of transformation? If not, it could well be argued that, whatever transitional problems remain, the Westphalia System has run its course, and is now unambiguously an obstacle to the realization of a just and functioning world. Such is the argument that Susan Strange presented in a posthumously published article with a punning title, 'The Westfailure System' (Strange, 1999). Strange's argument is worth examining in its own terms, but it is also interesting because of its author – Strange was a, if not 'the', leading figure in British IR for a generation, a realist, admittedly rather unorthodox, who was resolutely opposed to normative theory, or indeed most other kinds of theory; the fact that, at the end of her life, she could draw such radical conclusions about the legitimacy of the system is, in itself, telling (C. Brown, 1999c).

It should be said at the outset that while she had little sympathy for what she regarded as the 'globaloney' of globalization theory, she was convinced that the world had changed of late (Strange, 1994 and 1998). Strange was first and foremost an international political economist, and her understanding of the Westphalia System was that it grew up with the sovereign state and the market economy in symbiosis. The sovereign state provided the context for capitalism, while capitalism provided successful sovereign states with the wherewithal to prosper. Her general point, a commonplace of the literature more generally, is that the market economy has now extended itself in the world to the point where this symbiotic relationship has been broken. The territorial sovereign state is no longer capable of performing the role it once did. There are three particular points where this incapacity is most striking and damaging to human welfare.

First, a particular concern of Strange throughout her life, the global financial system is now beyond the control of any government and of the institutions that governments have created to attempt monetary management. Strange sees the creation and regulation of credit as the central international economic task. In the last resort, trade will look after itself – the giant corporations which dominate global production have an interest in world trade, and the efforts of such bodies as the WTO to regulate and control trade are of secondary importance to the motivations of these companies, who are well able to look after their own interests – but international monetary relations require supervision that a system of territorially based sovereign states can no longer supply. The destruction of Barings Bank in 1995 and the Asian collapse of 1997 are simply straws in the wind, indicators of what may be to come. On her account – and contrary to those for whom capitalism itself is the problem, who would welcome crisis on the basis that the worse the state of the world economy, the better the prospects for revolution – the economic collapse that a full-scale global financial crisis would create would be generally harmful to everyone's welfare; the potential inability of the system to manage and regulate the creation of credit means that, even in its own terms, it faces failure. However, the other two areas of 'Westfailure' she identifies are more obviously and directly disastrous.

The inability of a system of sovereign states to cope with the consequences of environmental degradation is the second such failure.
Global economic growth has taken place without reference to environmental consequences such as global warming, ozone layer depletion
and the loss of irreplaceable scarce resources, and the international
system has proved unable to prevent the situation from getting worse
in many areas, much less actually reverse these harmful consequences.
The reason for this inability is clear: the system of sovereign states
allows, even encourages, individual states to act selfishly. It will take a
collective effort to reverse environmental degradation, but the worst
polluters will have to make the biggest effort, and the present system
allows them to dodge their responsibilities; the effective impossibility
of sanctioning the most powerful countries – who are also the biggest
polluters – means that steps to avoid catastrophe rely upon the good
will of those states and their willingness to adopt an enlightened, long-
term definition of their self-interest. The environmental politics of the
last few years makes it clear that this cannot be relied upon. Moreover,
those poorer states which are not yet polluting at the level of the US,
Japan and Western Europe because of their poverty have no incentive
to adopt clean but expensive technology unless a collective effort is
made to compensate them for their restraint, and, again, this is not
something that can be expected to happen under the present system.

Even more directly contrary to general human welfare, third, Strange
points to a double failure of humanitarianism; on the one hand, the
present economic order works to increase global inequality, with the
least advantaged left ever further behind to face a future of malnutrition, poverty and, probably, increasingly violent civil strife, while on the
other, inequalities within 'successful' states grow worse, as the possibility that domestic welfare states can protect their peoples from the
restructurings forced on them by global capitalism recedes. Whatever
possibility there might once have been that the state could act as an
agent for social justice is being undermined by the logic of an economic
system that is out of human control and serving no general interest. The
only true beneficiaries of the present system are a transnational business
elite who run the giant corporations that provide the driving force
behind the hegemony of neo-liberalism (Van der Pijl, 1998).

This is a powerful indictment of the Westphalian order, and from a
writer who could not be accused of promoting an unrealistic, utopian
vision of the world. Part of the force of the indictment comes precisely
from the fact that no easy solution to these ills is offered, indeed, no
solution at all is on offer. If accepted as valid, Strange's indictment
addresses directly the central question posed by this book, and the
three key terms embedded in its title. As has been apparent since the
beginning of this work, its central question is whether 'sovereignty',

'rights' and 'justice' are notions that can be reconciled one with another, and, if so, on what terms. It has frequently been argued that reconciliation is not possible – that the rights of states are in direct contradiction to the rights of individuals, and that global social justice is not achievable in a world of sovereign states. But, powerful arguments have also been presented against this cosmopolitan viewpoint; it has been argued that the rights of individuals can only be guaranteed if the rights of political communities are respected, and that amongst the rights of communities is the right to be different, that the system of sovereign states prevents the emergence of an unhealthy destruction of cultural diversity.

It may be the case that the impact of globalization is now deciding this debate, not necessarily by coming down conclusively on one side but by rendering its terms irrelevant (Linklater, 1999). Cosmopolitans and communitarians were to be found on both sides of the security cordon at Seattle and Genoa; who could be more cosmopolitan than Mike Moore, the New Zealander who currently heads the WTO, or less cosmopolitan than José Bové, the French anti-globalization campaigner? Questions central to the old debate such as the relationship between our obligations to fellow citizens and those to a wider humanity begin to look secondary in the face of the difficulty in identifying *any* kind of source of moral agency in a world increasingly dominated by impersonal forces. Part of the irrationalism of the anti-globalization (actually anti-global capitalism) campaigners is a reflection of this sense of impotence – to 'oppose globalization' by trashing the local branch of Starbucks is tantamount to acknowledging that there is no effective action that can be taken to oppose globalization. However, the problem here is not simply one of agency, tactics or even strategy; the very goals of Strange's anti-Westfailure politics and the anti-globalization movement more generally are unclear.

What is to be done?

Once upon a time, those who opposed the capitalist world order had a clear sense of where they wanted to go. Marxists – and, for that matter, socialists more generally – knew that they wanted to replace capitalism with an economic system that was not based on the profit motive or on market forces. The ultimate goal of those who explicitly identified with Marx and Lenin was 'communism', a system where scarcity had been abolished and which would be reached via 'socialism', a fully planned industrial economy. Western social democrats focused on the establishment of a planned, mixed economy under which those capitalists who remained in business would be obliged to co-ordinate their activities under the auspices of some kind of democratically established and controlled planning body – in any event, public utilities and major industrial concerns would be under public ownership, and their decisions as to what to produce would be taken in the general interest. Both Marxists and social democrats generally favoured industrial society. Building on the paeans of praise for the world-transforming activities of the bourgeoisie that are to be found in the *Communist Manifesto*, communists anticipated the abolition of scarcity which would eventually follow once the processes of industrialization were allowed to develop free from the logic of capitalist accumulation. More prosaically, Western social democrats wished to deliver to their working-class constituencies the kinds of consumer goods that the rich took for granted and that could only be made available via mass production.

Two features of this thumbnail sketch are striking – how powerful these ideas were a generation or two ago, and how antediluvian they seem today. Of course, there are still Marxist groups around, and 'real' socialist parties abound, but the action has moved elsewhere. Whatever sympathy there might be for the remaining communist countries – North Korea, Cuba – virtually no one sees them as models for the rest of the world. Those democratic socialist parties in Europe that have survived and prospered under current conditions have largely done so by dropping virtually all of the features that would have identified them as socialist a generation ago, preferring 'third way' politics and electoral success to ideologically pure oblivion (Giddens, 2000). More to the point, few of the diverse ideologies of the campaigners against global capital draw upon the revolutionary traditions of the last two centuries. 'Subcomandante Insurgente Marcos', the leader of the Chiapas rebellion in Mexico, may have ideological roots that go back to Mao, Che Guevara and the various theories of 'people's war' of the 1960s, but it appears that the mobilization he has achieved is largely based on ethnic and traditional factors (Harvey, 1998; Marcos et al., 2001). Environmentalists can find little in the Marxist/socialist tradition to support their concerns, while trade unionists are obliged to sanitize their past in order to make contact with their new friends in the anti-globalization movement – the best example of this new consciousness being the demonstration by US steel workers at the WTO in 1999, which involved dumping imported steel into Seattle harbour for the benefit of the TV cameras; in order to preserve their environmentalist credentials, they were then obliged to undump the steel and dispose of it elsewhere.

If not an old-style revolution, then what? Different groups have their own models of the future which only rarely have any degree of ideological coherence. Labour unions are usually simply protectionist – which is one of the reasons why the governments of the newly industrializing countries (NICs) take such a jaundiced view of the antiglobalization campaigns; these governments are equally suspicious of well-meaning campaigns directed against sweatshops and child labour in the 'South'. Abolish child labour without making alternative provision for the children involved and all that will be achieved is the lowering of the competitiveness of the NICs; force Nike's subcontractors to pay North American wages in the Philippines or Vietnam and the sweatshops will indeed close, because investment in those countries will cease to be profitable. About the only anti-globalization group that does have a clear vision of the future are the 'deep green' environmentalists – but since this vision involves a dramatically reduced world population to allow the achievement of self-sufficiency and ecological balance via traditional agricultural methods, it tends not to be widely circulated outside of the websites and journals of the movement. There are, of course, consistent anti-capitalists in the anti-globalization movement, including the various anarchist groups who attend meetings such as the Genoa Summit in home-made body armour with the clear intention of taking on the police and the British 'wombles' who, in similar attire, attempt to loot and pillage. But, as these groups illustrate, there are ways of being anti-capitalist that are, in no sense, progressive – by their violent tactics these rioters demonstrate a closer affinity with the (equally anti-capitalist) fascist movements of contemporary Europe such as the British National Party or the French National Front than with any 'left' movement.

More representative of the general lack of ideology of the antiglobalization coalition is the slogan painted on the lead banner at one of the major demonstrations in London on May Day 2001 – 'Replace Capitalism with Something Nicer'. One profoundly hopes that this was actually meant to be funny, but, intentionally or not, it provides quite a good summary of much of the popular anti-globalization literature. Campaigners such as Naomi Klein and Noreena Hertz condemn the dominance of global brands, and the undemocratic influence of giant firms but without providing any convincing picture of how, in the long run, this influence could be diminished. Their remedies tend to focus on effective anti-monopoly legislation to break up the corporate giants and the establishment of moves towards higher levels of local self-government and trade union rights in the workplace, along with the kind of international redistribution of income and wealth advocated by writers such as Brian Barry and Thomas Pogge, and discussed earlier in this book – or, to put it differently, they support the idealized global social democracy envisaged by the *Brandt Report* at the end of the 1970s. There are practical problems here – is it actually likely that Western workers will voluntarily open up markets for Southern competitors? Can it really be envisaged that Western tax-payers will be prepared to authorize the kind of transfers of wealth that would replace the profit-oriented investments in the NICs of today's giant corporations? But more fundamental is the lack of attention to the dynamics of capitalism. The kind of locally restricted capitalism envisaged by these campaigners seems more or less guaranteed to break out of the bounds imposed upon it as soon as it can.

The French campaigners, José Bové, François Dufour and Anna de Casparis, in a similar general work, maintain that *The World is Not For Sale* (Bové et al., 2001). Bové, a French farmer who came to prominence as a result of his campaign against McDonald's in France, delivers a rhetorically powerful attack on the assumption that money is the only thing that matters, defending the importance of the preservation of local communities seen as at risk – as by Klein and Hertz – from giant corporations such as 'McDo's'. But – again as with Klein and Hertz – the French writers do not envisage an end to capitalism as such, merely the control of its global representatives. Instead, local French capitalists and socially responsible French farmers are seen as the antidote to excessive greed, not a wholly convincing vision of a better future.

As with Strange's 'Westfailure' article, these books succeed because they appear to diagnose an ill, rather than because of any positive position they advocate. There clearly is today a widespread popular sense that the 'runaway world' identified by Anthony Giddens is undermining things that are generally valued, such as a sense of community and a sense of personal security, and that many features of the contemporary world economy are manifestly unjust (Giddens, 1999). Pinning these evils on giant corporations seems to make a lot of sense, and the fact that these authors have no remedy for the disease they diagnose can in turn simply be interpreted as further evidence of the power of these corporations. In a way this is reassuring. Nothing is going to change, so it doesn't really matter that most of the readers of *No Logo* continue to buy their DKNY jeans and Nike trainers. After all, what difference can it make?

What has gone wrong here? The key feature of much of the anti-globalization literature is that it is backward-looking, apparently intent on creating a better yesterday, a sanitized version of the past in which socially responsible organic farmers, outward-looking owners of corner-shops and friendly local pubs worked together to provide the people with wholesome food and harmless entertainment – as opposed to the cheap meat and unnecessarily wide range of cheeses available in the modern supermarket, or the tawdry entertainment provided by the BBC, Channel 4, MTV and so on. The general public may be cynical about television and worried about food scares, but they are unwilling to buy into this utopia, even as they acknowledge the strength of the critique of the present upon which it is based. Perhaps what is required is a forward-looking critique of globalization – an account of the ills of the present that finds within those ills the basis for a better world, but a better world going forward not back. There are some indications that such a critique is emerging both from left-of-centre politicians – see, for example, the defence of the WTO and the G8 launched by Clare Short, the Labour Government's left-leaning International Development Minister – and from writers previously located much further to the left, such as Antonio Negri (Hardt and Negri, 2000).

In defence of globalization and some aspects of global capitalism

Any morally serious defence of globalization has to be addressed primarily to the issues of rights and justice that run through this book, that is, to the inequalities that exist in the current system – but before approaching this task a few words on some topics that are not of great moral significance but that are, nonetheless, important to the lives of the majority of ordinary people may be appropriate. The key point, hinted at above, is that a great many of the changes associated with the growing strength of global capitalism have been enormously positive for the majority of the citizens of the advanced industrial world. Even not very good supermarkets generally extend the range of goods available to lower-income groups by comparison with the council estate-based general stores they have replaced. Franchises such as McDonald's and Burger King represent an advance – certainly in hygiene and probably nutritionally – on some of the older cafes they have driven out of business in Britain, and the fact that it is now easy to buy a good cup of coffee in British cities is because of the spread of chains such as Starbucks and Coffee Republic, although, admittedly, this point may be less applicable to countries with a better-developed food culture such as France. Satellite and cable TV provides more and better mass entertainment than has been generally available in the past – and the fact that most of this entertainment is not based on high culture is hardly surprising: popular entertainment rarely, if ever, has been. The middle classes may regard package holidays in Spain with disdain, but at least the weather is usually better than Margate or Blackpool. The motor car provides ordinary people with mobility that even their immediate forefathers could not have dreamed of; the near universal spread of refrigerators and washing machines has cut out the daily drudge of shopping for perishables and washing factory-stained clothes by hand. All of these changes are the product of global capitalism, and all come with associated down-sides, but only the children of privilege – whose mothers were spared the drudgery of washing and shopping, whose parents could afford the time to have 'proper' holidays and had the cash to ensure access to high culture and the education to appreciate it – could deny that they have made things better for ordinary people.

There are also genuine issues of choice involved here. French intellectuals may deplore the fact that many of their fellow countrymen and women would rather see an American blockbuster than the latest locally produced movie but, on the assumption that they are not actually herded into the cinema by US Marines, is it actually anyone else's business how they choose to spend their leisure time? Can it really be the duty of the French state to exclude the American films that their own citizens want to see on the grounds that they are not good for them? If ordinary people wish to spend their spare cash on branded clothes, even when the latter are no different from generic items save in price, is it really Naomi Klein's business to tell them not to? Perhaps Klein would have been happier in the days of my childhood in 1950s Britain when there were far fewer logos but it was immediately obvious from the clothes they wore what class people came from, and only the middle classes and their betters were expected to be interested in fashion – the hostility of the middle classes then to 'teddy boys' was largely about telling these working-class kids not to aspire to a dress sense.

Of course, these are side-issues, and not terribly important in the wider scheme of things – most people in the world today, including many within the advanced industrial world, do not have any disposable income to speak of – but even so it is worth registering a protest against the puritanism of many in the anti-globalization movement, and, in particular, against their, perhaps unconscious, class bias against the pleasures of ordinary people. Still, the key issue is not the politics of the wearing of Calvin Klein jeans, but rather the international political economy of leisure wear in general, where it is made, by whom and for what wages. Can the contemporary, neo-liberal, international economy, which distributes the good things of life so unevenly, be defended? This is an uncomplicated question that invites an unqualified 'no', so perhaps it should be rephrased to allow for a more nuanced position – is the current world economy reformable so that it could deliver a more just world? Or are there practical alternatives to current arrangements that would deliver higher levels of social justice? Here the answers are indeed less clear-cut.

The first thing that has to be said is that it is already the case that the neo-liberal 'Washington Consensus' that governed IMF conditionality and World Bank loans in the early 1990s, and required of poor countries that they prioritize low inflation, end price controls, cut government spending and open themselves to the world economy, is widely regarded as having failed even within the community of IMF/World Bank/US Treasury officials who created it in the first place. It is now generally recognized that there have been very few 'success stories' for the Washington Consensus and plenty of examples of increased suffering for ordinary people, when cuts in government spending were usually targeted on the poor, and the ending of price controls on basic foodstuffs added to the misery. Figures such as Joseph Stiglitz, until 1999 Chief Economist at the World Bank, and Ravi Kanbur, until his resignation in 2000 the Editor-to-be of the *World Development Report 2000*, have acknowledged that this is so and moved towards developing a post-Washington Consensus (Stiglitz, 1998). Such a new consensus is, of course, unlikely to satisfy the critics of globalization, but it does indicate a greater degree of flexibility than the IMF and World Bank are usually credited with. Even so, the reforms will not get to the heart of the matter – it is not so much the details of the policies advocated by the Washington institutions that the protestors object to, but rather the assumptions that underlie these policies. What are these assumptions, and can they actually be defended?

The first premise of neo-liberalism is that there is no substitute for the market economy. Liberals have, of course, always believed this, but the collapse of communism in the 1980s has given this position wider credibility; if there is one clear lesson to be learnt from the Soviet experiment it is that once the early stages of industrialization have been gone through, the command economy cannot be made to work – and even at the early stages, five-year plans and the like require unacceptable levels of state coercion. The range of variables which need to be kept in play for a modern complex planned economy to work is simply too large to be modelled even using the most advanced computers – and this is so even without taking into consideration issues such as consumer choice (Nove, 1983 and 1991). Different kinds of market economy are available, but some kind of market is a necessity; since the emergence of industrial society, the most persistent opponents of liberal capitalism from left and right have argued that it is both possible and desirable to replace the impersonal forces of the market by conscious human control – they were wrong, and this error has enormous significance for the evolution of human society and the prospects for revolution. Richard Rorty captures this significance very crisply when he remarks that '[if] you still long for total revolution, for the Radical Other on a world historical scale, the events of 1989 show that you are out of luck' (Rorty, 1998, p. 229). This is not quite right; a revolution based on the socialization of poverty, the kind of primitive communism created by Pol Pot in his mercifully brief reign in Cambodia, is still possible – but this is not the kind of Radical Other that progressive thinkers have sought for the last two hundred years.

The second assumption of neo-liberal thought, and liberalism in general, is that free trade will benefit the poor – this is perhaps the most important bone of contention between those on different sides of the barricades at Seattle and Genoa. The central point is that poor countries, precisely because they are poor, by definition have lower labour costs; if they can combine this feature with reasonable levels of education and political stability then, left to its own devices, the international division of labour will work to channel capital in their direction and, in the medium-to-long run, this will work to equalize wages and general levels of development. The result will be to transfer some kinds of production from the rich world to the poorer world; metal-bashing workers in the advanced industrial world will have to retrain and it may be difficult for them to find work. It is easy to see why trade unions in the North will resist this trend, but what is very difficult to understand is why those who claim to have the interests of the South at heart will support them in their resistance. Southern governments also find this difficult to understand, which is why they are so deeply suspicious of the anti-globalization movement, who seem so adept at finding reasons why measures that would benefit the South are, really, undesirable. The ethical case against agricultural protection by the North is even more clear-cut; again, it is easy to see why heavily subsidized European farmers might want to exclude competition from the South, less easy to see why this should be regarded as a progressive position.

In so far as they have a coherent position, the opponents of free trade object to the fact that it will lead to production for the world market in Southern countries rather than production oriented towards local needs – the argument is that the poor in these countries would benefit more from a successful subsistence economy than they would from a trading economy. In the short run this might well be true, but the longer-term result of such a subsistence economy would be to deny the peoples of the South access to the kind of living standards that their Northern counterparts take for granted – if the peoples of the South are themselves prepared to forgo these living standards, then they have a right to do so, but it is much less clear that Northern well-wishers (or comparatively well-off Southern elites) should be allowed to take this decision on their behalf. The debate over the value to the poor of an open economy is closely related to the third basic assumption of current neo-liberal thought, which is that the basic problem of the less-developed countries is a lack of development capital and that such capital can only flow to these countries in sufficient quantities via private capital markets. Aid budgets are dwarfed by the amounts of money that private corporations and banks have at their disposal, and would be even in the unlikely event that there was sufficient political support in the North for them to be multiplied tenfold. The only way that the South will get access to the development capital it needs is via global private capital markets, and this fact has important implications in a number of areas. It suggests that pressure should be put on global firms to change the kind of investments they make rather than to prevent them from operating in the South at all. It also suggests that any solution to the 'debt crisis' in the least-developed countries that involves a write-off of debt must be drawn up in such a way that it does not act as a disincentive to future private lending.

If some of the most basic assumptions of neo-liberalism seem to be broadly right, ought not the programme to be endorsed as a whole? The problem is that while the model set out above may well be correct in its essentials, current political realities make it difficult for the poor to gain the theoretical benefits that it promises. It is difficult to persuade the poor of the benefits of free trade while the rich are protectionist; even though the theoretical argument in favour of open markets is still valid in such circumstances, the political rhetoric of 'fair trade' and counter-protectionism is very powerful. More to the point, a great deal of the difficulty with the neo-liberal model lies in the weakness of state structures in many parts of the South; for example, the kind of political stability needed to attract investment simply does not exist in much of sub-Saharan Africa, likewise the necessary educational and technical skills. Moreover, strong states are needed not just to attract capital but to ensure that the terms under which it is invested are as favourable to the poor as possible – here it is not so much the strength of the state that is important, but the integrity of elites, their willingness or unwillingness to be bought off by global firms.

There is a more general point here – market economies everywhere and always require strong, relatively incorruptible state authorities if they are to form the economic basis for a just society. Free trade and open markets are a recipe for continual change and upheaval, and strong states are needed to manage this process and to ensure that the losers are protected from its consequences – that their living standards are maintained in the short run and that they have the opportunity to retrain and find different kinds of work in the longer run. The adherents of contemporary neo-liberalism tend too readily to forget this requirement, but an international aid policy genuinely oriented to the poor would be one that promoted responsible, capable and democratic political authorities in poor countries, backed up by active civil societies. To its credit, Britain's Department for International Development has attempted to reorient much of the aid it disburses along these lines; this is 'democracy promotion' in a full sense, rather than the formal notion of spreading democratic institutions usually understood by that term (DFID, n.d.; M. Cox et al., 2000).

The posited need for strong state authorities takes the argument back to the themes of this book, but, before leaving behind neo-liberalism, some other caveats need to be made to the general support offered above for the key elements of the neo-liberal model. Most important, the fact that markets and private capital are essential features of the model tells us rather less than most adherents of neo-liberalism assume it does. There are lots of ways of organizing a market economy, from the social-democratic approaches of classic Scandinavian politics, via the successful social market of post-1945 (West) Germany, to such neo-liberal models as contemporary New Zealand. Similarly, there are different ways of organizing private enterprises, from the classic multinational corporation to the producer co-operatives that in countries such as Denmark have competed successfully in world markets. Moreover, the case for private enterprise in general has proved quite compatible with the public ownership of basic utilities in a great many successful capitalist economies. In short, there are genuine choices to be made here, even if the choice of a fully socialized economy is currently off the menu.

A second caveat is summarized by the term 'currently' in the last sentence. The dismal failure of the regimes of really existing socialism suggests that, for the moment, there is no alternative to some kind of market-based economy, but tells us much less about the longer-term trajectory of the system. A socialism based on global wealth rather than the socialization of poverty may, one day, become a practical possibility – and such was, of course, the basis for Marx's writing a century and a half ago. Marx himself and the early Marxists were always clear that they were not producing an emotional, moralizing, romantic critique of capitalism focusing on the sins of the latter and based on nostalgia for a simpler, purer rural past; they would have been horrified at the turning against progress so characteristic of the contemporary anti-globalization movement. Of course, faith in the future of scientific socialism was easier when science itself was less suspect and when the environmental problems that would come with economic growth were not understood – but one suspects that thinkers true to the spirit of Marx would embrace globalization and look to 'science' to solve the problems its successes have created.

Sovereignty, rights and justice in a post-Westphalian global politics

If strong state authorities are the solution to a great many of the ills of globalization, does this not constitute an endorsement of Westphalian norms, of the rights of states in a sovereignty-based system? No, because the sovereign state is not a synonym for the strong state. The possession of an effective administration and bureaucracy, the ability to shape events in the public interest and to shield one's people from the worst consequences of uncontrolled market forces is only contingently related to the legal status of being sovereign. Obviously, if one state is effectively under the control of another its ability to perform these functions will be severely impaired – but this says nothing about situations in which sovereignty is pooled and shared. It is certainly arguable that the various individual countries that make up the European Union are far more effective, far stronger, as a result of their membership of a body which undoubtedly involves the loss of sovereignty than they would be if they were to try to preserve their sovereignty and act in the world independently of each other – and it is noticeable that, for example, most British 'Eurosceptics' tacitly acknowledge that this is so, by their plans to become part of another wider grouping as members of the North American Free Trade Area, or at least, as super-loyal American allies.

Equally, the strong state is not necessarily a threat to the rights of the individual. Again, the European example is instructive; the European Convention on Human Rights certainly limits what states can do, thus interfering with their sovereignty, but it is by no means clear that they are prevented from acting in the interests of their peoples thereby. The kind of effective state administration that is needed to manage the impact of globalization ought not to be considered hampered by measures that defend the rights of the individual – just to the contrary, the best justification for a strong state is precisely that it can protect the rights of the individual. However, lest this all seem a little too good to be true, it is clear that strong and effective state administrations do have an impact on the relationship between the universal and the particular, between the interests of particular communities and the interests of humanity as a whole. Neo-liberalism asserts that, ultimately, these interests are identical, but that is in the very long run, and, as Lord Keynes famously remarked, in the long run we are all dead. In the meantime, in the here and now, there is a clear problem; the changes that accompany globalization are painful and one of the things that effective states can, and do, do is to try to ensure that this pain is borne by someone other than their own citizens. Comparatively well-organized states whose governments are responsive to the immediate needs of their peoples – and who want to be re-elected – will resist painful steps if they can, even when, in the longer run, their peoples have an interest in the goals that such steps are oriented towards. It is ultimately for this reason that successive American administrations have been unwilling to tackle the issue of the environment effectively, although, of course, the lobbying activities of US energy companies has reinforced this unwillingness. Here we can return to Strange's diagnosis of Westfailure. The Westphalian sovereignty system legitimates this kind of self-interestedness, and hampers the development of intergovernmental mechanisms to cope with problems of environmental degradation. Strange perhaps underestimates the extent to which states are capable, given sufficient will, of developing projects to protect their own citizens from the immediate impact of globalization, but she is surely right to argue that, under current conditions, the capacity of states to co-operate to solve collective problems is massively sub-optimal.

The theorists of global democracy discussed in the last chapter wish to push beyond Westphalia by developing global institutions that are democratically based and capable of overriding the legal autonomy of the states whose short-run conception of their own interests stands in the way of the development of solutions to the global problems identified by Strange (Held, 1995; Archibugi and Held, 1995; Archibugi et al., 1998). As suggested there, the problem with this position is that there is a degree of circularity to the case in its favour – a sense that the world constitutes a community is required before a global democracy could be effective, yet such a sense is unlikely to emerge in the absence of some kind of global democracy. Contemporary liberal democracies emerged from pre-democratic state structures; by analogy, global democracy would require the existence of a global state-structure that could be democratized. Most commentators have assumed that the emergence of such a world empire is both implausible and undesirable. However, some of the more interesting theorists of globalization contest this judgement; the title of Michael Hardt and Antonio Negri's recent book, *Empire*, conveys their sense that the world is being reshaped by globalization into an empire, albeit of a different kind from past examples. Their belief in the possibility of a genuine global democracy rests on this characterization (Hardt and Negri, 2000).

This is, however, a judgement that applies in the long run, and we must live in the here and now – apart from anything else, we have no way of knowing how long the long run will be. An astute Roman of the age of Claudian emperors might well have expressed doubts as to the long-term sustainability of Roman rule, but it would be two to three hundred years before his descendants noticed that the long term was about to become the short term. Today's international order is certainly based on the very tense, uneasy, unstable and frequently counterproductive co-existence and interaction of territorially based political units on the one hand, and increasingly deterritorialized economic and social systems on the other. There is no doubt but that this leads to the kind of impasses identified by Strange – and perhaps justifies describing the current order as a failure – but there is no reason to think that a new order which will resolve the tension is likely to emerge in the near future. Some write of our age as an 'interregnum', a period between two orders, the old state-centric system and a new, global, political order. The frame of reference here is quasi-Marxist, the underlying thought being that one social formation has exhausted its possibilities but still has the resources to delay the emergence of its successor (M. Cox et al., 2000). Perhaps so, but this is no help to us in setting a timescale for the emergence of the new order. It may be implausible that the Westphalia System will survive the twenty-first century, but then implausibility attaches to any prediction one might make about the course of events over the next hundred years. Intelligent science-fiction writers are probably a better guide to the future than either Westphalian or post-Westphalian international political theorists.

In any event, although it would be difficult to exaggerate the extent and pace of socio-economic change over the last two decades, it is very easy to exaggerate the degree of ideological cohesion of the Westphalia System *before* the era of globalization. A great deal of the commentary on globalization assumes that the thought of the Westphalian era – with the exception of a few radicals who can be discounted – was firmly statist and sovereignty-oriented, and thus that challenges to the sovereign state, for example, in the name of human rights, are a product of the last few decades. Part of the purpose of this book has been to dispel such assumptions. Sovereignty, rights and justice have been contested terms since the beginnings of the Westphalia System; what it means to be a sovereign state has never been something that has been uncontested – except perhaps in the minds of some realist writers in the immediate aftermath of the Second World War who, unfortunately, still far too often provide the picture of international relations theory used by its critics. Some things have changed: the development of a global capitalist economy has introduced levels of inequality not experienced in the classic Westphalian order, and the accompanying transformation of a European into a world system has created a level of cultural diversity that is equally unprecedented. However, it is striking how valuable the resources of Westphalian political theory have been for coping with these changes. Critics of the existing order such as Habermas, Held and Linklater draw on Kantian internationalism for inspiration; Walzer, the most successful defender of the rights of political communities, owes many of his best points to John Stuart Mill. Asian critics of the Western nature of human rights discourse readily accept other Western notions such as the right to national self-determination and the importance of the sovereign equality of states.

In short, there is no reason to think that the pre-globalization debates and arguments summarized and assessed in this book have lost their relevance. Ultimately, the justification for any kind of political theory is that it addresses, clarifies and brings into focus real issues that affect the lives of ordinary people, and it is as certain as one can be about anything that the questions of sovereignty, rights and justice discussed here will remain on this, the real agenda of world politics, for the foreseeable future.

Bibliography

Adler, E. 1997: Seizing the Middle Ground. *European Journal of International Relations*, 3, 319–64.

Albert, M., Jacobson, D. and Lapid, I. (eds) 2001: *Identities, Borders and Orders*. Minneapolis: University of Minnesota Press.

Allen, T. and Styan, D. 2000: A Right to Interfere? Bernard Kouchner and the New Humanitarianism. *Journal of International Development*, 12, 825–42.

American Journal of International Law, 1999a: Developments in International Criminal Law. 93, 1–123.

American Journal of International Law, 1999b: Editorial Comments: Nato's Kosovo Intervention. 93, 824–63.

American Political Science Review, 1997: Forum on Neo-Realism. 91, 899–936.

Anderson, B. 1983: *Imagined Communities*. London: Verso.

Angell, N. 1909: *The Great Illusion*. London: Weidenfeld & Nicolson.

Anscombe, G. E. M. 1981: *The Collected Philosophical Papers: Vol. 3 Ethics, Religion and Politics*. Oxford: Blackwell.

Appadurai, A. 1996: *Modernity at Large: Cultural Dimensions of Globalization*. Minneapolis: University of Minnesota Press.

Archibugi, D. and Held, D. (eds) 1995: *Cosmopolitan Democracy*. Cambridge: Polity.

Archibugi, D., Held, D. and Kühler, M. (eds) 1998: *Re-imagining Political Community: Studies in Cosmopolitan Democracy*. Cambridge: Polity.

Arrighi, G., Hopkins, T. and Wallerstein, I. 1989: *Anti-systemic Movements*. London: Verso.

Ashley, R. K. 1984: The Poverty of Neorealism. *International Organization*, 38, 225–86.

Baldwin, D. A. (ed.) 1993: *Neorealism and Neoliberalism: The Contemporary Debate*. New York: Columbia University Press.

Barber, B. 1996: *Jihad vs. McWorld*. New York: Ballantine Books.

Barkawi, T. and Laffey, M. 1999: The Imperial Peace: Democracy, Force and Globalisation. *European Journal of International Relations*, 5, 403–34.

Barkun, S. and Cronin, B. 1994: The State and the Nation; Norms and the Rules of Sovereignty in International Relations. *International Organization*, 48, 107–30.

Barnard, F. M. 1965: *Herder's Social and Political Thought*. Oxford: Clarendon Press.

Barnard, F. M. 1969: *J. G. Herder on Social and Political Culture*. Cambridge: Cambridge University Press.

Barry, B. 1973: *The Liberal Theory of Justice*. Oxford: Clarendon Press.

Barry, B. 1982/1989: Humanity and Justice in Global Perspective. In B. Barry, *Democracy, Power and Justice*, Oxford: Clarendon Press.

Barry, B. 1989: *Theories of Justice*. Hemel Hempstead: Harvester Wheatsheaf.

Barry, B. 1994: *Justice as Impartiality*. Oxford: Oxford University Press.

Barry, B. 1998: International Society from a Cosmopolitan Perspective. In Mapel and Nardin (1998).

Barry, B. 1999: Statism and Nationalism: A Cosmopolitan Critique. In Shapiro and Brilmayer (1999).

Barry, B. 2000: *Culture and Equality*. Cambridge: Polity.

Barry, B. and Goodin, R. E. (eds) 1992: *Free Movement*. Hemel Hempstead: Harvester Wheatsheaf.

Bauer, J. and Bell, D. A. (eds) 1999: *The East Asian Challenge for Human Rights*. Cambridge: Cambridge University Press.

Baylis, J. and Smith, S. (eds) 2001: *Globalisation and World Politics*, 2nd edn. Oxford: Oxford University Press.

Beck, U. 1999: *World Risk Society*. Cambridge: Polity.

Beitz, C. R. 1979/2000: *Political Theory and International Relations*, 1st/2nd edns. Princeton: Princeton University Press.

Beitz, C. R. 1983: Cosmopolitan Ideas and National Sovereignty. *Journal of Philosophy*, 80, 591–600.

Beitz, C. R. 1994: Cosmopolitan Liberalism and the States System. In C. Brown (1994c).

Beitz, C. R. 1999: Social and Cosmopolitan Liberalism. *International Affairs*, 75, 515–30.

Beitz, C. R. 2000: Rawls's Law of Peoples. *Ethics*, 110, 669–96.

Beitz, C. R. et al. 1985: *International Ethics*. Princeton: Princeton University Press.

Belich, J. 1996: *Making Peoples*. Auckland, NZ: Penguin.

Bell, D. 2000: *East Meets West: Human Rights and Democracy in East Asia*. Princeton: Princeton University Press.

Bell, L. S., Nathan, A. J. and Peleg, H. (eds) 2001: *Negotiating Culture and Human Rights*. New York: Columbia University Press.

Bentham, J. 1960: *Principles of Morals and Legislation*. Oxford: Basil Blackwell.

Bentham, J. 1962: Principles of International Law. *Works*, 2. New York: Russell & Russell.

Berlin, I. 1969: Two Concepts of Liberty. In I. Berlin, *Four Essays on Liberty*, Oxford: Oxford University Press.

Best, G. 1994: *War and Law Since 1945*. Oxford: Oxford University Press.

Blair, T. 1999: Doctrine of the International Community. Speech in Chicago, 22 April.

Bodin, J. 1992: *On Sovereignty*. Ed. Julius Franklin. Cambridge: Cambridge University Press.

Bohnman, J. and Lutz-Bachmann, M. (eds) 1997: *Perpetual Peace: Essays on Kant's Cosmopolitan Ideal*. Cambridge, MA: MIT Press.

Booth, K. 1991: Security in Anarchy: Utopian Realism in Theory and Practice. *International Affairs*, 67, 527–45.

Booth, K. and Smith, S. (eds) 1994: *International Relations Theory Today*. Cambridge: Polity.

Booth, K. (ed.) 2000: The Kosovo Tragedy: The Human Rights Dimension. *Special Issue International Journal of Human Rights*, 4, nos 1 and 2. (Reprinted as K. Booth (ed.) 2001: *The Kosovo Tragedy: The Human Rights Dimension*. London: Frank Cass.)

Boucher, D. (ed.) 1997: *The British Idealists*. Cambridge: Cambridge University Press.

Boucher, D. 1998: *Political Theories of International Relations*. Oxford: Oxford University Press.

Boucher, D. and Kelly, P. (eds) 1998: *Social Justice: From Hume to Walzer*. London: Routledge.

Bové, J., Dufour, F. and de Casparis, A. 2001: *The World is Not for Sale*. London: Verso.

Bowden, M. 1999: *Black Hawk Down*. New York: Bantam Books.

Bozeman, A. B. 1960: *Politics and Culture in International History*. Princeton: Princeton University Press.

Braudel, F. 1972: *The Mediterranean and the Mediterranean World in the Age of Philip II Vols I and II*. London: Collins.

Brewer, A. 1990: *Marxist Theories of Imperialism: A Critical Survey*. London: Routledge.

Brilmayer, L. 1989: *Justifying International Acts*. Ithaca, NY: Cornell University Press.

Brown, C. 1985: Development and Dependency. In M. Light and A. J. R. Groom (eds), *International Relations*. London: Pinter Press.

Brown, C. 1992a: *International Relations Theory: New Normative Approaches*. Hemel Hempstead: Harvester Wheatsheaf.

Brown, C. 1992b: 'Really-Existing Liberalism', and International Order. *Millennium: Journal of International Studies*, 21, 313–28.

Brown, C. 1994a: Critical Theory and Postmodernism in International Relations. In A. J. R. Groom and M. Light (eds), *Contemporary International Relations*. London: Pinter Press.

Brown, C. 1994b: 'Turtles All the Way Down': Antifoundationalism, Critical Theory, and International Relations. *Millennium: Journal of International Studies*, 23, 213–38.

Brown, C. (ed.) 1994c: *Political Restructuring in Europe: Ethical Perspectives*. London: Routledge.

Brown, C. 1994d: On the Idea of an International Community. In Booth and Smith (1994).

Brown, C. 1995a: International Theory and International Society: The Viability of the Middle Way. *Review of International Studies*, 21, 183–96.

Brown, C. 1995b: The End of History. In Danchev (1995).

Brown, C. 1997/2001: *Understanding International Relations*, 1st/2nd edns. London: Macmillan/Palgrave.

Brown, C. 1997: Review Essay: Theories of International Justice. *British Journal of Political Science*, 27, 273–9.

Brown, C. 1998: International Social Justice. In Boucher and Kelly (1998).

Brown, C. 1999a: History Ends, Worlds Collide. *Review of International Studies: Special Issue 'The Interregnum'*, 25, 45–57. (Reprinted as M. Cox, K. Booth and T. Dunne (eds) 2000: *The Interregnum*. Cambridge: Cambridge University Press.)

Brown, C. 1999b: Universal Human Rights: A Critique. In Dunne and Wheeler (1999).

Brown, C. 1999c: Susan Strange: A Critical Appreciation. *Review of International Studies*, 25, 531–5.

Brown, C. 2000a: Cultural Diversity and International Political Theory. *Review of International Studies*, 26, 199–213.

Brown, C. 2000b: On the Borders of (International) Political Theory. In N. O'Sullivan (ed.), *Political Theory in Transition*, London: Routledge.

Brown, C. 2000c: Cosmopolitanism, World Citizenship and Global Civil Society. *Contemporary Research in Social and Political Philosophy: Special Issue Human Rights and Cultural Diversity*, 3, 7–27. (Reprinted as S. Caney and P. Jones (eds) 2001: *Human Rights and Cultural Diversity*. London: Frank Cass.)

Brown, C. 2000d: A Qualified Defence of the Use of Force for Humanitarian Reasons. In Booth (2000).

Brown, C. 2000e: John Rawls, *The Law of Peoples*, and International Political Theory. *Ethics and International Affairs*, 14, 125–32.

Brown, C. 2000f: Human Rights and Human Dignity: An Analysis of the Human Rights Culture and its Critics. In Patman (2000).

Brown, C. 2001a: World Society and the English School: An International Society Perspective on World Society. *European Journal of International Relations* (forthcoming).

Brown, C. 2001b: Human Rights. In Baylis and Smith (2001).

Brown, C. 2001c: Ethics, Interests and Foreign Policy. In Smith and Light (2001).

Brown, C., Nardin, T. and Rengger, N. J. (eds) 2002: *International Relations in Political Thought: Texts in International Relations*. Cambridge: Cambridge University Press.

Brown, D. E. 1991: *Human Universals*. New York: McGraw Hill.

Brown, M. E., Lynn-Jones, S. M. and Miller, S. (eds) 1995: *The Perils of Anarchy: Contemporary Realism and International Security*. Cambridge, MA: MIT Press.

Buchanan, A. 1991: *Secession*. Boulder, CO: Westview Press.

Buchanan, A. 2000: Rawls's Law of Peoples: Rules for a Vanished Westphalian World. *Ethics*, 110, 697–721.

Bull, H. 1976: Martin Wight and the Theory of International Relations. *British Journal of International Studies*, 2, 101–16.

Bull, H. 1977/1995: *The Anarchical Society*. London: Macmillan.

Bull, H. 1984a: *Justice in International Relations: The Hagey Lectures*. Waterloo, Ontario: University of Waterloo.

Bull, H. (ed.) 1984b: *Intervention in World Politics*. Oxford: Oxford University Press.

Bull, H. and Watson, A. (eds) 1984: *The Expansion of International Society*. Oxford: Clarendon Press.

Burchill, S. and Linklater, A. (eds) 1996: *Theories of International Relations*. London: Macmillan.

Burke, E. 1906: *Letters on a Regicide Peace, Collected Works*, vol. 6. London: Longman.

Buruma, I. 1984: *Behind the Mask*. New York: Pantheon Books.

Bush, President G. 1990: Towards a New World Order, Address before a Joint Session of Congress, September 11. *US Department of State Dispatch*, 17.9.90, 91–4.

Butterfield, H. 1953: *Christianity, Diplomacy and War*. London: Epworth.

Butterfield, H. and Wight, M. (eds) 1966: *Diplomatic Investigations*. London: George Allen and Unwin.

Buzan, B. 1996: The Timeless Wisdom of Realism. In Smith, Booth and Zalewski (1996).

Campbell, D. 1993: *Politics without Principle: Sovereignty, Ethics, and the Narratives of the Gulf War*. Boulder CO: Lynne Rienner.

Campbell, D. 1998: *National Deconstruction: Violence, Identity and Justice in Bosnia*. Minneapolis: University of Minnesota Press.

Caney, S., George, R. and Jones, P. (eds) 1998: *National Rights, International Obligations*. Boulder, CO: Westview Press.

Caney, S. and Jones, P. (eds) 2001: *Human Rights and Cultural Diversity*. London: Frank Cass.

Canovan, M. 2000: Patriotism is not Enough. *British Journal of Political Science*, 30, 413–32.

Carens, J. 1992: Migration and Morality: A Liberal Egalitarian Perspective. In Barry and Goodin (1992).

Carr, E. H. 1939: *The Twenty Years Crisis*. London: Macmillan.

Carroll, J. 1993: *Humanism*. London: Fontana Press.

Cassen, R. (ed.) 1986: *Does Aid Work?*. Oxford: Clarendon Press.

Castells, M. 1996/7: *The Information Age: Economy, Society and Culture*, 3 vols. Oxford: Blackwell.

Ceadal, M. 1987: *Thinking about War and Peace*. Oxford: Oxford University Press.

Charlesworth, H. and Chinkin, C. 2000: *The Boundaries of International Law: A Feminist Analysis*. Manchester: University of Manchester Press.

Chomsky, N. 1994: *World Orders, Old and New*. London: Pluto Press.

Chomsky, N. 1999: *The New Military Humanism*. London: Pluto Press.

Clark, G. and Sohn, L. B. 1966: *World Peace through World Law*. Cambridge, MA: Harvard University Press.

Clark, I. 1999: *Globalisation and International Relations Theory*. Oxford: Oxford University Press.

Clarke, W. and Herbst, J. (eds) 1997: *Learning from Somalia: The Lessons of Armed Humanitarian Intervention*. Boulder, CO: Westview Press.

Clausewitz, C. 1976: *On War*. Trans. and ed. Michael Howard and Peter Paret. Princeton: Princeton University Press.

Cobden, R. 1903: *The Political Writings of Richard Cobden*. London: T. Fisher Unwin.

Cochran, M. 2000: *Normative Theory and International Relations*. Cambridge: Cambridge University Press.

Cohen, J. (ed.) 1996: *For Love of Country: Debating the Limits of Patriotism. Martha Nussbaum and Respondents*. Boston: Beacon Press.

Cohen, J., Howard, M. and Nussbaum, M. (eds) 1999: *Is Multiculturalism Bad for Women? Susan Moller Okin and Respondents.* Princeton: Princeton University Press.

Cohen, R. 1994: Pacific Unions: A Reappraisal of the Theory that 'Democracies Do Not Go To War With Each Other'. *Review of International Studies*, 20, 207–23.

Coker, C. 1994: *War in the Twentieth Century.* London: Brassey's.

Coker, C. 1998: *War and the Illiberal Conscience.* Boulder, CO: Westview Press.

Coleman, J. 2000: *A History of Political Thought from the Middle Ages to the Renaissance.* Oxford: Blackwell.

Cook, R. (ed.) 1994: *Human Rights of Women: National and International Perspectives.* Philadelphia: University of Pennsylvania Press.

Coomaraswamy, R. 1994: To Bellow Like a Cow: Women, Ethnicity and the Discourse of Rights. In Cook (1994).

Connolly, W. E. 1983: *The Terms of Political Discourse.* Oxford: Martin Robertson.

Connolly, W. E. 1987: The Dilemma of Legitimacy. In W. E. Connolly, *Politics and Ambiguity.* Madison, WI: University of Wisconsin Press.

Connolly, W. E. 1988: *Political Theory and Modernity.* Oxford: Blackwell.

Connolly, W. E. 1991: *Identity/Difference: Democratic Negotiations of Political Paradox.* Ithaca, NY: Cornell University Press.

Connolly, W. E. 1995: *The Ethos of Pluralization.* Minneapolis: University of Minnesota Press.

Connolly, W. E. 2000: Speed, Concentric Circles and Cosmopolitanism. *Political Theory*, 28, 596–618.

Cotton, J. 2001: Against the Grain: The East Timor Intervention. *Survival*, 43, 127–42.

Cox, M. (ed.) 2000: *E. H. Carr: A Critical Appraisal.* Basingstoke: Palgrave/ Macmillan.

Cox, M., Booth, K. and Dunne, T. (eds) 1999: *The Interregnum.* Cambridge: Cambridge University Press.

Cox, M., Ikenberry, J. and Inoguchi, T. (eds) 2000: *American Democracy Promotion: Impulses, Strategies and Impacts.* New York: Oxford University Press.

Cox, R. 1981: Social Forces, States, and World Orders: Beyond International Relations Theory. *Millennium: Journal of International Studies*, 10, 126–55.

Crawford, J. (ed.) 1988: *The Rights of Peoples.* Oxford: Clarendon Press.

Daadler, I. 2000: *Getting to Dayton: The Making of America's Bosnia Policy.* Washington, DC: The Brookings Institute.

Danchev, A. (ed.) 1995: *Fin de Siècle: The Meaning of the Twentieth Century.* London: I. B. Tauris.

Danchev, A. and Halverson, T. (eds) 1996: *International Perspectives on the Yugoslav Conflict.* Basingstoke: Macmillan.

Danish Institute for International Affairs, 1999: *Humanitarian Intervention: Legal and Political Aspects.* Copenhagen.

DeCosse, D. (ed.) 1992: *But Was it Just?* New York: Doubleday.

de Maistre, J. 1965: *Selected Works of Joseph de Maistre.* Ed. Jack Lively. London: Allen and Unwin.

Department for International Development (DFID) n.d.: *Making Government Work for Poor People.* www.dfid.gov.uk.

Der Derian, J. 1992: *Antidiplomacy: Spies, Terror, Speed and War*. Oxford: Blackwell.

Des Forges, A. 2000: Shame: Rationalising Western Apathy on Rwanda. *Foreign Affairs*, 79, 141–4.

Deudeny, D. 1996: Binding Sovereigns: Authorities, Structures and Geopolitics in Philadelphia Systems. In T. J. Biernteker and C. Weber (eds), *State Structure as Source Construct*, Cambridge: Cambridge University Press.

Deudeny, D. and Ikenberry, J. G. 1999: The Nature and Sources of Liberal International Order. *Review of International Studies*, 25, 179–96.

Dicken, P. 1992: *Global Shift: The Internationalisation of Economic Activity*. London: Chapman and Hall.

Donagan, A. 1977: *A Theory of Morality*. Chicago: University of Chicago Press.

Donnelly, J. 1993: *International Human Rights*. Boulder, CO: Westview Press.

Donnelly, J. 1998: Human Rights: A New Standard of Civilisation. *International Affairs*, 74, 1–24.

Donnelly, J. 2000: *Realism and International Relations*. Cambridge: Cambridge University Press.

Dowty, A. 1987: *Closed Borders*. New Haven: Yale University Press.

Doyle, M. 1983: Kant, Liberal Legacies and Foreign Policy, Parts I and II. *Philosophy and Public Affairs*, 12, 205–35 and 323–53.

Doyle, M. 1986: Liberalism and World Politics. *American Political Science Review*, 80, 1151–70.

Dunne, T. 1995: The Social Construction of International Society. *European Journal of International Relations*, 1, 367–89.

Dunne, T. 1998: *Inventing International Society*. London: Macmillan.

Dunne, T. and Wheeler, N. 1996: Hedley Bull's Pluralism of the Intellect and Solidarism of the Will. *International Affairs*, 72, 91–107.

Dunne, T. and Wheeler, N. (eds) 1999: *Human Rights in Global Politics*. Cambridge: Cambridge University Press.

Dunne, T. and Wheeler, N. 2001: The Australian-led Intervention in East Timor. *International Affairs*, 77, 805–27.

Edkins, J. 1999: *Poststructuralism and International Relations*. Boulder, CO: Lynne Rienner.

Edkins, J., Persram, N. and Pin-Fat, V. (eds) 1999: *Sovereignty and Subjectivity*. Boulder, CO: Lynne Rienner.

Elshtain, J. B. (ed.) 1981: *Public Man, Private Woman*. Oxford: Martin Robertson.

Elshtain, J. B. 1987: *Women and War*. Brighton: Harvester Wheatsheaf.

Elshtain, J. B. (ed.) 1991: *Just War Theory*. Oxford: Blackwell.

Elshtain, J. B. 1998: *Women and War* Ten Years After. *Review of International Studies*, 24, 447–60.

Elster, J. 1992: *Local Justice*. New York: Russell Sage Foundation.

Ethics 2000: Symposium on Martha Nussbaum's Political Philosophy, 111, 5–140.

Ethics and International Affairs 1997: Twenty Years of *Just and Unjust Wars*, 11, 3–104.

Ethics and International Affairs 2000: The Meaning of Kosovo, 14, 3–65.

Finnemore, M. 1996: Constructing Norms of Humanitarian Intervention. In P. Katzenstein (ed.), *The Culture of National Security*. New York: Columbia University Press.

Finnis, J. 1980: *Natural Law and Natural Rights*. Oxford: Clarendon Press.

Finnis, J. 1996: The Ethics of War and Peace in the Catholic Natural Law Tradition. In Nardin (1996).

Finnis, J., Boyle, J. and Grisez, G. 1987: *Nuclear Deterrence, Morality and Realism*. Oxford: Clarendon Press.

Forsyth, M. G., Keens-Soper, H. M. A. and Savigear, P. (eds) 1970: *The Theory of International Relations*. London: Allen and Unwin.

Foucault, M. 1986: What is Enlightenment?. In P. Rabinow (ed.), *The Foucault Reader*. Harmondsworth: Penguin.

Fox, W. R. T. 1985: E. H. Carr and Political Realism: Vision and Revision. *Review of International Studies*, 11, 1–16.

Frank, A. G. 1971: *Capitalism and Underdevelopment in Latin America*. Harmondsworth: Penguin.

Frank, A. G. and Gills, B. (eds) 1993: *The World System: Five Hundred Years or Five Thousand Years*. London: Routledge.

Frank, T. 2001: *One Market Under God*. London: Secker & Warburg.

Freedman, L. 2000: Victims and Victors: Reflections on the Kosovo War. *Review of International Studies*, 23, 335–58.

Freud, S. 1985: *Civilization, Society and Religion*. Harmondsworth: Penguin.

Fritz, J.-S. and Lensu, M. (eds) 2000: *Value Pluralism, Normative Theory and International Relations*. Basingstoke: Macmillan.

Frost, M. 1996: *Ethics in International Relations*. Cambridge: Cambridge University Press.

Frost, M. 1998: A Turn not Taken: Ethics in International Relations at the Millennium. *Review of International Studies*, Special Issue, 124–46.

Frost, M. 2000: Reply to Peter Sutch. *Review of International Studies*, 26, 477–83.

Fukuyama, F. 1989: The End of History. *The National Interest*, 16, 3–16.

Galtung, J. 1971: A Structural Theory of Imperialism. *Journal of Peace Research*, 13, 81–94.

Gandhi, M. K. 1996: *Selected Political Writings*. Ed. Denis Dalton. Indianapolis: Hackett.

Gellner, E. 1988: *Plough, Sword and Book: The Structure of Human History*. London: Collins Harvill.

Gellner, E. 1994: *Conditions of Liberty: Civil Society and its Rivals*. London: Hamish Hamilton.

Geras, N. 1998: *The Contract of Mutual Indifference*. London: Verso.

Ghandhi, P. R. 2000: *Blackstone's Human Rights Documents*, 2nd edn. London: Blackstone Press.

Giddens, A. 1985: *The Nation-State and Violence*. Cambridge: Polity.

Giddens, A. 1999: *The Runaway World*. Cambridge: Polity.

Giddens, A. 2000: *The Third Way and its Critics*. Cambridge: Polity.

Gill, S. (ed.) 1993: *Gramsci, Historical Materialism and International Relations*. Cambridge: Cambridge University Press.

Gilpin, R. 1984: The Richness of the Tradition of Political Realism. *International Organization*, 38, 287–304.

Goldstein, J. and Keohane, R. O. (eds) 1993: *Ideas and Foreign Policy*. Ithaca, NY: Cornell University Press.

Gong, G. C. 1984: *The Standard of 'Civilisation', in International Society*. Oxford: Oxford University Press.

Goodin, R. 1995: Government House Utilitarianism. In R. Goodin, *Utilitarianism as a Public Philosophy*. Cambridge: Cambridge University Press.

Gourevitch, P. 1998: *We wish to inform you that tomorrow we will be killed with our families: Stories from Rwanda*. New York: Farrar, Straus and Giroux.

Gow, J. 1997: *Triumph of the Lack of Will: International Diplomacy and the Yugoslav War*. London: C. Hurst & Co.

Gowa, J. 1999: *Ballots and Bullets: The Elusive Democratic Peace*. Princeton: Princeton University Press.

Gray, C. 2000: No Good Deed Shall Go Unpunished. In Booth (2000).

Grieco, J. M. 1988: Anarchy and the Limits of Cooperation: A Realist Critique of the Newest Liberal Institutionalism. *International Organization*, 42, 485–508.

Griffiths, M. 1992: *Realism, Idealism and International Politics: A Reinterpretation*. London: Routledge.

Guzzini, S. 2000: A Reconstruction of Constructivism in International Relations. *European Journal of International Relations*, 6, 147–82.

Haass, R. 2000: *Intervention*, 2nd edn. Washington, DC: The Brookings Institute.

Habermas, J. 1973: *Legitimation Crisis*. Boston: Beacon Hill.

Habermas, J. 1984: *The Theory of Communicative Action*, vols I and II. Cambridge: Polity.

Habermas, J. 1987: *The Philosophical Discourses of Modernity*. Cambridge: Polity.

Habermas, J. 1994: *The Past as Future*. Cambridge: Polity.

Habermas, J. 1999: Bestialität und Humanität. *Die Zeit*, 18, 29 April.

Hall, J. A. (ed.) 1995: *Civil Society*. Cambridge: Polity.

Hall, R. B. 1999: *National Collective Identity: Social Constructs and International System*. New York: Columbia University Press.

Halliday, F. 1992: An Encounter with Fukuyama. *New Left Review*, 193, 89–95.

Halliday, F. 1994: *Rethinking International Relations*. London: Macmillan.

Hanson, V. D. 1989: *The Western Way of War: Infantry Battle in Classical Greece*. New York: Knopf.

Hardin, G. 1974: Lifeboat Ethics. *Psychology Today*, 8.

Hardin, R. and Mearsheimer, J. J. (eds) 1985: *Ethics*, Special Issue on Nuclear Deterrence and Disarmament, 95, 3.

Hardt, M. and Negri, A. 2000: *Empire*. Cambridge, MA: Harvard University Press.

Harvey, N. 1998: *The Chiapas Rebellion*. Durham, NC: Duke University Press.

Hasenclever, A., Mayer, P. and Rittberger, V. 1997: *Theories of International Regimes*. Cambridge: Cambridge University Press.

Hegel, G. F. W. 1956: *Philosophy of History*. New York: Dover.

Hegel, G. F. W. 1991: *Elements of the Philosophy of Right*. Cambridge: Cambridge University Press.

Held, D. 1991: *Political Theory Today*. Cambridge: Polity.

Held, D. 1995: *Democracy and the Global Order*. Cambridge: Polity.

Held, D. et al. 1999: *Global Transformations*. Cambridge: Polity.

Held, D. et al. (eds) 2000: *The Global Transformations Reader*. Cambridge: Polity.

Helms, J. 2000/2001: American Sovereignty and the UN. *The National Interest*, 62, 31–4.

Herskovits, M. 1973: Cultural Relativism and Cultural Values. In J. Ladd (ed.), *Ethical Relativism*. Belmont, CA: Wadsworth.

Hertz, N. 2001: *The Silent Takeover*. London: Heinemann.

Hilferding, R. 1981: *Finance Capital*. Ed. Tom Bottomore. London: Routledge, Kegan Paul.

Hill, C. 1989: 1939: the Origins of Liberal Realism. *Review of International Studies*, 15, 319–28.

Hinsley, F. H. 1963: *Power and the Pursuit of Peace*. Cambridge: Cambridge University Press.

Hinsley, F. H. 1966: *Sovereignty*. London: Hutchinson.

Hirst, P. and Thompson, G. 1999: *Globalization in Question: The International Economy and the Possibilities of Governance*. Cambridge: Polity.

Hobbes, T. 1946: *Leviathan*. Ed. with an introduction by M. Oakeshott. Oxford: Basil Blackwell.

Hobhouse, L. J. 1918: *The Metaphysical Theory of the State*. London: George Allen and Unwin.

Hochschild, A. 1998: *King Leopold's Ghost*. New York: Houghton Mifflin Co.

Hoffmann, S. 1977: An American Social Science: International Relations. *Daedalus*, 106, 41–61.

Hoffmann, S. 1981: *Duties Beyond Borders*. Syracuse, NY: Syracuse University Press.

Hoffmann, S. and Fidler, D. 1991: *Rousseau on International Relations*. Oxford: Clarendon Press.

Holbraad, C. 1970: *Concert of Europe*. London: Longman.

Hollis, M. and Smith, S. 1991: *Explaining and Understanding International Relations*. Oxford: Clarendon Press.

Holt, T. 1997: *The Walled Orchard*. London: Warner Books.

Hume, D. 1987: *Essays: Moral, Political and Literary*. Indianapolis: Liberty Classics.

Huntington, S. 1993a: The Clash of Civilisations. *Foreign Affairs*, 72, 22–49.

Huntington, S. 1993b: Response: If not Civilisations, What? *Foreign Affairs*, 72, 186–94.

Huntington, S. 1996: *The Clash of Civilizations and the Remaking of World Order*. New York: Simon and Schuster.

Hurrell, A. 1990: Kant and the Kantian Paradigm in International Relations. *Review of International Studies*, 16, 183–205.

Hutton, W. 1995: *The State We're In*. London: Cape.

Ignatieff, M. 2000: *Virtual War*. New York: Metropolitan Books.

Independent International Commission on Kosovo, 2000: *The Kosovo Report*. Oxford: Oxford University Press.

International Affairs 1999: Special Anniversary Issue: International Justice, 75.

Jackson, R. 1990: *Quasi-States: Sovereignty, International Relations and the Third World*. Cambridge: Cambridge University Press.

Jackson, R. 2000: *The Global Covenant*. Oxford: Oxford University Press.

Johnson, J. T. 1975: *Ideology, Reason and the Limitation of War: Religious and Secular Concepts, 1200 to 1740*. Princeton: Princeton University Press.

Johnson J. T. 1981: *Just War Tradition and the Restraint of War*. Princeton: Princeton University Press.

Jones, C. 1999a: *Global Justice: Defending Cosmopolitanism*. Oxford: Oxford University Press.

Jones, C. 1999b: Patriotism, Morality and Global Justice. In Shapiro and Brilmayer (1999).

Jones, P. 1994: *Rights*. Basingstoke: Macmillan.

Jones, P. 1998: Political Theory and Cultural Diversity. *Critical Review of International Social and Political Philosophy*, 1, 28–62.

Jones, R. W. 1999: *Security, Strategy and Critical Theory*. Boulder, CO: Lynne Rienner.

Joy, B. 2000: Why the Future Doesn't Need Us. *Wired*, 8.04, 238–62.

Judah, T. 2000: *Kosovo: War and Revenge*. New Haven: Yale University Press.

Kaldor, M. and Vojevoda, I. (eds) 1998: *Democratisation in Central and Eastern Europe*. London: Pinter Press.

Kaufman, C. D. and Pape, R. A. 1999: Explaining Costly International Moral Action: Britain's Sixty Year Campaign against the Slave Trade. *International Organisation*, 53, 361–8.

Keohane, R. O. (ed.) 1985: *Neorealism and its Critics*. New York: Columbia University Press.

Keohane, R. O. 1989: *International Institutions and State Power*. Boulder, CO: Westview Press.

Klein, N. 2001: *No Logo*. London: Flamingo.

Klinghoffer, A. 1998: *The International Dimension of Genocide in Rwanda*. New York: New York University Press.

Knorr, K. and Rosenau, J. N. (eds) 1969: *Contending Approaches to International Politics*. Princeton: Princeton University Press.

Krasner, S. D. 1985: *Structural Conflict: The Third World Against Global Liberalism*. Berkeley: University of California Press.

Krasner, S. D. 1999: *Sovereignty: Organized Hypocrisy*. Princeton: Princeton University Press.

Kratochwil, F. 1989: *Rules, Norms and Decisions*. Cambridge: Cambridge University Press.

Kratochwil, F. 1995: Sovereignty as *Dominion*: Is there a Right of Humanitarian Intervention?. In Lyons and Mastanduno (1995).

Kratochwil, F. 2000: Constructing a New Orthodoxy? Wendt's *Social Theory of International Politics* and the Constructivist Challenge. *Millennium: Journal of International Studies*, 29, 73–101.

Kratochwil, F. and Lapid, Y. (eds) 1996: *The Return of Culture and Identity in International Relations Theory*. Boulder, CO: Lynne Rienner.

Krause, M. (ed.) 1989: *Relativism*. Notre Dame, IN: University of Notre Dame Press.

Kubalkova, V., Onuf, N. and Kowert, P. 1998: *International Relations in a Constructed World*. Armonk, NY: M. E. Sharpe.

Kuper, A. 2000: Rawlsian Global Justice. *Political Theory*, 28, 640–74.

Kuperman, A. 2000: Rwanda in Retrospect. *Foreign Affairs*, 79, 94–118.

Kymlicka, W. 1995a: *Multicultural Citizenship*. Oxford: Oxford University Press.

Kymlicka, W. (ed.) 1995b: *The Rights of Minority Cultures*. Oxford: Oxford University Press.

Kymlicka, W. and Norman, W. (eds) 2000: *Citizenship in Diverse Societies*. New York: Oxford University Press.

Laberge, P. 1998: Kant on Justice and the Law of Nations. In Mapel and Nardin (1998).

Lacher, H. 2000: Historicising the Global: Capitalism, Territoriality and the International Relations of Modernity. Ph.D. thesis: University of London.

Lawson, S. 1998: Democracy and the Problem of Cultural Relativism. *Global Society*, 12, 251–70.

Lenin, V. I. 1968: The State and the Revolution, and Imperialism: Highest Stage of Capitalism. *Selected Works*. Moscow: Progress Publishers.

Linklater, A. 1981/1990: *Men and Citizens in the Theory of International Relations*. London: Macmillan.

Linklater, A. 1990: *Beyond Realism and Marxism: Critical Theory and International Relations*. London: Macmillan.

Linklater, A. 1992: The Question of the Next Stage in International Relations Theory: A Critical Theoretic Approach. *Millennium: Journal of International Studies*, 21, 77–98.

Linklater, A. 1998: *The Transformation of Political Community*. Cambridge: Polity.

Linklater, A. 1999: The Evolving Spheres of International Justice. *International Affairs*, 75, 473–82.

Lipschutz, R. D. 1996: *Global Civil Society and Global Environmental Governance*. Albany, NY: State University of New York Press.

List, F. 1966: *The National System of Political Economy*. London: Frank Cass.

Loescher, G. 1993: *Beyond Charity: International Co-operation and the Global Refugee Crisis*. New York: Oxford University Press.

Long, D. and Wilson, P. (eds) 1995: *Thinkers of the Twenty Years Crisis: Interwar Idealism Reassessed*. Oxford: Clarendon Press.

Luttwak, E. 1999: Give War a Chance. *Foreign Affairs*, 78, 36–45.

Luxemburg, R. 1951: *The Accumulation of Capital*. London: Routledge and Kegan Paul.

Lyons, G. M. and Mastanduno, M. (eds) 1995: *Beyond Westphalia?*. Baltimore: Johns Hopkins Press.

MacIntyre, A. 1981: *After Virtue*. Notre Dame, IN: University of Notre Dame Press.

MacKinnon, C. 1989: *Towards a Feminist Theory of the State*. Cambridge, MA: Harvard University Press.

MacKinnon, C. 1993: Crimes of War, Crimes of Peace. In Shute and Hurley (1993).

MacMillan, J. 1996: Democracies Don't Fight: A Case of the Wrong Research Agenda. *Review of International Studies*, 22, 275–99.

Mahbubani, K. 1992: The West and the Rest. *The National Interest*, 28, 3–13.

Makinda, S. M. 1993: *Seeking Peace from Chaos: Humanitarian Intervention in Somalia*. Boulder, CO: Lynne Rienner.

Mandelbaum, M. 1999: A Perfect Failure. *Foreign Affairs*, 98, 2–8.

Mann, M. 1986/1993: *The Sources of Social Power*, vols I and II. Cambridge: Cambridge University Press.

Mannheim, K. 1936/1960: *Ideology and Utopia*. London: Routledge and Kegan Paul.

Mapel, D. 1992: Military Intervention and Rights. *Millennium: Journal of International Studies*, 20, 41–53.

Mapel D. and Nardin, T. (eds) 1998: *International Society*. Princeton: Princeton University Press.

'Marcos, Subcomandante' et al. 2001: *Our Word is Our Weapon*. London: Serpent's Tail.

Marx, K. 1969: *The Eastern Question*. Ed. E. Marx Aveling and E. Aveling. London: Frank Cass.

Matilal, B. K. 1989: Ethical Relativism and Confrontation of Cultures. In M. Krause (1989).

Mayall, J. (ed.) 1996: *The New Interventionism: 1991–94*. Cambridge: Cambridge University Press.

Mayer, J., Boli, J. and Thomas, G. 1997: World Society and the Nation-State. *American Sociological Review*, 62, 171–90.

Mazzini, G. 1907: Duties of Man. In *Mazzini's Essays*, London: Everyman's Library, Dent.

McGrew, A. et al. 1992: *Global Politics: Globalisation and the Nation State*. Milton Keynes: Open University Press.

Mearsheimer, J. 1994/1995: The False Promise of International Institutions. *International Security*, 19, 5–49. (And collected in M. E. Brown et al. (1995)).

Melvern, L. 2000: *A People Betrayed: The Role of the West in Rwanda's Genocide*. London: Zed Books.

Mill, J. S. 1972: *Utilitarianism, On Liberty and Representative Government*. London: Dent.

Mill, J. S. 1984: A Few Words on Non-intervention. In *Collected Works of John Stuart Mill, vol. 21. Essays on Equality, Law and Education*. Toronto: University of Toronto Press.

Millennium: Journal of International Studies 2000: Seattle December 1999, 29, 103–40.

Miller, D. 1995: *On Nationality*. Oxford: Oxford University Press.

Miller, D. and Walzer, M. (eds) 1995: *Pluralism, Justice and Equality*. Oxford: Oxford University Press.

Mohamed, M. Bin and Ishihara, S. 1996: *The Voice of Asia: Two Leaders Discuss the Coming Century*. Tokyo: Kodansha International Ltd.

Monbiot, G. 2000: *Captive State*. Basingstoke: Macmillan.

Moore, J. (ed.) 1998: *Hard Choices: Moral Dilemmas in Humanitarian Intervention*. Lanham, MD: Rowman and Littlefield.

Moore, M. (ed.) 1998: *National Self-Determination and Secession*. Oxford: Oxford University Press.

Morgenthau, H. J. 1948: *Politics Among Nations*. New York: Knopf.

Mouffe, C. 1993: *The Return of the Political*. London: Verso.

Murray, A. 1996a: The Moral Politics of Hans Morgenthau. *The Review of Politics*, 58, 81–107.

Murray, A. 1996b: *Reconstructing Realism*. Edinburgh: Keele University Press.

Nagel, T. 1985: War and Massacre. In Beitz et al. (1985).

Nardin, T. 1981: Distributive Justice and the Criticism of International Law. *Political Studies*, 29, 232–44.

Nardin, T. 1983: *Law, Morality and the Relations of States*. Princeton: Princeton University Press.

Nardin, T. 1989: The Problem of Relativism in International Ethics. *Millennium: Journal of International Studies*, 18, 140–61.

Nardin, T. (ed.) 1996: *The Ethics of War and Peace*. Princeton: Princeton University Press.

Nardin, T. and Mapel, D. (eds) 1992: *Traditions of International Ethics*. Cambridge: Cambridge University Press.

Neufeld, M. 1995: *The Restructuring of International Relations Theory*. Cambridge: Cambridge University Press.

Nicholson, M. 1996: *Causes and Consequences in International Relations: A Conceptual Survey*. London: Pinter Press.

Niebuhr, R. 1932: *Moral Man and Immoral Society*. New York: Charles Scribner's Sons.

Norman, R. 1995: *Ethics, Killing and War*. Cambridge: Cambridge University Press.

Nove, A. 1983: *The Economics of Feasible Socialism*. London: Allen and Unwin.

Nove, A. 1991: *The Economics of Feasible Socialism Revisited*. London: Unwin Hyman.

Nussbaum, M. 1993: Non-relative Virtues: An Aristotelian Approach. In Nussbaum and Sen (1993).

Nussbaum, M. 1997: Kant and Cosmopolitanism. In Bohman and Lutz-Bachman (1997).

Nussbaum, M. 1999: The Professor of Parody: The Hip Defeatism of Judith Butler. *The New Republic*, 22 February, 37–45.

Nussbaum, M. 2000: *Women and Human Development*. Cambridge: Cambridge University Press.

Nussbaum, M. and Glover, J. (eds) 1995: *Women, Culture and Development*. Oxford: Clarendon Press.

Nussbaum, M. and Sen, A. (eds) 1993: *The Quality of Life*. Oxford: Clarendon Press.

Oakeshott, M. 1975: *On Human Conduct*. Oxford: Clarendon Press.

Oakeshott, M. 1991: Political Discourse. In *Rationalism in Politics and other Essays*, new and expanded edn, Indianapolis: Liberty Press.

O'Brien, C. C. 1962: *To Katanga and Back: A UN Case History*. London: Hutchinson.

Ohmae, K. 1990: *The Borderless World*. London: Collins.

O'Neill, O. 1986: *Faces of Hunger*. London: Allen and Unwin.

O'Neill, O. 1991: Transnational Justice. In Held (1991).

O'Neill, O. 1994: Justice and Boundaries. In C. Brown (1994c).

O'Neill, O. 2000: *Bounds of Justice*. Cambridge: Cambridge University Press.

Onuf, N. 1989: *World of Our Making*. Columbia, SC: University of South Carolina Press.

Pangle, T. L. and Ahrendorf, P. J. 1999: *Justice and Nations: On the Moral Basis of Power and Peace*. Lawrence, KA: University of Kansas Press.

Parekh, B. 1999: Moral Diversity and the Search for Non-Ethnocentric Universalism. In Dunne and Wheeler (1999).

Parekh, B. 2000: *Rethinking Multiculturalism*. Basingstoke: Macmillan.

Parkinson, F. 1977: *The Philosophy of International Relations*. Beverley Hills, CA: Sage.

Paskins, B. and Dockrill, M. 1979: *The Ethics of War*. London: Duckworth.

Patman, R. (ed.) 2000: *Universal Human Rights*. Basingstoke: Macmillan.

Pelcynski Z. (ed.) 1971: *Hegel's Political Philosophy*. Oxford: Oxford University Press.

Peters, J. S. and Wolper, A. (eds) 1995: *Women's Rights, Human Rights: International Feminist Perspectives*. New York: Routledge.

Peterson, S. 2000: *Me Against My Brother: At War in Somalia, Sudan and Rwanda*. London: Routledge.

Peterson, V. S. 1990: Whose Rights? A Critique of the 'Givens' in Human Rights Discourse. *Alternatives*, 15, 303–44.

Pilger, J. 1999: Under the influence: The real reason for the United Nations' intervention is to maintain Indonesian control. *Guardian*, 21 September.

Plant, R. 1983: *Hegel: An Introduction*. Oxford: Blackwell.

Pocock, J. G. A. 1975: *The Machiavellian Moment: Florentine Political Thought and the Atlantic Republican Tradition*. Princeton: Princeton University Press.

Pogge, T. 1989: *Realizing Rawls*. Ithaca, NY: Cornell University Press.

Pogge, T. 1994a: Cosmopolitanism and Sovereignty. In C. Brown (1994c).

Pogge, T. 1994b: An Egalitarian Law of Peoples. *Philosophy and Public Affairs*, 23, 195–224.

Pogge, T. 1998: A Global Resources Dividend. In D. A. Crocker and T. Linden (eds), *Ethics of Consumption: The Good Life, Justice and Global Stewardship*, Lanham, MD: Rowman & Littlefield.

Polanyi, K. 1975: *The Great Transformation*. Boston: Beacon Books.

Porter, B. 1968: *Critics of Empire: British Radical Attitudes to Colonialism in Africa, 1895–1914*. London: Macmillan.

Porter, B. (ed.) 1972: *The Aberystwyth Papers*. Oxford: Oxford University Press.

Powell, R. 1991: Absolute and Relative Gains in International Relations Theory. *American Political Science Review*, 85, 1303–20.

Powell, R. 1994: Anarchy in International Relations: The Neoliberal-Neorealist Debate. *International Organisation*, 48, 313–34.

Prospect 1999: Debate on Kosovo: Robert Skidelsky and Michael Ignatieff. June, 16–21.

Prunier, G. 1995: *The Rwanda Crisis, 1959–94: History of a Genocide*. New York: Columbia University Press.

Ramsbotham, O. and Woodhouse, T. 1996: *Humanitarian Intervention in Contemporary Conflict*. Cambridge: Polity.

Ramsey, P. 1968: *The Just War*. New York: Charles Scribner's Sons.

Rawls, J. 1971/1999: *A Theory of Justice*, 1st and 2nd (revised) edns. Oxford: Oxford University Press.

Rawls, J. 1993: The Law of Peoples. In Shute and Hurley (1993).

Rawls, J. 1995: *Political Liberalism*. Cambridge, MA: Harvard University Press.

Rawls, J. 1999a: *Collected Papers*. Cambridge, MA: Harvard University Press.

Rawls, J. 1999b: *The Law of Peoples*. Cambridge, MA: Harvard University Press.

Reich, R. 1992: *The Work of Nations*. New York: Vintage.

Reiss, H. (ed.) 1970: *Kant's Political Writings*. Cambridge: Cambridge University Press.

Renan, E. 1939: What is a Nation?. In A. Zimmern (ed.), *Modern Political Doctrines*. London: Oxford University Press.

Rengger, N. J. 1988: Serpents and Doves in Classical International Theory. *Millennium: Journal of International Studies*, 17, 215–25.

Renteln, A. D. 1990: *International Human Rights: Universalism vs. Relativism*. London: Sage.

Review of International Studies 1999a: *Special Issue: the Interregnum*, 25. (Also published as M. Cox, K. Booth and T. Dunne (eds) 1999: *The Interregnum*. Cambridge: Cambridge University Press.)

Review of International Studies 1999b: Forum on Andrew Linklater's *The Transformation of Political Community*, 25, 139–75.

Review of International Studies 2000: Forum on Alexander Wendt's *Social Theory of International Politics*, 26, 123–80.

Riley, P. 1983: *Kant's Political Philosophy*. Totowa, NJ: Rowman Littlefield.

Rivkin, D. B. and Casey, L. A. 2000/2001: The Rocky Shoals of International Law. *The National Interest*, 62, 35–46.

Roberts, A. 1993: Humanitarian War. *International Affairs*, 69, 429–49.

Roberts, A. 1999: Nato's 'Humanitarian War' over Kosovo. *Survival*, 41.

Roberts, A. and Guelff, R. (eds) 2000: *Documents on the Laws of War*. Oxford: Oxford University Press.

Roberts, A. and Kingsbury, B. (eds) 1993: *United Nations, Divided World: the UN's Role in International Relations*. Oxford: Oxford University Press.

Robertson, R. 1995: Glocalization: Time-Space and Homogeneity-Heterogeneity. In M. Featherstone, S. Lash and R. Robertson (eds), *Global Modernities*, Thousand Oaks, CA: Sage.

Rorty, R. 1993: Human Rights, Rationality and Sentimentality. In Shute and Hurley (1993).

Rorty, R. 1998: The End of Leninism, Havel, and Social Hope. In *Truth and Progress: Philosophical Papers Vol. 3*, Cambridge: Cambridge University Press.

Rose, M. 1998: *Fighting for Peace: Bosnia, 1994*. London: The Harvill Press.

Rosenberg, J. 1994: *The Empire of Civil Society*. London: Verso.

Rosenthal, J. 1991: *Righteous Realists*. Baton Rouge, LA: University of Louisiana Press.

Rosenthal, J. (ed.) 1999: *Ethics and International Affairs*. Washington, DC: Georgetown University Press, for Carnegie Council for Ethics and International Affairs.

Ruggie, J. G. 1998: *Constructing the World Polity*. London: Routledge.

Russett, B. 1993: *Grasping the Democratic Peace: Principles for a Post-Cold War World*. Princeton: Princeton University Press.

Sakakiba, E. 1995: The End of Progressivism: A Search for New Goals. *Foreign Affairs*, 74, 8–15.

Sandel, M. 1982: *Liberalism and the Limits of Justice*. Cambridge: Cambridge University Press.

Scanlon, T. M. 1982: Contractualism and Utilitarianism. In A. Sen and B. Williams (eds), *Utilitarianism and Beyond*. Cambridge: Cambridge University Press.

Scanlon, T. M. 1999: *What We Owe to Each Other*. Cambridge, MA: Harvard University Press.

Schmidt, B. 1998: *The Political Discourse of Anarchy: A Disciplinary History of International Relations*. Albany, NY: State University of New York Press.

Schmitt, C. 1996: *The Concept of the Political*. Chicago: University of Chicago Press.

Scholte, J. A. 2000: *Globalisation*. London: Macmillan.

Schweller, R. 1999: Fantasy World. In *Review of International Studies* (1999b).

Searle, J. 1995: *The Construction of Social Reality*. London: Allen Lane.

Seaton, A. 1999: Serbia, 'Ethnic War' and the Media. *Political Quarterly*, 70, 254–70.

Sellar, W. C. and Yeatman, R. J. 1930: *1066 And All That*. London: Methuen.

Sen, A. 1977: Rational Fools: A Critique of the Behavioural Foundations of Economic Theory. *Philosophy and Public Affairs*, 6, 317–44.

Sen, A. 1982: *Poverty and Famine*. Oxford: Clarendon Press.

Sen, A. 2000a: *Development and Freedom*. Cambridge: Cambridge University Press.

Sen, A. 2000b: East and West: the Reach of Reason. *New York Review of Books*, XLVII, 12, 20 July.

Shapiro, I. and Brilmayer, L. (eds) 1999: *Global Justice* NOMOS XLI. New York: New York University Press.

Shawcross, W. 2000: *Deliver us from Evil: Peacekeepers. Warlords and a World of Endless Conflict*. London: Bloomsbury.

Shue, H. 1983: *Basic Rights: Famine, Affluence and United States Foreign Policy*. Princeton: Princeton University Press.

Shute, S. and Hurley, S. (eds) 1993: *On Human Rights*. New York: Basic Books.

Singer, P. 1985: Famine, Affluence and Morality. In Beitz et al. (1985).

Smith, K. E. and Light, M. M. (eds) 2001: *Ethics and Foreign Policy*. Cambridge: Cambridge University Press.

Smith, M. J. 1986: *Realist Thought from Weber to Kissinger*. Baton Rouge, LA: University of Louisiana Press.

Smith, S. 1992: The Forty Years Detour. *Millennium: Journal of International Studies*, 21, 489–506.

Smith, S., Booth, K. and Zalewski, M. (eds) 1996: *International Theory: Post-Positivist Perspectives*. Cambridge: Cambridge University Press.

Spiro, P. J. 2000: The New Sovereigntists. *Foreign Affairs*, 79, 9–15.

Steiner, H. 1992: Libertarianism and the Transnational Migration of People. In Barry and Goodin (1992).

Steiner, H. 1994: *An Essay on Rights*. Oxford: Blackwell.

Steiner, H. 1999: Just Taxation and International Re-distribution. In Shapiro and Brilmayer (1999).

Steiner, H. J. and Alston, P. (eds) 2000: *International Human Rights in Context: Law, Politics, Morals – Texts and Materials*, 2nd edn. Oxford: Clarendon Press.

Sterne, L. 1967: *A Sentimental Journey through France and Italy*. London: Penguin.

Stiglitz, J. 1998: *More Instruments and Broader Goals: Moving towards the Post-Washington Consensus*. Helsinki: UN University.

Strange, S. 1994: Wake up Krasner! The World *has* Changed. *Review of International Political Economy*, 1, 209–19.

Strange, S. 1996: *The Retreat from the State*. Cambridge: Cambridge University Press.

Strange, S. 1998: Globaloney. *Review of International Political Economy*, 5, 704–11.
Strange, S. 1999: The Westfailure System. *Review of International Studies*, 25, 345–54.
Sutch, P. 2000: Human Rights as Settled Norms: Mervyn Frost and the Limits of Hegelian Human Rights Theory. *Review of International Studies*, 26, 215–31.
Tang, J. H. (ed.) 1994: *Human Rights and International Relations in the Asia-Pacific Region.* London: Pinter Press.
Taylor, C. 1971: Interpretation and the Sciences of Man. *Review of Metaphysics*, 25, 3–51.
Taylor, C. 1975: *Hegel.* Cambridge: Cambridge University Press.
Taylor, P. and Groom, A. J. R. 1992: *The UN and the Gulf War, 1990–1991: Back to the Future.* London: Royal Institute of International Affairs.
Teschke, B. 1998: Geopolitical Relations in the European Middle Ages: History and Theory. *International Organization*, 52, 325–58.
Thomas, C. 1987: *In Search of Security: The Third World in International Relations.* Brighton: Wheatsheaf Books.
Thompson, J. 1992: *Justice and World Order.* London: Routledge.
Thucydides 5th Century BC/1998: *The Pelopennesian War.* Trans. S. Lattimore. Indianapolis: Hackett.
Tickner, J. A. 1989: Hans Morgenthau's Principles of Political Realism: A Feminist Reformulation. *Millennium: Journal of International Studies*, 17, 429–40.
Tilly, C. (ed.) 1975: *The Formation of National States in Western Europe.* Princeton: Princeton University Press.
Tippett, M. 1991: *Those Twentieth Century Blues: An Autobiography.* London: Hutchinson.
Toffler, A. and Toffler, H. 1993: *War and Anti-War.* Boston: Little, Brown.
Tomlinson, J. 1999: *Globalization and Culture.* Cambridge: Polity.
Treitschke, H. von 1916/1963: *Politics.* Abridged and ed. by Hans Kohn. New York: Harcourt, Brace and World.
Tuck, R. 1999: *The Rights of War and Peace.* Cambridge: Cambridge University Press.
Tully, J. 1995: *Strange Multiplicity.* Cambridge: Cambridge University Press.
Van der Pijl, K. 1998: *Transnational Classes and International Relations.* London: Routledge.
Van Evera, S. 1999: *Causes of War: Power and the Roots of Conflict.* Ithaca, NY: Cornell University Press.
Van Ness, P. (ed.) 1999: *Debating Human Rights: Critical Essays from the US and Asia.* London: Routledge.
Vincent, R. J. 1974: *Nonintervention and International Order.* Princeton: Princeton University Press.
Vincent, R. J. 1986: *Human Rights and International Relations.* Cambridge: Cambridge University Press.
Viroli, M. 1995: *For Love of Country.* Oxford: Clarendon Press.
Walker, R. B. J. 1993: *Inside/Outside: International Relations as Political Theory.* Cambridge: Cambridge University Press.
Wallace, W. 1999: The Sharing of Sovereignty: The European Paradox. *Political Studies*, 47, 503–21.

Wallerstein, I. 1974: *The Modern World System*, vol. I. London: Academic Press.

Waltz, K. 1959: *Man, the State and War*. New York: Columbia University Press.

Waltz, K. 1979: *Theory of International Politics*. Reading, MA: Addison-Wesley.

Waltz, K. 1990: Realist Thought and Neorealist Theory. *Journal of International Affairs*, 44, 21–37.

Waltz, K. 1997: Evaluating Theories. *American Political Science Review*, 91, 913–18.

Waltz, K. 1998: An Interview with Kenneth Waltz (conducted by Fred Halliday and Justin Rosenberg). *Review of International Studies*, 24, 371–86.

Walzer, M. 1965: *The Revolution of the Saints*. Cambridge, MA: Harvard University Press.

Walzer, M. 1977/1992: *Just and Unjust Wars*, 1st and 2nd edns. New York: Basic Books.

Walzer, M. 1983: *Spheres of Justice*. London: Martin Robertson.

Walzer, M. 1987: *Interpretation and Social Criticism*. Cambridge, MA: Harvard University Press.

Walzer, M. 1990: The Communitarian Critique of Liberalism. *Political Theory*, 8, 6–23.

Walzer, M. 1994a: Notes on the New Tribalism. In C. Brown (1994c).

Walzer, M. 1994b: *Thick and Thin: Moral Argument at Home and Abroad*. Notre Dame, IN: University of Notre Dame Press.

Walzer, M. (ed.) 1995: *Toward a Global Civil Society*. Providence, RI: Berghahn Press.

Warren, B. 1980: *Imperialism: Pioneer of Capitalism*. London: New Left Books.

Watson, A. 1992: *The Evolution of International Society: A Comparative Historical Analysis*. London: Routledge.

Weiss, T. G. 1999: *Military-Civil Interactions: Intervening in Humanitarian Crises*. Lanham, MD: Rowman and Littlefield.

Weller, M. 1999a: The Rambouillet Conference. *International Affairs*, 75, 211–51.

Weller, M. 1999b: On the Hazards of Foreign Travel for Dictators and Other Criminals. *International Affairs*, 75, 599–618.

Welsh, J. M. 1995: *Edmund Burke and International Relations*. London: Macmillan.

Wendt, A. 1992: Anarchy is What States Make of It: The Social Construction of Power Politics. *International Organization*, 46, 391–426.

Wendt, A. 1999: *Social Theory of International Politics*. Cambridge: Cambridge University Press.

Wheeler, N. J. 1992: Pluralist and Solidarist Conceptions of International Society: Bull and Vincent on Humanitarian Intervention. *Millennium: Journal of International Studies*, 21, 463–87.

Wheeler, N. J. 2000: *Saving Strangers*. Oxford: Oxford University Press.

Wight, M. 1966: 'Why there is no international theory' and 'Western values in international relations'. In Butterfield and Wight (1966).

Wight, M. 1946/1978: *Power Politics*. Leicester: Leicester University Press.

Wight, M. 1977: *Systems of States*. Leicester: Leicester University Press.

Wight, M. 1991: *International Theory: The Three Traditions*. Ed. G. Wight and B. Porter. Leicester: Leicester University Press.

Williams, H. 1983: *Kant's Political Philosophy*. Oxford: Blackwell.

Williamson, R. (ed.) 1998: *Some Corner of a Foreign Field: Intervention and World Order*. Basingstoke: Macmillan.

Woodward, P. A. (ed.) 2001: *The Doctrine of Double Effect: Philosophers Debate a Controversial Moral Principle*. Notre Dame, IN: University of Notre Dame Press.

Zakaria, F. 1994: Culture is Destiny: A Conversation with Lee Kuan Yew. *Foreign Affairs*, 73, 109–26.

Zakaria, F. 1997: The Rise of Illiberal Democracy. *Foreign Affairs*, 76, 22–43.

Zartman, W. I. (ed.) 1994: *Collapsed States: The Disintegration and Restoration of Legitimate Authority*. Boulder, CO: Lynne Rienner.

Index

Bold numbers indicate key pages on the subject